W9-ATN-804

NEW ENGLAND'S
B E S T - L O V E D
D R I V I N G
T O U R S

IDG Books Worldwide, Inc.
An International Data Group Company
Foster City, CA ■ Chicago, Il ■ Indianapolis, IN ■ New York, NY

Written by Kathy Arnold and Paul Wade

Additional research: Lans Christensen, Gael May McKibben, Tom
Arnold and Harlan Levy

First published 1997
Revised second edition 1999

Edited, designed and produced by AA Publishing.

Published by AA Publishing

Published in the United States by IDG Books Worldwide, Inc.
An International Data Group Company
909 Third Avenue, New York, NY 10022

Frommer's is a registered trademark of Arthur Frommer.
Used under license.

ISBN 0-7645-6366-1
ISSN 1520-9911

Cataloging-in-Publication Data is available from the Library of
Congress.

Color separation: Daylight Colour Art, Singapore

Printed and bound by G. Canale
& C. s.p.a., Torino, Italy

Below: *fall on the
Mohawk Trail*

CONTENTS

ABOUT THIS BOOK

This book is not only a practical touring guide for the independent traveler, but is also invaluable for those who would like to know more about New England.

It is divided into the 6 states, each with its own city and driving tours. The driving tours start and finish in those cities which we consider to be the most interesting centers for exploration.

There are special features on Boston and the American Revolution, the beauty of the Fall, and the rich heritage of the arts and the surrounding seas.

Each tour has details of the most interesting places to visit en route. Boxes catering for special interests follow some of the main entries – for those whose interest is in history, or walking, or those who have children. There are also boxes which highlight scenic stretches of road and which give details of special events, crafts and customs.

The simple route directions are accompanied by an easy-to-use map at the beginning of each tour, along with a chart showing how far it is from one town to the next in miles and kilometers. This can help you to decide where to take a break and stop overnight. (All distances quoted are approximate.)

Before setting off, it is advisable to check with the information center listed at the start of the tour for recommendations on where to break your journey, and for additional information on what to see and do, and when best to visit.

Torrington, Connecticut

Tour Information
See pages 165–73 for addresses, telephone numbers and opening times of the attractions mentioned in the tours, including telephone numbers of tourist offices.

Accommodations
See pages 163–4 for a list of recommended hotels for each tour.

Motoring
For information on aspects of motoring in New England see pages 159–60.

INFORMATION FOR NON-U.S. RESIDENTS

Banks
Banks are usually open Mon–Fri 9–3. Many have extended hours until 5pm (or 8–9pm on Thu) and on Sat from 9–2, or later.

Although foreign currency can be changed at big hotels or airports, U.S. dollar travelers' checks are recommended as they are readily accepted as cash everywhere from restaurants to gas stations.

Credit Cards
Major credit cards are accepted in New England. However, many small bed and breakfasts or remote small shops will accept only cash or travelers' checks. If you have a major credit or charge card, you may be able to obtain cash from an ATM.

Currency
The American unit of currency is the dollar, consisting of 100 cents. All the notes are green, are the same size and have similar designs, so be careful. They range from one to two, five, ten, 20, 50 and 100 dollars. Coins are in demoninations of one cent, (penny), 5 cents (nickel), 10 cents (dime), 25 cents (quarter) and ... rarely, a silver dollar.

Customs Regulations
Non-U.S. residents may take in 200 cigarettes or 50 cigars, a liter of alcohol and $100 worth of gifts. Customs officials are very strict about banning any fresh meat, fruit, plants and, of course, drugs (unless on prescription).

Electricity
Standard voltage is 110–120V, 60 cycles AC, using flat two-pin plugs. Bring the right adaptor.

Emergency Telephone Numbers
If you have an emergency, telephone the police at 911 who will put you in touch with the right

service. Otherwise, dial "0" and consult the operator.

Entry Regulations

Citizens of most European countries, plus Japan and New Zealand, no longer need visas as long as they are visiting the U.S. for business or tourist purposes. For a stay not exceeding 90 days, and provided that a return or onward ticket is held, only a valid passport is required. Check with your travel agent before travelling, since American immigration officials are very strict.

Health Matters

It is essential to have adequate health insurance before travelling to the U.S. While hospitals are usually excellent, treatment can be expensive. It may be delayed or refused without proof of proper insurance. Your hotel will be able to recommend a doctor or hospital. Alternatively, call the local hospital. No special inoculations are required. See also page 159.

Post Offices

Stamps for postcards and letters are on sale in many shops and hotels; for larger packages, go to a post office. It is cheaper to send postcards and aerograms than letters. See also page 161.

Public Holidays

See page 159 and **New England Calendar of Events**, pages 160–1.

Telephones

Each state has several area codes, with new ones opening up all the time as telecommunications expand. Pay phones require 5, 10 and 25 cent coins, so use a telephone card for convenience. To call abroad, dial 011, then the country code:
Australia 61, Canada 1, New Zealand 64, U.K. 44.

Time

New England is on Eastern Standard Time (EST), 5 hours behind the U.K., 6 hours behind mainland Europe, and 15 hours behind Sydney, Australia.

Daylight Saving Time alters the time by one hour from March or April to October or November.

Travelers Aid Society

The Travelers Aid Society, at 711 Atlantic Avenue, Boston, Massachusetts 02111 (tel: 617/542 7286), is dedicated to helping travelers. Staff provide crisis intervention, counseling, referrals to community sources, and emergency financial assistance to travelers in crisis. Travelers Aid volunteers at Logan Airport (tel: 617/567 5385) and the Greyhound Bus Terminal, South Station (tel: 617/737 2880) will help you to find an address, a hospital, lost luggage, a way to get money from home, or the solution to any other travel dilemma.

Useful Addresses

DestINNations (for inn reservations), 572 Route 28, West Yarmouth, MA 02673 (tel: 508/790 0577); (elsewhere in U.S.A. and Canada) 800/333 4667; (in U.K.) North America Travel Service (tel: 0113 243 0000).
Bed and Breakfast Agency of Boston, 47 Commercial Wharf, Boston, MA 02110. Tel: (in U.K.) 0800 895128 (in U.S.A. and Canada) 800/248 9262.
New England Bed and Breakfast, Box 1426, Waltham MA 02154 (tel: 617/244 2112).
Central Reservation Service of New England, 300 Terminal C, Logan Airport, Boston 02128 (tel: 617/569 3800 or 800/332 3026.

Lobster pots at Mystic Seaport

MASSACHUSETTS

After 380 years of permanent European settlement, Massachusetts has acquired a "little history." Here, the Pilgrims landed and built their communities. A century and a half later, patriotic passion exploded in a series of events culminating in the American Revolution. Not surprisingly, that heritage has been preserved. Conservation has encompassed old houses and bridges, churches and farms, even entire villages.

Massachusetts is known as the Bay State because of the gaping Atlantic gulf enclosed by the flexed arm of Cape Cod. The shape of the state ensures a variety of landscapes. It stretches from the storm-tossed Atlantic to the rolling, wooded hills of the Berkshires, with the rich meadows of the Connecticut Valley in between.

The seasons are distinct: crisp, clear winter days melting into an explosion of spring greenery and flowers, followed by muggy, soporific summers and, finally, the fall with its dazzling multi-colored leaves (see pages 102–3).

Massachusetts, especially around Boston, was also America's cultural cradle (see pages 56–7). Artists and writers, poets and musicians have long been drawn together by the web of academia. Harvard University, founded in 1636, is the oldest American institute of higher learning, but there are numerous other colleges to be found throughout the state, as well as boarding schools (called "prep schools" because they prepare students for college).

Outdoor festivals of music and drama are a bonus for visitors during the summer months.

But the region's focus always returns to history. Many of America's most treasured icons are here, from Plymouth Rock to Boston's Old North Church and Concord's historic bridge. Thanksgiving is celebrated with justifiable pride; after all, the tradition of eating turkey and pumpkin pie was "invented" here. They even have the cranberry bogs nearby to provide the accompanying sauce.

Concord is a beautiful town with a rich and varied history

Tour 1

*"Listen, my children, and you
   shall hear,
Of the midnight ride of
   Paul Revere ..."*

Paul Revere is one of the best-known messengers in history, thanks to Henry Wadsworth Longfellow's poem. His ride from Boston to warn the Americans that the British were on the march has become legendary. The patriots assembled and took on the trained soldiers, first in Lexington and then in Concord. All the British wanted to do was capture the rebels' arms cache; they had no idea that the skirmishes of April 19, 1775 would spark the American Revolution. In both towns, historic sites have been preserved, while the visitor information centers provide details of "who did what and when." The route for this tour also has a literary focus. In the 19th century, Concord was the home of some of the best-known writers of the day: Henry David Thoreau, Louisa May Alcott, Nathaniel Hawthorne and Ralph Waldo Emerson.

Tour 2

Although Cape Cod has long been recognized as a playground for Bostonians, the North Shore, with its rugged, rocky outcrops is also a popular place to relax by the sea. Add to that atmospheric fishing villages and the gruesome history of witches in Salem, and this drive is fun as well as scenic. The sparkling light has long attracted artists, especially in Rockport. Castles and underwater rocks, whales, frozen peas and even clam chowder are threads in the rich tapestry of America's history which unravels along this shoreline drive.

Tour 3

Cape Cod enjoys a mystique matched by few holiday destinations. The names of its 300-year-old villages are reminders of English fishing ports, its history peopled with Indians and fishermen, whalers and sea captains. On Cape Cod Bay, the sands are

sheltered and the water is warmer than on the Atlantic Ocean shore, where strong waves buffet the dunes of the Cape Cod National Seashore. This 40-mile (60km) coastline stretches from the elbow of the peninsula up to Provincetown, known for its bohemian lifestyle. The popularity of the Cape has taken its toll: roadside development sprawls around Hyannis on the south shore and traffic can be bumper to bumper on summer weekends. Off season, it is easier to get away from it all, and find what aficionados call "the old Cape Cod."

Tour 4

Western Massachusetts has an intriguing mixture of the rural and sophisticated, the historic and eccentric. The rolling Berkshire Hills inspired authors

Chatham Light, Cape Cod. Lighthouses are a unique part of New England's heritage

such as Herman Melville and Edith Wharton, and attracted millionaires, who built vacation homes away from the seaside. Now the hills resound to summer festivals of music and theater. Attractive towns and villages range from Deerfield, with its perfectly preserved 17th-century houses, to Williamstown with its excellent college and astonishing art collection. Stockbridge thrives on its "traditional America" image, ably reinforced by *Saturday Evening Post* cover artist Norman Rockwell, whose paintings are on display here. Drive down lazy back roads to old covered bridges arching over rocky streams; there are surprises around every corner.

BIRTHPLACE OF A NATION

The American perspective of the War of Independence is simple: the Colonists were oppressed by King George III and Parliament and justifiably rebelled. The issues were a little more complex. In the early days, there were no "states" as such. The Colonies differed in population and style of government: some depended on fishing and trade, others on farming and tobacco. Although links with the Mother Country were strong for economic and cultural reasons, the Colonists had become increasingly independent-minded during the century-and-a-half since the first settlers arrived.

A turning point in American history was the defeat of the French and the Indians in the war from 1756 to 1763. This gave the New Englanders, and the colonies along the coast to the south, a vision of vast lands stretching westwards and a sense of "new" country to be developed. Relations with Britain, however, became strained when Parliament decided that the colonies should help pay for the seven years of war; after all, the English reasoned, they were defending Colonial lands. Moreover, a 10,000-strong army was still needed to protect the Colonies. A monopoly on trade was proclaimed, restricting Colonists to dealing only with Britain and other British possessions (notably the West Indies). Further, a ban was issued on new settlements west of the Appalachians.

Although these restrictions rankled, what inflamed Colonial passions was direct taxation. Traditionally, Britain had raised money by customs duties on shipping; the Stamp Act in 1765 set a new precedent. This placed a charge on all contracts, deeds, newspapers and legal documents. Protests forced its repeal within a year, but other revenue-raisers followed, only to be repealed. Parliament decided to stand firm on one, however. That was the tax on tea.

After the French and Indian War, economic times were hard for the Colonists, and the new rules hurt financially. But the Colonists also protested on prin-

ciple. "No taxation without representation" was the cry at public meetings and in pamphlets. Articles questioned the legality of such taxes, claiming that they infringed the charters of some of the Colonies.

Boston was an important focus of militant feelings, which periodically exploded into riots. One relatively minor event, on March 5, 1770, became a legend. A lone British sentry on duty at the Custom House was harassed by a crowd. Reinforcements arrived, but the mob continued to bait the soldiers, heckling them and throwing stones. Shots were fired; five Colonists died. This incident became known as the "Boston Massacre" and was used by leaders such as Samuel Adams to whip up emotions.

Three years later, in December, came one of the most colorful incidents of the era, the Boston Tea Party. As a protest against the tax of 3 pence per pound on tea, about a hundred men, disguised as Native

Americans, boarded the newly arrived HMS *Dartmouth*. Its cargo of 300 chests of tea was thrown overboard. In response, General Gage and four British regiments were sent to Boston, and the port was closed down in 1774.

Below: the Boston Massacre, in which five Colonists died
Bottom: the "Sons of Liberty," disguised as Mohawk Indians, throw East India Company tea into the water

The scene was set for the smoldering coals of resentment to be ignited. In April, 1775, it was reported to General Gage that farmers in Concord, a small village west of Boston, were stockpiling firearms. He ordered 700 British troops to march out, confiscate and destroy the Patriots' illegal cache. On route, they skirmished with the Minute Men (locals who could be ready "in a minute" to fight) in Lexington before being outnumbered in Concord. Instead of withdrawing in an orderly manner, the British confronted the militiamen, lost three soldiers and had to beat a hasty, undignified retreat to Boston.

cost was hundreds of lives. The psychological victory belonged to the Americans. King George III replied savagely by declaring the colonies to be in rebellion. Mercenaries were hired in Europe and transported across the Atlantic to augment the troops.

Not all the Colonists were ready for war. About one-third remained loyal to the crown and another third were neutral. The rest, however, were vociferous and demanded to sever links with the Mother Country. Further British attacks on Falmouth (now Portland, Maine) in October, 1775 and on Norfolk, Virginia in January, 1776, only

Boston, never to return. Fighting, however, continued elsewhere. In May, representatives of all 13 Colonies met in Philadelphia, Pennsylvania. Freedom was the agenda of this Continental Congress. A short document drafted by Thomas Jefferson of Virginia set out the grievances and proclaimed that "these united colonies are, and of right ought to be, free and independent states." This was the Declaration of Independence, accepted unanimously by the delegates and signed on July 4, 1776.

Liberty did not come immediately, however. War raged for five years and even after the

Some 20,000 Minute Men rushed to Boston, penning the British forces in. In May, 1775, artillery powder and ammunition captured at Fort Ticonderoga in New York State was hauled overland by the Colonists and used to capture Bunker Hill. Although the Redcoats soon stormed and recaptured it, the

served to fan the fury. *Common Sense*, a pamphlet written by Thomas Paine, became a best seller, with 120,000 copies sold in January, 1776 alone. Although he was an Englishman who had lived in the Colonies for only a year, he argued strenuously for independence. In March, 1776, the British withdrew from

The citizens of Lexington re-enact the events of April 19 1775

formal British surrender in 1781, London refused to recognize the Colonies' independence. Finally, in September, 1783, a peace treaty was signed in Paris, acknowledging that a new nation had been born.

TOUR
1

Lexington & Concord

Concord and Lexington are two of the most famous towns in the United States, due to the skirmishes between locals and British soldiers in 1775 that triggered the American Revolution. Concord has an additional claim to fame: it was home to some of the great writers of 19th-century America. Today, Lexington feels like a residential suburb of Boston, while Concord has retained more of its historical flavor. The main theme of this route is liberty and literature, but at the end of the drive, the focus is strictly contemporary.

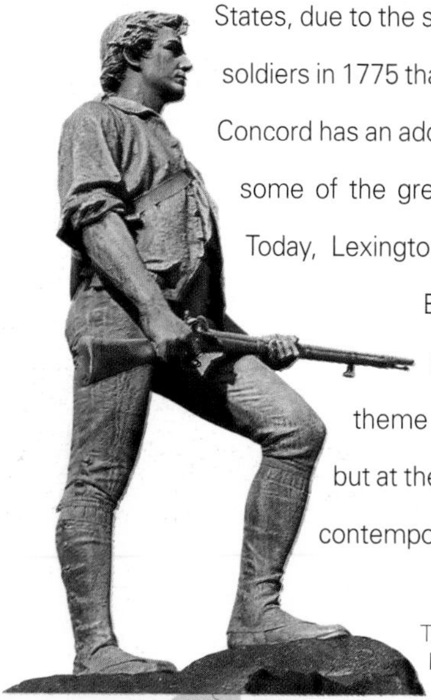

The Minute Man Statue on Lexington Green

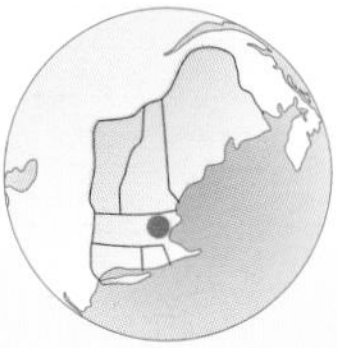

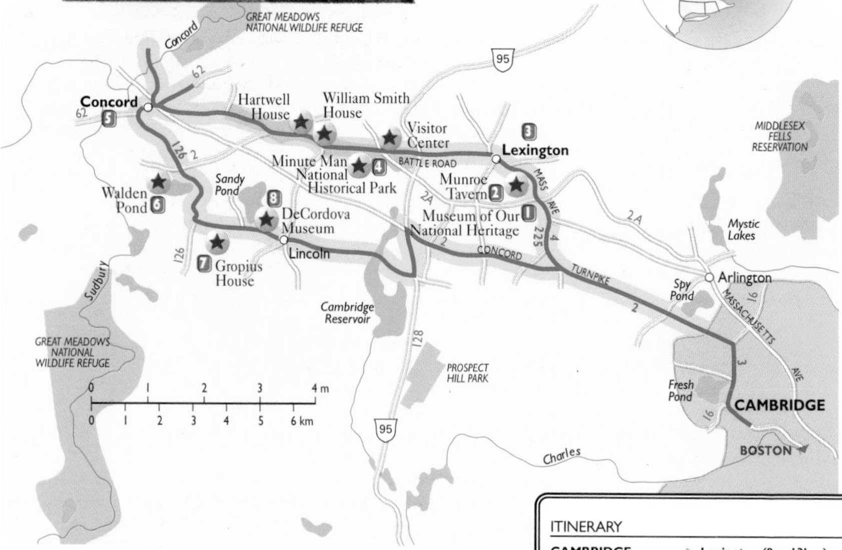

GREAT MEADOWS NATIONAL WILDLIFE REFUGE
Concord
62
95
Concord 5
Hartwell House
William Smith House
Visitor Center
3 Lexington
MIDDLESEX FELLS RESERVATION
126
2
Minute Man National Historical Park 4
BATTLE ROAD
Munroe Tavern 2
MASS AVE
Walden Pond 6
Sandy Pond
8 DeCordova Museum
Museum of Our National Heritage 1
2A
225
4
Mystic Lakes
Lincoln
CONCORD
TURNPIKE
7 Gropius House
Arlington
Spy Pond
MASSACHUSETTS AVE
16
Sudbury
Cambridge Reservoir
128
GREAT MEADOWS NATIONAL WILDLIFE REFUGE
PROSPECT HILL PARK
Fresh Pond
3
0 1 2 3 4 m
0 1 2 3 4 5 6 km
95
CAMBRIDGE
Charles
BOSTON

ITINERARY	
CAMBRIDGE	▶ **Lexington (8m-13km)**
LEXINGTON	▶ **Concord (6m-10km)**
CONCORD	▶ **Cambridge (16m-26km)**

1 DAY • 30 MILES • 49KM

FOR HISTORY BUFFS

The Colonists had no regular army. What they did have, however, were militia, small forces of volunteers pledged to be ready at a minute's notice, giving rise to the the name "Minute Men." Although mainly farmers, the men also hunted for game, using "rifled" guns which were more accurate than the British muskets. Like modern guerilla fighters, the Colonists tended to disappear into the country-side, rather than march along roads as the British did. In any case, British soldiers were easy to spot, because of the bright red coats they wore.

Headquarters of the Lexington Minute Men, 1775

▶ *i* *Cambridge Visitor Information Booth, Harvard Square*

▶ *From Cambridge, take the Fresh Pond Parkway (**Routes 16** and **3**) to **Route 2** west. Take this for 3 miles (5km) and then exit onto **Routes 4** and **225**. At the first stop sign, turn left onto Massachusetts Avenue (always known as "Mass Ave"). This was the route taken by Paul Revere on his way to Lexington. At the junction with the **2A**, turn left onto **2A West** to reach the Museum of Our National Heritage.*

❶ Museum of Our National Heritage

This is a bright and airy museum with great displays and special exhibitions, and it provides a splendid introduction to the sites along the rest of the tour. But it's not all about the Revolution. The lively exhibitions cover all aspects of American culture, from Women of the Wild West to toys, costume and arts and crafts, and there is a full program of concerts, films, lectures and activities.

▶ *Return to the Massachusetts Avenue junction and turn left to reach Munroe Tavern.*

❷ Munroe Tavern

On the afternoon of April 19, 1775, this fine old pub (1695) was the site of the temporary hospital and headquarters for British soldiers retreating from the battle at Concord. Fourteen years later, George Washington dined here in an upstairs room, while on tour in New England. Today it is the headquarters of the Lexington Historical Society.

▶ *Follow Massachusetts Avenue for about a mile (1.5km), straight into Lexington to the triangular green.*

❸ Lexington

This cradle of the American Revolution is dotted with significant sites, not least of which is Battle Green. Here, a bronze statue of Captain John Parker stands on a stone cairn, facing the line of the British approach. Behind him the Lexington militia would have stood. "Ye villains, ye rebels, disperse!" ordered the arrogant Major John Pitcairn. Faced by the superior numbers and strength of the

British, Parker wisely told his men: "Don't fire unless fired upon, but if they mean to have a war, let it begin here!"

A shot rang out, no-one knows from where. Suddenly fire was exchanged; two British soldiers and eight Minute Men were killed or wounded. Seven of them are buried under the Revolutionary Monument further along on the Green. The British, having beaten off this minor attack, marched on towards Concord.

In the nearby Visitor Center there is a diorama giving an overview of the events of that day. Next door to it is Buckman Tavern, a handsome three-story tavern (1690) where, in the early hours of April 19, 1775, several Lexington Minute Men had gathered to drink ale. Around 4am came the news that 700 British troops were just minutes from the Green. Bells rang out, drums rolled and the Minute Men, under the command of

Captain John Parker, filed out of the tavern. As the sun rose, they assembled on the Green, more as a protest than looking for a fight. The Tavern looks exactly as it did in 1775, with bar orders chalked on the tap room wall. The front door has a hole in it, allegedly from a bullet shot during the encounter.

From here go to the right of the Green and turn right on Hancock Street. Number 36 is the Hancock-Clarke House, where, at around 1am on April 19, 1775, John Hancock and Samuel Adams were awakened by a knock on the door. Paul Revere had arrived to warn these two important leaders of the patriots' cause that the British were on the march. This 1698 house is furnished as it would have been on that fateful night.

Lexington's First Parish Church

Among the memorabilia you can see Major Pitcairn's pistols (see previous page) and the drums belonging to Minute Man William Drummond.

▶ *Leave Lexington on Massachusetts Avenue and follow it west (where it becomes Battle Road) for 2 miles (3km). Turn right onto* **Route 2A** *and drive to the Minute Man National Historical Park.*

4 Minute Man National Historical Park
Although the actual road followed by the British troops has been largely covered over by Route 2A, a small section has been preserved in the Minute Man National Historical Park. About half a mile (800m) beyond the Visitor Center is the site where Paul Revere was

SPECIAL TO...

The events of April 19, 1775 are re-enacted each year on Patriots' Day. At sunrise, latter-day Minute Men from communities around Concord march through the woods much as their ancestors did. Historically accurate 1775 uniforms are *de rigueur*, both for the "farmers" and the "Redcoats." In a brief but moving ceremony near the Old North Bridge, officials from Britain and America pay their respects to those who died, as the *Last Post* rings out. Later in the day, skirmishes are cheerfully re-enacted, with much rattling of drums and piping of fifes. Nowadays, the holiday falls on the Monday closest to April 19, to make a long weekend.

captured by a British patrol. His fellow messenger, Dr. Samuel Prescott, eluded them and rode on to Concord. In another half mile (800m), a narrow winding section of the original Battle Road bears off to the right. This is a typical "two rod road," named because of the 32-foot (10m) distance between the stone walls on either side of the road (a rod measures 16 feet/ 5m). Here, the William Smith House, the remains of the Hartwell House, and the Ephraim Hartwell Tavern all reflect the style of architecture and the methods of construction used in the buildings of Colonial Massachusetts.

[i] *Minute Man Visitor Center, Route 2A, Lexington*

▶ *Drive to the intersection of Battle Road and **Route 2A**, turn right and continue to Concord.*

🖪 Concord

Concord was founded in 1635, and is redolent with history, from its historic houses (many with date plaques) to its reminders of the Revolution, to its literary heritage.

The approach to the center of Concord is along Lexington Avenue, where two historic properties were once the homes of famous writers. The Wayside, with its distinctive red brick chimneys, was originally the home of the muster master, whose job was to summon the Minute Men if the British attacked. In the 19th century, it became first the residence of the Alcott family, then in 1852, Nathaniel Hawthorne bought it and changed the name from Hillside to The Wayside. He completed *Tanglewood Tales* in his study in the tower at the top of the house.

A little way farther up the street is Orchard House, to which the Alcott family moved after leaving The Wayside. It was here that Louisa May wrote much of *Little Women*. Researchers for the 1992 movie

of the book took photographs and made sketches here, then built a house in Canada especially for the filming. It was not an exact replica, however, and those taking the guided tour may notice a number of differences, particularly in the bedrooms. Carefully preserved furnishings and costumes reflect the family's 20 years here.

Closer to the town center, take a left onto the Concord Turnpike for the Concord Museum. This is a fine example

Orchard House, the home of novelist Louisa May Alcott

of a small museum, and it encompasses all aspects of Concord's history in a particularly engaging way. Relics of the Revolution include Paul Revere's signal lantern and the sword that belonged to Colonel Barrett, commander of the Concord militia. Literary mementos include Louisa May Alcott's tea kettle and doll, Henry David Thoreau's bed, writing desk and rocking chair from his cabin at Walden Pond (see overleaf), and Ralph Waldo Emerson's study, brought from his former home across the street and reconstructed here.

When Emerson's original house was destroyed by fire in 1872, the philosopher-poet's reaction was unusual, to say the least: "But isn't it a lovely blaze!" was all he said. Sent away to recover from the shock, he returned after a year to find that his home had been rebuilt by his friends and neighbors. Emerson's life here was characterized by "plain living and high thinking" but is less remembered for his essays than for quotes such as, "If a man can write a better book, preach a better sermon, or make a better mousetrap than his neighbor, though he builds his house in the woods, the world will beat a path to his door." The reconstructed house is exactly as he left it – except for the study, of course.

Off Concord's Green, along Route 62, is Sleepy Hollow Cemetery, every bit as peaceful as it sounds. Here, on top of "Author's Ridge" are the last resting places of Louisa May Alcott, Ralph Waldo Emerson and Nathaniel Hawthorne. The grave of Henry David Thoreau is marked by a simple headstone, inscribed with only one word: "Henry."

The most famous site in Concord is undoubtedly the Old North Bridge on Liberty Street, the "rude bridge" where, on April 19, 1775, "... the embattled farmers stood, And fired the shot heard round the world." These words are from the *Concord Hymn*, written by Emerson in 1837 to celebrate the completion of the Battle Monument. One of the most powerful American icons, it was sculpted by Daniel Chester French, who also created the figure of Abraham Lincoln for the Lincoln Memorial in Washington D.C.

On the day of the battle, some 400 Minute Men were waiting here to confront the 700

tired and worried British Regulars. As they advanced across the bridge, the famous shot rang out. The sloping fields would have looked much as they do now, though the bridge is a modern replica. Across the river, at the edge of an open field, stands the Old Manse. It was from a window of this three-story wooden house that the parson, William Emerson, watched the bloody events. He was the grandfather of Ralph Waldo Emerson, who lived here as a little boy. In later years the house was rented to Nathaniel Hawthorne, and some of his possessions are still there, including his writing desk.

ⓘ *Concord Chamber of Commerce Visitor Kiosk, Heywood Street; North Bridge Visitor Center, Liberty Street*

▶ *Leave Concord following the sign for **Route 2A**, from the Green. After a short distance, turn right on Heywood Street, then left on Walden Street (**Route 126**). Continue for 1 mile (2km), crossing **Route 2**, to the Walden Pond parking lot.*

⑥ Walden Pond

Henry Thoreau came here and "lived alone, in the woods, a mile from any neighbor, in a house I had built myself, on the shore of Walden Pond." This two-year "back to nature" experience was the basis of his most famous work, *Walden*, published in 1854. Seeking the solitude that he found may be difficult in summer, when families swim and picnic at "this pond ... so remarkable for its depth and purity ... a clear and deep well, half a mile long and a mile and three quarters in circumference ..." A replica of his cabin is conveniently close to the parking lot; to avoid the crowds, walk around to the far side of the water, where a cairn marks the site of the real cabin. The pond is surrounded by the 304-acre (122-hectare) Walden Pond State Reservation.

▶ *Follow **Route 126** south for a short distance to Baker Bridge Road and turn left. At No. 68 is the Gropius House.*

⑦ Gropius House

This is the home of the German architect Walter Gropius, founder of the Bauhaus Movement, who moved to America in 1937 and lectured at Harvard for 14 years. The house was far ahead of its time, combining traditional architecture with the innovative use of modern materials, such as welded steel, glass blocks, and chrome. Its furnishings are also interesting, and the house contains works of modern art.

▶ *Continue to the end of the road and turn right onto Sandy Pond Road. On the left is the DeCordova Museum.*

⑧ DeCordova Museum

Dedicated to the work of contemporary American artists, this museum is located in 35

The Old North Bridge, actually a modern replica

Lexington & Concord

SPECIAL TO...

Around 1845, Concord was the literary epicenter of America, with four of the country's most revered writers living near one another. Ralph Waldo Emerson (1803–82) was a philosopher, poet and magnetic speaker. Today, he is best remembered for the *Concord Hymn*, encapsulating the events of the Old North Bridge (see page 14).

In 1837, he struck up a friendship with Henry Thoreau (1817–62). Thoreau came to live in Concord and spent two years in a small cabin that he constructed himself at the edge of Walden Pond. It was here that he wrote his most memorable book, *Walden*. The Salem-born novelist Nathaniel Hawthorne (1805–64), a Concord resident for a few years, was also part of the group. At that time, though Louisa May Alcott (1832–88) was just a child, she was already writing poems and romantic stories.

acres (14 hectares) of open fields and woods overlooking Sandy Pond. Around 60 sculptures are displayed outside in natural settings, and in summer outdoor jazz concerts are staged here. The museum shop sells original works of art.

▶ *Return to Sandy Pond Road, turn left and drive to the first*

RECOMMENDED TRIPS

Canoes can be rented at the South Bridge Boathouse (on Main Street, Concord) for trips through Concord and the Great Meadows National Wildlife Refuge. Although there are 18 miles (29km) of navigable water, the paddle to the North Bridge and back is an easy two hours and is an excellent way to see parts of the town that haven't changed significantly since the Revolution.

If paddling is not your style, you can take the marked nature trail (3 miles/5km) in the wildlife refuge.

intersection. Cross Lincoln Road, and continue on Trapelo Road for 2½ miles (4km) to Route 128. Go north on Route 128 to Route 2 east, the first exit, and return to Cambridge.

FOR HISTORY BUFFS

"March with the Corps of Grenadiers and Light Infantry ... to Concord, where you will seize and destroy all Artillery, Ammunition, Provisions, Tents, Small Arms, and all Military Stores ... but you will take care that the Soldiers do not plunder the Inhabitants, or hurt private property."

Unfortunately the orders of General Gage were leaked to patriots in Boston and, as the British prepared to cross the Charles River on the night of April 18, two lanterns appeared in the belfry of the Old North Church. A waiting Paul Revere saw the signal and set off on horseback to tell the men of Lexington and Concord to be ready.

The North
Shore

One famous seaport after another follows the curve of the coast north of Boston, from the towns of Gloucester and Marblehead, to Salem and Newburyport. There are hundreds of handsome old houses, and dozens of high-quality museums and art galleries.

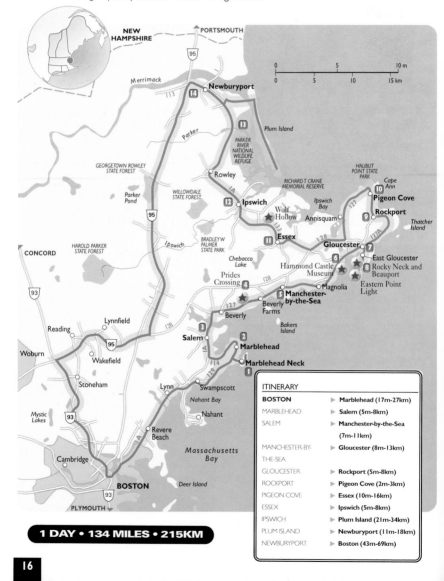

ITINERARY		
BOSTON	▶	**Marblehead** (17m-27km)
MARBLEHEAD	▶	**Salem** (5m-8km)
SALEM	▶	**Manchester-by-the-Sea** (7m-11km)
MANCHESTER-BY-THE-SEA	▶	**Gloucester** (8m-13km)
GLOUCESTER	▶	**Rockport** (5m-8km)
ROCKPORT	▶	**Pigeon Cove** (2m-3km)
PIGEON COVE	▶	**Essex** (10m-16km)
ESSEX	▶	**Ipswich** (5m-8km)
IPSWICH	▶	**Plum Island** (21m-34km)
PLUM ISLAND	▶	**Newburyport** (11m-18km)
NEWBURYPORT	▶	**Boston** (43m-69km)

1 DAY • 134 MILES • 215KM

i *Boston Common Visitor Information Center, 147 Tremont Street*

▶ *Leave Boston via the Callahan Tunnel, and follow **Route 1A** to Lynn. After 8 miles (13km), pass a rotary (roundabout), and bear right onto Carroll Parkway. Follow **Route 129** along the sea wall to Swampscott, and bear right onto Puritan Road, for 1 mile (1.5km) until it rejoins **Route 129**. Go right on **Route 129** to Ocean Avenue and turn right to Marblehead Neck.*

Marblehead attracted fishermen from Cornwall, England, in 1629.

❶ Marblehead Neck

On the road across the causeway, look right for a view of the Boston skyline. To the left, a fleet of sailboats sits anchored in Marblehead harbor. Bear right and follow signs for the Bike Route for about 2 miles (3km) to Chandler Hovey Park and the lighthouse. From the park there are spectacular views all the way to Manchester and Gloucester harbors. Marblehead Neck itself is all quiet residential streets.

▶ *Return to **Route 129** and turn right to Marblehead.*

❷ Marblehead

The up-hill-and-down-dale style of Marblehead's old town reflects the West of England origins of the fishermen who settled here in 1629. On Front Street, the oldest houses cluster round the harbor of what was soon known as the "greatest Towne for fishing in New England." As the seafarers developed a thriving overseas trade, so the merchants built bigger and better houses. Jeremiah Lee Mansion is a fine example: a Georgian mansion, built in 1768 and now home to

the Marblehead Historical Society. Marblehead sailors played a vital role in the Revolution, and a local boat, the *Hannah*, takes pride in being America's first warship. Today luxury yachts fill the moorings.

i *Information Booth, Pleasant and Spring streets*

▶ *Leave Marblehead on **Route 114**, then join **Route 1A North** and drive 5 miles (8km) to Salem.*

❸ Salem

One short period of hysteria in the 17th century singled Salem out from the rest of the North Shore coastal ports. Now, more than 300 years later, witchcraft trials and executions have become big business. Those wanting to relive the gruesome spectacles can visit the Witch Museum, Witch Village and Witch House, but there is much more to see in this historic town. The fine mansions were so impressive that future-president John Adams wrote in 1766: "the houses are the most elegant and grand that I have seen in any of the maritime towns." Examples can be found on Chestnut, Essex and Federal streets.

The Pioneer Village is a re-

Statue of Puritan Roger Conant, who founded Salem in 1626, outside the Salem Witch Museum

created 17th-century fishing village, complete with period homes, gardens, and live animals. Costumed guides show how the early settlers lived, and there is lots of visitor participation.

The Peabody Museum, arguably America's oldest museum, was started in 1799 by a group of sea captains wishing to display their souvenirs from far-flung voyages. The richest and most impressive section is the Asian Export Art Collection which contains beautiful oriental objects, which were made specifically for sale to the West.

The town's nautical traditions are portrayed in the admirable Salem Maritime National Historic Site that snakes along the harbor front.

ⓘ *New Liberty and Essex streets*

FOR HISTORY BUFFS

Salem comes from the Hebrew word *Shalom*, meaning peace. But the calm of Salem was shattered in 1692 when several young girls began to have fits and accused three women of casting spells on them. Panic followed, other accusations were made, and before common sense prevailed, 19 people had been hanged, and one man, Giles Grey, was crushed by rocks. The hysteria was stamped out the following year, when the governor ordered all the "witches" to be released from prison, probably because his wife had been one of the accused!

▶ Take **Route 1A North** across the bridge over Beverly Harbor, and follow **Route 127** through Beverly for 4 miles (6km) to the Prides Crossing railroad station.

❹ Prides Crossing

When the railroad from Beverly was extended to Manchester in 1840, it crossed land once owned by the Pride family, who supposedly received the grant in the early 1700s from the King of England. The route was used by wealthy Bostonians who left the city and came out to spend the summers by the water in their large mansions. The railroad depot still has separate benches marked for use by Democrats and Republicans. Now, residents of this small village make the trip in and out of Boston every day by car.

▶ Continue on **Route 127** for 3 miles (5km) into the center of Manchester-by-the-Sea.

❺ Manchester-by-the-Sea

Originally settled by Englishmen from Manchester, the town's name was amended recently to emphasize its position at the head of a pretty harbor, graced with its flotilla of sailboats. On one side of the town square is First Parish Church, built in 1807, with a clock face on each side of its distinctive steeple. Visitors come in summer, not just to walk along the waterfront, but also to spend the day on Singing Beach, where the wind "sings" as it whistles along the sand.

▶ *Continue on **Route 127** for 3 miles (5km), then bear right for Magnolia. Continue for 2 miles (3km) through the town center and up the hill on Norman Avenue to Hammond Castle.*

6 Hammond Castle Museum

Whenever you use a remote control button to switch television channels or open the garage from your car, the man to thank is Dr. John Hammond (1888–1965). This genius thought up over 800 inventions and was granted 400 patents, mainly to do with electronics. His quirky mind is reflected in the clifftop mansion he built in 1926, which incorporates bits of European buildings: there is an archway built with lava rock from Mount Vesuvius, and a Roman bath. There are even secret passages and a laboratory. His vast 8,200-pipe organ stands in an impressive hall where concerts are given at weekends. Hammond is buried on the grounds with two of his cats and, as requested, poison ivy grows over his grave.

▶ *Return to **Route 127** and continue for 2 miles (3km) to Gloucester.*

7 Gloucester

The first landmark in town to meet your eye is *The Man at the Wheel*, the statue of a ship's pilot staring out towards the mouth of the harbor. The statue was set in place in 1923 to commemorate Gloucester's 300th birthday, and as a reminder that the town continues to be a working port, America's oldest. Although fishing boats still chug in, ready to sell their catch, the fleet has decreased in recent years.

However, the maritime tradition attracts tourists, not just for the annual Schooner Festival in early September, but throughout the summer for whale-watching excursions. The Cape Ann Historical Museum is a tribute to artist Fitz Hugh Lane, who lived out his life here. Not surprisingly, he specialized in seascapes.

i *Stage Fort Park Information Center, Hough Avenue*

FOR CHILDREN

A great way to take children sightseeing in Gloucester is on a Moby Duck tour. Amphibious vehicles transport you around land-based attractions then plunge straight into the water to explore the maritime sights of this famous seafaring town. Children will also enjoy a tour of the schooner *Adventure*, moored in the harbor. A national historic landmark, it was the town's last fishing schooner.

SPECIAL TO...

There really was a Cap'n Birdseye. As early as 1912, Clarence Birdseye of Gloucester was intrigued to see how the Inuit people of Labrador preserved their food by freezing it. By 1924, he had perfected the bulk deep-freezing technique that is taken for granted today. The Freezing Company concentrated on fruit and vegetables in the early days, but as demand for his products grew, Birdseye needed to speed up the process, so he invented the multiple plate freezer, which is still used. In the 1950s, the company developed fish sticks, or fish fingers, a great favorite with children.

The pier at Gloucester
Inset: *The Man at the Wheel*

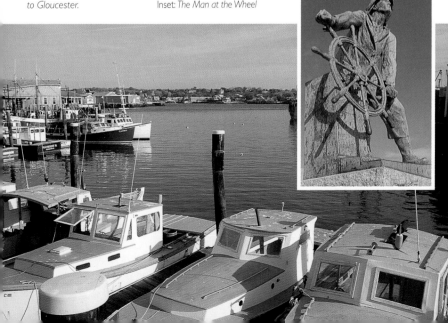

WHALEWATCHING...

Up and down the coast of New England, boats still set off to hunt for whales. Unlike the 19th century, however, the purpose is not to shoot the majestic mammals with harpoons, but with cameras. Tours depart regularly from Boston, but they also leave from Salem and Gloucester on the North Shore, from Portsmouth, New Hampshire and from Cape Cod towns such as Provincetown. The favorite places for spotting whales are the Stellwagen Bank and Jeffreys Ledge, both popular feeding grounds. Harbor porpoises and Atlantic white-sided dolphins, relatives of the whales, are also abundant, and have teeth rather than the baleen plates of the whales.

RIGHT WHALES

Named by Yankee whalers, because they were the "right" whales to catch, this is the most endangered species in the world. The whales are easily recognized by the callosities, crusty growths, on their backs. Reaching up to 50 feet and 60 tons (16m and 61,000kg), they can be spotted offshore from April to January.

HUMPBACK WHALES

The name comes from their habit of arching their backs before diving. They are also known to "breach," leaping clear out of the water, a particularly impressive sight, since humpbacks grow up to 50 feet (16m) long and 30 tons (30,500kg) in weight. They are resident off New England from spring to fall.

FIN WHALES

The largest whales in New England waters are also the most common. Reaching 70 feet (21m) in length and 50 tons (51,000kg), fin whales can be identified by their dorsal fin, as well as the white chevron on their backs. Like the humpbacks, they are resident from spring to fall.

SPECIAL TO...

May 22 is Motif No. 1 Day in Rockport. It celebrates an old fishing shack, dating from the mid-1800s, that stands at the end of Bradley Wharf in Rockport Harbor. Local lore has it that, back in the 1920s, art teacher Lester Hornby was confronted by yet another student's sketch of this dark red hut, festooned with lobster traps and colorful lobster floats. "What? Motif number one again!" he exclaimed despairingly to the pupil. Would-be photographers and painters should walk to the end of the wharf to compose their own version of this picturesque icon.

▶ Follow **Route 127** for 1 mile (2km), then bear right onto East Main Street for Rocky Neck.

8 Rocky Neck and Beauport

Rocky Neck is a small settlement of working artists. The oldest such colony in the country, it has survived here since 1916. Some 30 people live on the tiny peninsula, with their studios in wood-shingled shacks. The roads are all one-way, narrow, and busy on weekends.

Further towards Eastern Point lighthouse is Beauport. From the turn of the century, big spenders such as R. T. Vanderbilt and J. D. Rockefeller, as well as such stars as Joan Crawford, came out here to consult Henry Davis Sleeper (1878–1934), *the* interior decora-

Rockport's harbor epitomizes coastal New England

tor of his day. In Beauport, his own summer home, he gave each of the 40 rooms a design theme, from the Lord Byron and Paul Revere Rooms to the China Trade and India Rooms. The house is now a museum, full of his collection of antiques and art.

▶ Return to Gloucester and follow signs for **Alternate Route 127A** to Rockport.

9 Rockport

As its name implies, Rockport's early fame was founded on rock, in particular the granite quarried for many of America's 19th-century monuments, bridges, and civic buildings. For the past century, however, Rockport has been better known for its artists' colony and the town is full of galleries and craft shops exhibiting their work, principally the Rockport Art Association's galleries on Main Street.

The heart of the action in this popular resort is Bearskin Neck, where old fishing lofts have been turned into studios and galleries, restaurants and shops selling souvenirs.

Despite this bohemian air, Rockport is "dry," so no liquor may be sold. Years before Prohibition, Hannah Jumper led 200 women of Rockport in the Hatchet Gang Raid of 1856. These militant teetotallers imposed their own ban on booze by smashing every cask, bottle, and flask they could find, and the men of Rockport haven't had the courage to ask for a drop ever since. Visitors need not despair: drinks may be enjoyed with a seafood meal – as long as diners bring their own bottles.

ⓘ Upper Main Street

▶ Leave town, rejoining **Route 127**, and follow signs for Pigeon Cove (2 miles/3km).

10 Pigeon Cove

Just off Route 127, this small community boasts an unusual building. At No. 52 Pigeon Hill Street stands the Paper House, built between 1922 and 1942 by Elis Stenman and his family. It took two decades and both the house and the furniture have been constructed out of 100,000 old newspapers. The walls are 215 sheets thick, the desk is made from the Christian Science Monitor, and a bookshelf uses only foreign papers!

▶ Continue on **Route 127** and after 1 mile (1.6km) is the turning for Halibut Point State Park. **Route 127** continues past rocky points of land and art galleries to the rotary (round-about) at **Route 128**. Go west on **Route 128**, then turn right onto **Route 133** west for Essex.

⓫ Essex

The 40 or so antique shops that line Main Street in this small, sleepy-looking town draw dealers and amateurs from all over America for the quality and excellent value of their wares. The small Shipbuilding Museum, also on Main Street, recalls the town's heyday in the days of sail.

SPECIAL TO...

Woodmans of Essex is credited with inventing fried clams back in 1916, and is still one of the best-known clam shacks in New England. "Woodie's" is known for serving fresh, delicious fried clams, clam cakes, and New England clam chowder made with milk, butter, lots of potatoes, and clams.

▶ Continue to Ipswich. **Route 133** north joins **Route 1A**.

⓬ Ipswich

Ipswich has several fine houses, particularly the 1640 John Whipple House, one of the oldest Puritan homes still standing, and the John Heard House. This Federal-style mansion retains its period furnishings and has collections of art, toys, carriages and sleighs.

Out of town, some 6 miles (10km) along Argilla Road, is the home of Chicago industrialist Richard T. Crane, on the crest of Castle Hill. This 59-room Great

House recalls the stately homes of England, with its 63-foot (18.9m) long gallery and 16-foot (4.8m) high ceilings. It is open for tours, and there are also concerts and an antique auto show on the grounds each summer. Down below, the 5-mile (8km) long beach is one of the most beautiful north of Cape Cod. Beware of the three weeks at the end of July and early August when the voracious, biting "greenhead" flies take over the strand.

▶ Continue north on **Route 133** and **Route 1A** for 11 miles (18km) to Hanover Street. Turn right for Plum Island and the Parker Refuge.

BACK TO NATURE

Located one mile north of the turn-off to Crane's Beach on Route 133, Wolf Hollow is home to 17 North American wolves. After listening to a presentation about this nearly extinct animal, visitors can watch the wolves as they respond to commands from their trainers. Fear not, for although they are at close range, a strong fence separates observers from the observed.

⓭ Plum Island and the Parker River National Wildlife Refuge

With its vast expanse of salt marsh, this is a major stopping point for birds migrating north and south each year. Early spring and late fall are the ideal times to see some of the 300 species. Stand on the observation platform built along the roads to observe cranes, herons and Canada geese.

Plum Island, first visited by Samuel de Champlain in 1601, is a 6-mile (10km) long beach that acts as a breakwater to the coastal towns. Stop on the access road and follow the boardwalks across the dunes, but remember that swimming is dangerous here because of the cold water and the strong undertows.

▶ Return to **Route 1A** and continue into Newburyport.

⓮ Newburyport

As in so many New England towns, the charming wooden houses of Colonial times were destroyed by fire and have been rebuilt in brick. A renovation program in the 1970s and 1980s tidied up the rundown sea front and restored the line-up of fine Federal and Greek Revival architecture. Now this ship-building town at the mouth of the Merrimack River is an attractive, if busy, place to spend time. The Custom House on Water Street is given over to a museum of all things maritime, including a re-creation of a ship's bridge.

Two centuries ago, the town commissioned Charles Bulfinch, the architect of the State House in Boston, to design the Courthouse on High Street. This street is often called "sea captain row," with mansions such as the three-story Cushing House, built in 1808 by John Cushing. His son, Caleb, was the first emissary sent by the United States to China, and his collection of fine porcelain, paintings, and cabinetware from China fills the 21 rooms.

ⓘ Merrimac Street

▶ Leave on High Street (**Route 113**) and follow signs to I–95 south and **Route 128**. (Do not take **Route 1**.) Take I–95 south, then west. After about 30 miles (48km), turn south onto I–93 for Boston.

RECOMMENDED WALKS

Halibut Point State Park is a delightful place to stop and stretch your legs, with well-maintained nature and walking trails. The point is not named for fish; it was originally called "Haul About Point" because sailing ships had to "come about" here and tack to sail around Cape Ann.

Cape Cod

2 DAYS • 241 MILES • 387KM

This 62-mile (100km) long peninsula is one of the country's eminent vacation playgrounds. Route 6A, the Old King's Highway, passes through 300-year-old communities where every other house seems to be a craft shop, antique store or bed and breakfast.

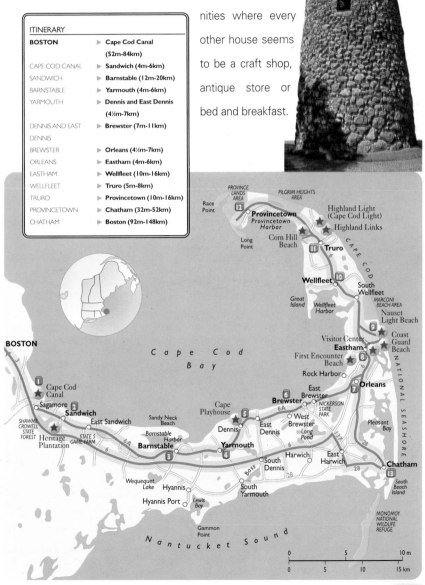

Fine example of Sandwich's famous glass, highly valued by collectors Page 23: Scargo Hill Observatory

ⓘ *Cape Cod Chamber of Commerce, Hyannis*

▶ *Leave Boston on* **Route 93**; *take* **Route 3** *south to the Sagamore Bridge, crossing the Cape Cod Canal.*

❶ Cape Cod Canal
Sailing from Boston around the outside of Cape Cod has always been dangerous. Indeed, even just a century ago, some 25 ships a year foundered on the 135-mile (216km) journey. Traders welcomed the opening of the canal in 1914, 300 years after Myles Standish of the Plymouth Colony first proposed the idea. Running 17 miles (28km) from Cape Cod Bay to Buzzard's Bay, the Canal is 160 yards (150m) wide. Nowadays, recreational yachtsmen take the short cut, watched by fishermen and cyclists on the Cape Cod Canal Bikepath.

ⓘ *70 Main Street, Buzzards Bay*

▶ *Now on* **Route 6A**, *continue to Sandwich (4miles/6km).*

❷ Sandwich
Sandwich reeks of old-world charm, due to its fine collection of 18th- and 19th-century houses, the Wren-like spire on the First Church of Christ, and tree-lined streets. Overlooking Shawme Pond is shingled Dexter Grist Mill, still in working order, and one of the oldest houses on the Cape, the 1654 Hoxie House. In classic "salt box" style, with diamond window panes, it contains 17th-century furniture, tools, and tableware inside. The Eldred House, next door, is now a museum dedicated to the children's author Thornton W. Burgess, best remembered for his *Peter Cottontail* stories. Despite its 300 years of history, however, Sandwich is no living museum: its lobster boats are

actually working vessels, handled by real fishermen.

▶ *Continue on* **Route 6A** *to Barnstable (12½ miles/20km).*

❸ Barnstable
Off the road to the left, 4 miles (6km) before Barnstable, Sandy Neck is a rich nature reserve where the dunes were trampled by U.S. soldiers training for the North African Desert campaign during World War II. When a north wind blows, watch for windsurfers skimming across Barnstable Harbor.

In town, drop into the Sturgis Library to see the original home of the Reverend John Lothrop, one of the first residents of the 1639 settlement. The library's genealogical records are useful for those searching out family roots, especially if they are descended from the Lothrops, who occupy much of the cemetery. The main industries in the 19th century were growing cranberries, and making bricks, some of which are now collector's items.

▶ *Continue on* **Route 6A** *to Yarmouth.*

4 Yarmouth

The Captain Bangs Hallet House reflects the affluence and sophistication of a successful sea captain's life in the 19th century. Situated near the Yarmouthport Post Office, its handsome Greek Revival façade hides the original 1740 structure. It is now the headquarters of the local historical society, and the starting point for pleasant walks through a nature preserve along the Botanic Trails of Yarmouth.

The 1680 Thatcher House and the 1780 Winslow-Crocker House next door, now run by the Society for the Preservation of New England Antiquities, are filled with high-quality furniture and household objects made in Colonial and Federal times by New England craftsmen.

i Yarmouth Area Chamber of Commerce, 657 Route 28, East Yarmouth

▶ Continue on **Route 6A** to Dennis and East Dennis.

5 Dennis and East Dennis

Few men can match Josiah Dennis' claim of having five villages named for him. This 17th-century Congregational minister is immortalized in East, West and South Dennis, as well as Dennisport and Dennis. In his home, the Josiah Dennis Manse, visitors can see his portable pulpit, watch weavers at work and browse round the small maritime museum. There is a 200-year-old schoolhouse on the grounds.

Not quite as ancient, but still the oldest summer theater in the U.S.A., is the Cape Playhouse, where Bette Davis worked as an usherette. Gregory Peck and Henry Fonda also started their acting careers here. Don't miss the Cape Museum of Fine Arts in the grounds, or the church-like building nearby which is actually an art deco cinema, complete with leather seats and a mural by 20th-century American artist Rockwell Kent.

Take time to see the lie of the land from the Scargo Hill

Observatory where, on a good day, you can see Provincetown, 20 miles (32km) to the north.

i Dennis Chamber of Commerce, Junction Routes 134 and 28, West Dennis

▶ Continue on **Route 6A** to Brewster (7 miles/11km).

6 Brewster

On and behind Route 6A, which doubles as Main Street in Brewster, stand the elegant clapboard houses of 19th-century sea captains. At the height of New England's trading with China, as many as 100 lived here, and many are buried in the graveyard next to the "Captains' Church," the First Parish Church. Memories and records of that era are in the Brewster Historical Society Museum at Spruce Hill, East Brewster.

Other museums worth a visit include the New England Fire and History Museum, which has a unique 1929 Mercedes-Benz fire engine, and reconstructions

You can watch the process of corn being ground at Brewster

FOR CHILDREN

The Cape Cod Museum of Natural History at Brewster is popular for its aquarium and lively exhibitions, lectures and tours explaining the Cape's bird and animal life. As well as two short trails in the wildlife sanctuary, the longer John Wing Trail is a fine walk to the unspoiled beach. Remember, though, to check times of tides before setting out. The museum also organizes nature trips by boat to the Monomoy Islands, a wildlife refuge off Chatham.

of a blacksmith's and an apothecary's. More souvenirs of yesteryear include the old Post Office and Barbershop at the 200-year-old windmill at West Brewster.

i Brewster Chamber of Commerce, Town Hall

BACK TO NATURE

The alewife, a type of herring, spawns in fresh water every three or four years. In spring, these silvery fish swim up the narrow Stony Brook creek, using the fish ladder to bypass the water-powered Grist Mill on Stony Brook Road, just north of Brewster, off Route 6A, and return to the ponds where they were conceived.

▶ *Continue on **Route 6A** to the Orleans roundabout.*

7 Orleans

The name rhymes with "beans," even though it commemorates the French Duke of Orléans, who fled here from the French Revolution in 1797. This busy town has been the "hub of the Outer Cape" for two centuries. Back then fish, and salt for preserving the catch, were shipped direct to Boston from tiny Rock Harbor on Cape Cod Bay.

▶ *Continue north for 4 miles (6km) on what is now **Route 6** to Eastham. Just before the town, the road to Fort Hill, on the right, provides panoramic views above the cupola-crowned Victorian house of whaling captain Edward Penniman.*

8 Eastham

The windmill opposite the Town Hall in Eastham, pronounced East-Ham, was built in Plymouth in 1688, rebuilt in Truro, then moved to its present site in 1808. The oldest windmill on the Cape, it is celebrated on Windmill Weekend in September. Samoset Road leads to Cape Cod Bay. Here, First Encounter Beach is the legendary site of the first meeting between the Pilgrims and the Native Americans. A metal plaque explains how arrows and musket fire were exchanged when the newcomers encountered the Indians, who remembered a slave trader kidnapping some of their people six years before. Don't expect to find any arrow-heads, though; the Pilgrims gathered up the arrows and sent them back to England as curiosities.

From here to Provincetown, the Cape is a landscape of steep dunes tufted with grass. On the Atlantic side, breakers pound the flat beaches while light-houses emphasize the sense of solitude.

At the Salt Pond Visitor Center, beyond Eastham, displays and films explain the ecology and wildlife of the 27,000-acre (10,900-hectare) Cape Cod National Seashore, a stretch of unspoiled coastline some 40 miles long (64km). A road leads to Coast Guard Beach where, in 1929, Henry Beston spent a year writing his classic nature journal, *The Outermost House*. The book is evocative, and perhaps more readable than Henry Thoreau's *Walden*. The beach is superb.

Eye-catching façade on Cape Cod

The Nauset Light serves as a reminder of the region's sea-faring heritage

Eastham Information Center, Route 6

▶ *Detour east to Coast Guard Beach, on Doane Road, then turn left on Ocean View Drive to Nauset Light Beach.*

SPECIAL TO...

The local Indians taught the Pilgrims how to cook shellfish and New Englanders still use the same method for a clambake on the beach. Dig a shallow pit into the sand, line it with stones and build a wood fire. When the wood has burned down, cover the hot stones with layers of damp seaweed, clean clams, more seaweed, corn on the cob and bluefish. Seal with a tarpaulin. Leave for an hour to steam, then uncover and eat.

9 Nauset Light Beach

As you drive through the typical scrub oak and pine that is the natural vegetation of Cape Cod, you will catch glimpses of the ocean to the right. You can venture down to a stretch of seemingly unending sandy beach, where the Atlantic waves thunder in, and you can get away from other people simply by taking a walk.

SCENIC ROUTES

The Cape Cod Central Railroad, complete with commentary, runs by cranberry bogs and marshes between Hyannis and the Cape Cod Canal. This should not be confused with the Cape Cod Rail Trail, where there is no longer a train. The Rail Trail follows the former Boston to Provincetown railroad route between South Dennis and Wellfleet. Here, the bed has been replaced by a smooth, 25-mile (40km) path. Its flatness makes it ideal for joggers, hikers, and cyclists.

▶ *Loop back to **Route 6** via Cable Road and Nauset Road to Wellfleet (7 miles/11km).*

10 Wellfleet

Famous for its oysters since Samuel de Champlain's Gallic taste-buds were tickled in 1606, this charming town, complete with picturesque harbor and photogenic old houses, now attracts artists, whose number is so great that their works fill its 22 art galleries. Fishing still goes

Wellfleet was once a Colonial whaling and cod fishing port

on, and the clock on the First Congregational Church reflects Wellfleet's nautical tradition by following ships' time, confusing landlubbers considerably by chiming, for example, two bells at one, five and nine o'clock. It is reportedly the only clock in the world to do so.

i *Wellfleet Chamber of Commerce, off Route 6, South Wellfleet*

FOR HISTORY BUFFS

"...I extend on behalf of the American people most cordial greetings and good wishes to you and all the people of the British Empire." President Theodore Roosevelt's trans-atlantic message to King Edward VII of England in 1903 was the first sent from Guglielmo Marconi's Wireless Telegraph Station in South Wellfleet.

At Orleans, the French Cable Station had already linked up with Brest in France in 1891. The stations were situated here because the Cape is one of the closest parts of the U.S. to Europe.

RECOMMENDED WALKS

The Great Island Trail is an 8-mile (13km) round-trip walk along a narrow spit of sand. The trail is covered at high tide, and has views up to Provincetown and down to Brewster. To get there, follow Holbrook Avenue from Wellfleet Center. Turn right on to Chequesset Road and drive past the dunes and salt ponds to the parking lot.

▶ Continue north on **Route 6** for 5 miles (8km) to Truro.

🕚 Truro

Originally named Dangerfield, this is a small, quiet neighbor-hood. On the way to North Truro, the Highland or Cape Cod Light is on South Highland Road. Standing on the site of the Cape's first lighthouse (1791), it has been damaged and restored, moved and rebuilt. The oldest golf course on the Cape, Highland Links, is nearby.

Back on Route 6, turn down Corn Hill Road for Corn Hill Beach where, in the parking lot, is a little taste of Pilgrim lore. Soon after the Pilgrim Father's arrival, Captain Myles Standish came across a cache of corn buried by an Indian in the sand. Desperate for food, he took it, but on meeting with the owner about a year later, Standish repaid him what was owed.

Further north, park the car and hike the short Pilgrim Spring Trail to the spot where legend has it that the Pilgrim Fathers first found "springs of fresh water" after their grueling transatlantic crossing.

▶ Continue north on **Route 6** to Provincetown (10 miles/16km).

🕛 Provincetown

Although the Vikings are reck-oned to have landed here long before, in AD 1004, this is where it all started for the Americans on November 11 or 21, 1620, depending on which calendar you use. The *Mayflower* dropped anchor in what is now Provincetown Harbor, after a 65-day voyage. Of the 102 passen-gers, one had died, but a baby had been born. Myles Standish, a soldier of fortune hired by the Pilgrims for protection, rowed ashore. These days, a rather unimpressive plaque on Commercial Street marks the event. After five weeks, the Pilgrims continued on their way, hoping to find a more hospitable site for settlement. They are remembered with the Pilgrim Monument, found in the center of town. Built in 1910, the gran-ite tower soars 252 feet (76m) high. The stairs are a real test of stamina, but climbers can read the plaques noting the founding dates of Massachusetts towns and *Mayflower* descendants. The reward is the observation plat-form at the top. The museum at the base tells the story of Provincetown.

The town's main industry of deep-water fishing for cod, mackerel and whales was estab-lished in the early 18th century. Although the fishing heyday passed over a century ago, 35 boats still go out each morning to supply New York and Boston with fresh fish, and whale watch-ing is a popular excursion in wintertime.

Today, in Provincetown, known almost universally as P-town, the fun begins after the day-trippers have gone home. Artists have been coming here since Charles Hawthorne arrived in 1899. He taught for 30 years and his painting, *Fish Cleaners*, can be seen in the Town Hall.

Edward Hopper and Jackson Pollock are among the famous who joined the amateurs, working in the dazzling light on the shore. Playwright Eugene O'Neill wrote and produced his earliest plays in what was, and still is, a surprisingly bohemian town where everyone comes to have a good time.

[i] *307 Commercial Street*

▶ *Return on Route 6, but before the Orleans rotary (round-about), turn off on Route 28 for Chatham (32 miles/52km).*

13 Chatham
Sitting right on Cape Cod's "elbow," Chatham relies on more than just tourism, thanks to its busy fishing fleet. The bounty of the sea is represented by the striking 1992 sculpture *Provider* on Fish Pier. Here, each afternoon, crates of flounder and

haddock, cod and halibut are transferred straight from the boats to waiting trucks. Take a walk along Main Street, with its clapboard houses, restaurants, shops, and 175-year-old Mayo House, the headquarters of the local historical society. Train buffs should head for the Railroad Museum in the 1887 depot, where there is a diorama of the railroad yard as it was in 1920.

[i] *533 Main Street*

▶ *Take Route 28 out of Chatham. Turn north on Route 137 and rejoin Route 6 at Exit 11. Follow Route 6 back to the Sagamore Bridge, then Route 3 to Route 93 and back to Boston.*

Provincetown, overlooked by the Center Methodist Church
Inset: cranberries at Plymouth

2 DAYS • 181½ MILES • 292KM

The Berkshire
Hills

The Berkshires were once the exclusive playground of the rich. Now these forested slopes are a vacation destination for everyone, particularly music lovers who are drawn to the numerous summer festivals.

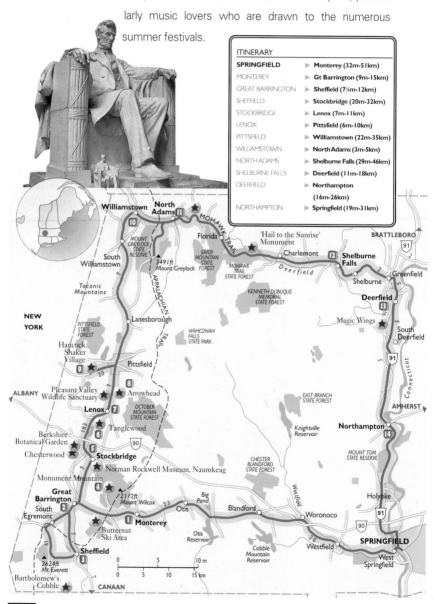

ITINERARY

SPRINGFIELD	▶	**Monterey (32m-51km)**
MONTEREY	▶	**Gt Barrington (9m-15km)**
GREAT BARRINGTON	▶	**Sheffield (7½m-12km)**
SHEFFIELD	▶	**Stockbridge (20m-32km)**
STOCKBRIDGE	▶	**Lenox (7m-11km)**
LENOX	▶	**Pittsfield (6m-10km)**
PITTSFIELD	▶	**Williamstown (22m-35km)**
WILLIAMSTOWN	▶	**North Adams (3m-5km)**
NORTH ADAMS	▶	**Shelburne Falls (29m-46km)**
SHELBURNE FALLS	▶	**Deerfield (11m-18km)**
DEERFIELD	▶	**Northampton (16m-26km)**
NORTHAMPTON	▶	**Springfield (19m-31km)**

*ℹ 1441 Main Street, Springfield;
Riverfront Park Information Center,
West Columbus Avenue*

SPECIAL TO...

Basketball was invented in
Springfield, and the town
boasts the Basketball Hall of
Fame. Desperate to exercise
bored young men during the
winter of 1891, Dr. James
Naismith nailed up a couple of
peach baskets in the gymnasium of the Springfield YMCA
and tossed them a soccer ball.
Basketball was born. At first,
the players had to put up a ladder to retrieve the ball every
time there was a score. Then
someone had a brilliant idea:
remove the bottom of the baskets. First accepted at the 1936
Olympics, basketball has
become the world's most
popular indoor sport.

FOR CHILDREN

South of Springfield on Route
159, the former Riverside Park
has been transformed by a
multimillion-dollar investment
into the Six Flags New England
theme park. It has terrifying
roller-coasters and free-fall
drop rides, the gentler Poison
Ivy Twisted Train and Loony
Tunes rides for younger
children, a spectacular Batman
show, a Bugs Bunny musical
and lots more to keep the
whole family happy all day.

▶ *From Springfield, take Route
20 west across the
Connecticut River, through
West Springfield, passing the
Exposition grounds, site of the
huge "Big E," New England's
largest fair, held every
September. Bear left on Route
23 west at Woronoco. Drive
through Blandford and Otis to
Monterey.*

❶ Monterey
The Mexican name of this town
honors General Zachary Taylor, a
hero in the Mexican-American
War (1846–8). So popular was
"Old Rough and Ready" Taylor
after his victories at Monterey
and Buena Vista, that one
Kentuckian predicted (correctly)
that the general would win the
1848 presidential election "by
spontaneous combustion." Born
in Virginia, Taylor had no known
connections with the village.

▶ *Continue on Route 23, past
the Butternut Ski Area.*

❷ Great Barrington
Local inventor William Stanley
assured that this small town
would have its place in the
history books. He first demon-
strated the potential of using
alternating current here in 1886
by lighting up 24 shops on the
main street. Stanley's system,
more efficient than Edison's
cumbersome direct current
lighting, led to more widespread
use of electricity. A lamp and
plaque in the small park at the
corner of Main and Cottage
streets tells the story.

On five Saturdays in summer,
St. James Church hosts the
Aston Magna Festival. It is the
oldest festival in America
devoted to baroque, classical and
early romantic music, all played
on period instruments.

▶ *Leave town on Route 7 and
head south for 7½ miles
(12km) to Sheffield.*

❸ Sheffield
Back in the 18th century, two
minor events helped shape

Monterey's One Room School
Opposite: Abraham Lincoln's
statue, Chesterwood Studio

BACK TO NATURE

About 1½ miles (2km) south of Sheffield, is one of several small, flat-topped hills known locally as "cobbles." Barthlomew's Cobble is a 500-million-year-old lump of limestone and quartzite, doubling as a nature reserve. The Ledges Interpretative Trail (20 minutes) winds through rugged, glacially formed rocks. Here, some 45 species of fern, many of them rare, grow in the summer. A small museum records some of the 900 types of plants and wildlife in the area.

American democracy. In 1773, the Sheffield Declaration demanded freedom for the individual, while in 1787, Shays' Rebellion ended here. Poor farmers, many of them Revolutionary War veterans, thought they were being overtaxed and rebelled under Captain Daniel Shays. The seven-month protest brought the end of imprisonment for debt, and also strengthened the case for federal and state laws. A century or so ago, local people carved a large slab of marble into a monument honoring the rebellion. It stands in a field north of the town. Today, antique shops line the main street.

▶ *Leave Sheffield west on Berkshire School Road to* **Route**

FOR HISTORY BUFFS

The charming wooden Ashley House in Sheffield is named after Colonel John Ashley who campaigned for The Sheffield Declaration of equal rights in the late 18th century. His slave, Mum Bet, is better remembered, since she used her master's arguments to gain her own freedom in 1783. The woodwork and paneling in Ashley's upstairs study show the skill of the craftsmen who built the house in 1735.

41 and turn north. Join **Route 23** *and take it through South Egremont to Great Barrington. Rejoin* **Route 7** *and head north to Monument Mountain.*

4 Monument Mountain

This jumble of huge boulders has long been a favorite for picnickers and hikers. Back in 1850, two of New England's best-known authors, Herman Melville and Nathaniel Hawthorne, first met here. Caught in a thunderstorm, they took shelter, drank champagne with their companions, and listened to a recitation of *The Story of the Indian Girl*. The poem relates the local legend of a love-lorn girl who leapt to her death from this mountain.

RECOMMENDED WALKS

Two trails lead to Squaw Peak, the 1,735-foot (520m) summit of Monument Mountain. The easier trail takes about an hour; follow the sign for Indian Monument. The longer hike (3 miles/5km) climbs through oaks, white pines, laurels and chestnuts, revealing mysterious caves under overhanging rocks and rushing streams. A fine view can be had from the top.

▶ *Continue north on* **Route 7** *to Stockbridge.*

5 Stockbridge

Stockbridge was created in 1722 as a well-meaning experiment by the London Society for the Propagation of the Gospel in Foreign Lands. The local Indians were invited to settle alongside the English colonists in the hope that they would become "civilized," and follow Christian and English customs. Despite the support given by the Indians during the Revolutionary War, the Colonial ambitions of the settlers put an end to the experiment.

Even today, the Berkshires remains picture-postcard pretty, with tall maples and elms. There isn't a telephone or electricity pole in sight, all the cables have been buried underground. The Red Lion Inn is the heart of the town, as it has always been since pre-Revolutionary days. Although this old coaching inn burned down last century, the Victorian replacement retains the wide porches, with rocking chairs for watching life pass by.

Installed in the old Linwood estate, the Norman Rockwell Museum has 600 of the illustrator's works, and contains his studio, which was moved here lock, stock, palette, and paintbrush. Rockwell's *Saturday*

Norman Rockwell's studio, in Stockbridge

Evening Post magazine covers made him a household name, and all 321 are here. Freckle-faced boys, cuddly grannies and Thanksgiving turkeys all appear bathed in the glow of nostalgia.

Near by is Chesterwood, the summer home and studio of sculptor Daniel Chester French. The best known of his 1,000 works on display are national symbols: the solemn, seated figure of Abraham Lincoln in the Lincoln Memorial in Washington D.C. and *The Minute Man* statue at the Old North Bridge in Concord, Massachusetts.

Besides attracting artists, the Berkshires became a resort for turn-of-the-century millionaires. Up Prospect Hill is Naumkeag, the Choate family's magnificent estate. The 23-room mansion vies for attention with the land-scaping. The birch walk alone is worth the entrance fee.

As you leave Stockbridge to continue the itinerary, look for the Berkshire Botanical Garden, 2 miles (3km) out of town at the junction of Routes 183 and 102. One of the oldest botanical gardens in the U.S., it is a beauti-ful and relaxing place to visit, with 15 acres (6 hectares) of colorful landscaped gardens that include water features, annual and perennial beds, vegetable plots, a children's garden and a woodland trail.

ℹ️ *Main Street*

▶ *Leave town on* **Route 102** *west. Turn right on* **Route 183** *north at the Berkshire Botanical Garden and continue north for 6 miles (10km) to Tanglewood.*

6 Tanglewood

The former country estate of the Tappan family is now synony-mous with music. Although the New York Symphony first performed here in 1934, it is the Boston Symphony Orchestra that has made Tanglewood its summer home since 1936. Over the years, millions have come to picnic on the grounds before listening to concerts in the 6,000-seat Koussevitzky Music Shed. Great conductors such as Leonard Bernstein and Seiii Ozawa have directed here. In 1994, the 1,200-seat Seija Ozawa Hall was added: the rear wall opens on to a grassy hillside. Jazz, folk and pop are also on the program, along with recitals by students from the prestigious Tanglewood summer music school. Also in the grounds is a reproduction of author Nathaniel Hawthorne's Little Red House, the summer cottage where he wrote *The Tanglewood Tales* and *The House of the Seven Gables*.

▶ *Follow* **Route 183** *to Lenox.*

7 Lenox

Because of the film *The Age of Innocence*, there has been renewed interest in the Pulitzer Prize-winning writer Edith Wharton (1862–1937). Visitors come to this attractive town which was the haunt of some of America's richest families more than a century ago. The Vanderbilts, Carnegies, and other stars of New York's upper crust summered in what they referred to as "Berkshire cottages." Some of these grand estates still exist, others are charming small hotels such as the Wheatleigh and the Blantyre. The Mount, Wharton's 35-room mansion, was built to

---

> ### SPECIAL TO...
>
> The 1969 film, *Alice's Restaurant*, was based on an incident that has become a leg-end. After folk singer Arlo Guthrie and friends had enjoyed their Thanksgiving dinner in an old church in Housatonic, they deposited the leftovers outside the Stockbridge town dump. Guthrie was arrested by Officer Obie, and ended up in jail. The conviction meant that Guthrie, a Vietnam protester, could not be drafted for the war. As for Alice and her restaurant, she had several in the area; one is now Naji's, off Stockbridge's Main Street.

Tanglewood's 1,200-seat Seiji Ozawa Hall

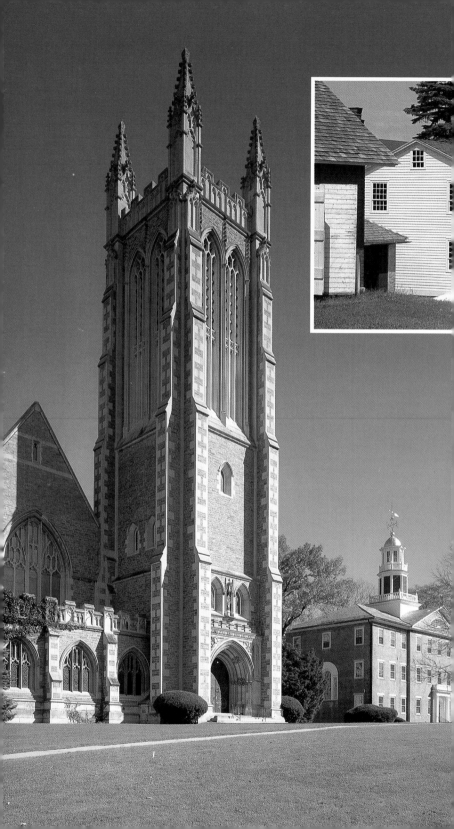

Williamstown's Gothic cathedral
Inset: Hancock Shaker Village

her own rigid specifications. She spent her happiest years here (1902–11), writing such novels as *Ethan Frome* in bed each morning. She delighted in looking east over the "outdoor rooms," the splendid gardens, and the pond that she designed. The grounds are now used for the popular alfresco productions of the resident performers, Shakespeare and Company.

i Chamber of Commerce, 75 Main Street

▶ *Continue north on **Route 7A/7** towards Pittsfield. On the right, just before the town, are signs for Arrowhead.*

8 Arrowhead

Author Herman Melville (1819–91) was inspired by the Berkshires. Between 1850 and 1863, he lived on this farm where the views reminded him of his seafaring days: "I look out of my window in the morning when I rise as I would out of the porthole of a ship in the Atlantic." He could see the humpbacked, whale-like shape of Mount Greylock, a constant influence as he wrote *Moby Dick*. The novel did not sell, so

Melville was forced to leave Arrowhead and take a job as a customs officer in New York. He died a poor man.

i Berkshire Common Level Plaza, Pittsfield; Park Square, Pittsfield

▶ *Continue north for 2 miles (3km) to Pittsfield, turn left on **Route 20** and drive 3 miles (5km) to Hancock Shaker Village.*

9 Hancock Shaker Village

The Shakers, a socialist Christian sect, are remembered for their use of dance in religious services, and their exquisitely simple but practical furniture and architecture. The last of the Shakers left Hancock in 1960, after 170 years, but their homes, workshops, herb gardens, and farm have been restored and revived.

Typical is the three-story round barn, built in 1826, where one man standing in the center can feed 54 cows with ease. Shaker food is served on Saturday nights in summer. The tranquility of the 1,200 acres (480 hectares) of meadows and woodlands clearly reinforces Hancock's original Shaker name: the City of Peace.

▶ *Return to Pittsfield and **Route 7**. Continue north for 22 miles (35km) to Williamstown on **Route 7**.*

10 Williamstown

Revolutionary soldier Colonel Ephraim Williams' gift of money ensured that both the town and college would bear his name. With that, he outdid earlier educational benefactors such as John Harvard and Nicholas Brown, who only have schools named for them. Today, Williams College is one of the country's most distinguished small colleges, and the town is one of the most attractive in New England.

There is plenty here for culture addicts. First on anyone's list should be the Sterling and Francine Clark Art

Institute, housed in a stunning white, marble, temple-like building. The art collection was created by the Singer sewing machine heir and his French wife and features works by European and American painters. Included are *At the Concert*, one of 30 paintings by Pierre Auguste Renoir; a study of Rouen Cathedral by Claude Monet, and *Rockets and Blue Lights* by J. M. W. Turner.

Next is the college's own Museum of Art, which concentrates on non-Western and ancient art. Contemporary works, such as Andy Warhol's yellow and black self-portrait are on display. For over 40 years, the Williamstown Theater Festival has attracted such star names as Paul Newman and Joanne Woodward to participate in the summer season.

i Routes 2 and 7

▶ *Drive east on **Route 2** for 4 miles (6.5km) to North Adams.*

11 North Adams

The term Museum of Contemporary Art will never be the same after you have been to the innovative new Massachusetts Museum of Contemporary Art (MASS MoCa). Contemporary in every sense of the word, the museum embraces a new approach to putting visual, performing and media arts on show. The whole process of creativity is explored here, and the center not only stages exhibitions and performances by renowned artists, but

---

BACK TO NATURE

Halfway between Lenox and Pittsfield is the Pleasant Valley Wildlife Sanctuary. With its hummingbirds and beavers, this is a delightful place for a stroll. Some 7 miles (11km) of marked trails meander through the 1,400 acres (560 hectares) of meadow and forest.

also shows work in progress in its art fabrication shops, production studios, performance rehearsals and the use of multimedia technologies. The museum is housed in a converted mill complex consisting of some 27 buildings, linked by covered bridges and elevated walkways.

▶ *Continue east on* **Route 2**.

🄬 Shelburne Falls

Hamlets dot this rugged road as it passes through forests and along the edges of gorges. Although little seems to have changed in Shelburne Falls since the gushing water drove

---

SPECIAL TO...

Three hundred years ago, Native Americans crossed the Berkshire Hills by walking a trail cut through the forest. Later, pioneer settlers broadened the route on their way through to what is now New York State. Opened in 1914 as one of America's first "scenic highways," the Mohawk Trail is a popular drive these days, especially in the fall (see pages 102–3). The Mohawk tribe is remembered with *Hail to the Sunrise*, the statue of a serene Indian brave, his arms raised to the east.

---

the mills, members of the local horticultural society did have the ingenuity to disguise a 400-foot (120m) long trolley bridge with a hanging flower garden, the Bridge of Flowers.

▶ *Continue to Greenfield and turn south on* **Route 5** *to historic Deerfield.*

🄭 Deerfield

Called simply "The Street," Deerfield's main thoroughfare is lined with the most impressive

The "Hail to the Sunrise" memorial at the entrance to the Mohawk Trail State Forest

collection of original Colonial houses in New England. The surrounding fields and absence of advertizing completes the film-set effect. A dozen of the 65 18th- and 19th-century houses are open to the public, revealing a potted history of early American interior decorating, from furniture to textiles and silverware.

For those in a hurry, the Memorial Hall Museum explains much of the town's rich, if violent, history. In 1675, Indians massacred farmers as they paused to eat grapes, giving a nearby stream its present name of Bloody Brook. In 1704, the French and Indians ravaged the town in the depths of winter, carrying off 112 prisoners to Canada.

The Indian House Door, with its gaping hole hacked by a tomahawk, is preserved in the Memorial Hall. The Hall was once used by students at the 200-year-old Deerfield Academy, a well-known boarding school. By contrast, the colors and restoration work in the Wells-Thorn House recall happier days. In 1774, residents raised a liberty pole, and declared their independence nine days before the historic Fourth of July, 1776.

ℹ️ *Routes 5 and 10, South Deerfield*

FOR CHILDREN

Butterflies never fail to delight children, and they are sure to be captivated by Magic Wings Butterfly Conservatory and Garden, which opened in the spring of 2000. Lush conservatory gardens house a variety of colorful, free-flying tropical butterflies and moths, and outdoor gardens have been planted specially to attract indigenous species.

▶ *You can either continue south for 16 miles (26km) on **Route 5** to Northampton or use the faster route, **I–91**.*

14 Northampton

With its mixture of industrial and educational heritage, Northampton is a pleasant, balanced sort of town. Little evidence remains that it was first settled in 1654. In the 1980s, a vigorous program of downtown renewal sprouted restaurants and boutiques. It is the home of one of America's first women's colleges, founded in 1875 by Sophia Smith, and Smith College is still one of the nation's most prestigious schools.

ℹ️ *99 Pleasant Street*

▶ *Return to I–91 south and drive to Springfield.*

Dwight House is a delightful example of early 18th-century architecture in Deerfield

FOR HISTORY BUFFS

"This is my letter to the world, that never wrote to me ..." penned the poet and recluse Emily Dickinson (1830–86) who lived in Amherst, northeast of Northampton, on Route 9. Of her 1,700 poems, only 11 had been published by the time she died. Hundreds were later found in her bedroom. Dickinson rarely left the house, but was a favorite with local children, lowering baskets of her home-baked gingerbread to them from her window. Most of her papers and belongings are kept at Harvard University and Amherst College, but her white dress hangs in her house. The garden at Amherst is a delight.

SPECIAL TO...

Sylvester Graham of Northampton was a health food fanatic who gave his name to Graham flour, a type of wholewheat flour which is more familiar when made into Graham Crackers.

BOSTON

With its unique blend of history and modern development, its "walkable" downtown and efficient public transport system, Boston is a delight for the visitor. Words like "sophisticated" and "civilized" are often used to describe this city that feels European but is the birthplace of American liberty. Balancing all this is a lively student population of over 250,000, from around 60 colleges and universities.

The city owes its foundation to the sea. When the Puritans settled here in 1630, they found poor soil, but a fine harbor. By 1700, only the ports of London and Bristol outranked Boston. Until 1755, Boston was the largest city in North America. Its place on the American stage, however, was guaranteed less by wealth and more by its independent thinkers, who had been in the forefront of the Independence movement (see pages 8–9).

Boston's great strength is that it has moved with the times. Soon after Independence, the rich merchants moved to the elegant estate developed on Beacon Hill where families such as the Cabots, Lodges, and Lowells established an almost European aristocracy in the land of democracy. These "Boston Brahmins," as historian Oliver Wendell Holmes dubbed them, considered themselves the "hub of the solar system," and the term "Hub" is one of many nicknames for the city.

When the city's vitality faded in the 1960s, a bold plan of urban renewal revitalized the downtown area. Faneuil Hall Market, once a decaying group of waterside warehouses, became a throbbing tourist attraction, with shops and restaurants.

The USS *Constitution*

As well as theater, music, and art galleries, sport plays a major part in the life of the city. The professional teams boast proud histories in the nation's four favorite sports: baseball (the Red Sox), ice hockey (the Bruins), basketball (the Celtics) and football (the New England Patriots). As for getting around, that is easy. "The T," as locals call the MBTA (Massachusetts Bay Transport Authority), was the country's first such subway system, opened in 1897.

Tour 5

The Boston Freedom Trail is a "must" for anyone interested in American history. A red line on the pavement leads visitors along the world's first self-guided walking tour of its kind. Along the route are buildings that played an important role in the uprising against British Colonial rule over 200 years ago. This is no dry re-run of history, however.

There is also tantalizing trivia, from America's oldest restaurant to the nation's oldest commissioned vessel. Plaques and cemeteries, sculpture and bullet marks are also pointed out to give an insight into the history of the city, known as the "Cradle of the American Revolution."

Tour 6

There is more to Boston than Revolutionary history. This walk shows off the contrasts in Boston, starting down by the water and the modern aquarium and ending at the top of the John Hancock Tower, with its panoramic views over the city. In between are the cobbled streets and Georgian front doors on Beacon Hill, the chic shops of Newbury Street, and the open-air elegance of the Public Garden. Always a city that has welcomed strangers, there are also moving tributes to Afro-Americans and victims of the Holocaust.

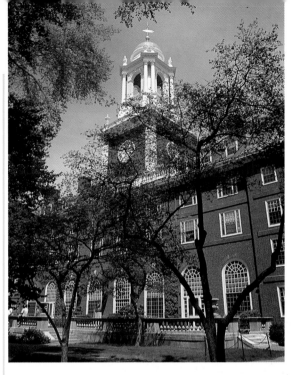

Tour 7

Harvard University is one of the world's great educational institutions. Its libraries and museums boast some of the finest collections in the world, housed in magnificent examples of architecture, from the 17th century to the present day. At the same time, the student body, which now includes the women of Radcliffe College, adds zest to Cambridge, where coffee shops and boutiques, bookstores and

Harvard University is one of the pre-eminent Ivy League establishments in the country

art galleries are a pleasure for students and visitors alike. With huge mature trees along the Charles River, and New England clapboard houses, Cambridge retains its own character, totally distinct from Boston, just a bridge or two away.

Boston's impressive skyline at night

The Boston
Freedom Trail

A local journalist, William Schofield, came up with the simple but effective idea of linking Boston's historically important sites with a walking trail. That was back in 1951. Since then, millions have taken the route, marked sometimes by a painted red line, at other times by red bricks.

HALF A DAY

Allow half a day, longer if you want to explore the Charlestown Navy Yard, located near the end of the Trail, home of the USS *Constitution*. Remember that in summer long lines build up to see this historic ship.

▶ *Start at the information booth on the Tremont Street side of Boston Common, near the Park Street MBTA stop.*

❶ Boston Common

Often called America's first public park, this common land in the very heart of Boston was set aside in 1634 for "the feeding of Cattell" and as a "trayning field" for militia. Once the cattle left around 1830, the Common was used for recreation and oration. In 1851, Amelia Bloomer, wearing her manly "bloomers," campaigned for women's rights.

In the coming century, charismatic speakers such as Martin Luther King, Jr. and Pope John Paul II have also addressed large crowds here. Today it is an area of lawns, trees, and even baseball diamonds.

▶ *Follow the red line to the State House.*

❷ State House

Built in 1795, this "new" seat of state government replaced the Old State House of 1713. The original red-brick structure was designed by Charles Bulfinch, the most able and sought-after architect of his day. His original dome of wood was replaced first with a copper one, then gilded with 23-carat gold leaf in 1874.

▶ *Just across Beacon Street is a large monument.*

❸ Shaw/54th Regiment Memorial

The lively bronze bas-relief by Augustus Saint-Gaudens pays tribute to the local black soldiers who volunteered to fight for the North in the American Civil War. Prejudice confined blacks to the ranks, but wealthy white Bostonian, Robert Gould Shaw, led what became the 54th Massachusetts Regiment. He was killed, along with 32 of his soldiers, in the assault on Fort Wagner, South Carolina. Their heroism inspired the 1989 film, *Glory*, which won three Academy Awards.

The Robert Gould Shaw/54th Regiment Memorial

▶ *Walk through the Common to Park Street Church.*

❹ Park Street Church

Founded in 1809, this is where anti-slavery campaigner William Lloyd Garrison made his first speech in 1829. Two years later, the hymn *America* was first sung on the steps, and it remains part of the church's Fourth of July tradition. It is ironic that the melody is the same as the British national anthem.

▶ *Adjacent to Park Street Church, facing Tremont Street, is the Old Granary Burying Ground.*

❺ Old Granary Burying Ground

Buried here are some of the best-known leaders of the patriot cause: John Hancock, Samuel Adams, John Otis, and Paul Revere (see page 11). One of the most popular graves, however, is that of Mary Goose, also called Elizabeth Vergoose, and supposedly the original Mother Goose. The mother and step-mother of a total of 20 children, she was buried here in 1757. Her son-in-law was

supposed to have published *Mother Goose's Melodies* (*Songs for the Nursery*).

▶ *Turn left on Tremont Street. Cross to King's Chapel, on the corner of School Street.*

❻ King's Chapel

Dating from 1749, King's Chapel was seen as a symbol of British rule in North America. The colony's governors worshiped in a special canopied pew. George Washington also used it in 1789; perhaps one reason that it has survived. Today's congregation follows a curious mixture of Church of England and Unitarian liturgy.

▶ *Walk down School Street. Behind the chapel is the graveyard.*

7 Burying Ground

This cemetery contains the graves of several historic figures, including Mary Chilton, the first of the *Mayflower* pilgrims to reach Plymouth Rock, and John Winthrop, first governor of the colony. Others buried here include William Dawes, who joined Paul Revere in his "midnight ride," as well as Elizabeth Pain, who provided the inspiration for Hester Prynne in Nathaniel Hawthorne's *The Scarlet Letter*. The oldest gravestone in Boston remembers William Paddy, who died in 1658.

▶ *Continue on School Street, passing Old City Hall.*

8 Globe Corner Bookstore

The name of the Old Corner Bookstore was changed after the *Boston Globe* bought the building, one of Boston's oldest. What started out as an apothecary shop in 1712, became famous in the mid-19th century as the publishers Ticknor and Fields. Their best-selling authors included Nathaniel Hawthorne, Henry Wadsworth Longfellow, Henry David Thoreau, and Julia Ward Howe, who penned *The Battle Hymn of the Republic*, the anthem of the North during the Civil War.

▶ *Turn right on Washington Street.*

9 Old South Meeting House

Standing in the quiet simplicity of this 1729 Congregational church, it is hard to imagine the fiery debates that inflamed political passions and led to the

The Globe Corner Bookstore was once the literary hub of Boston

Revolution. Back then, "Old South" was the largest space available for public assemblies. After the Boston Massacre in 1770, protesters marched from here to confront the lieutenant-governor. Over three years later came the meeting that triggered the Boston Tea Party (see page 8). Today, the second-oldest church in Boston is a museum recording those tumultuous days.

ⓘ *Boston National Park Visitors Center, 15 State Street*

▶ *Turn back and follow Washington Street past the Globe Corner Bookstore. Just before the Old State House, a walkway to the right leads to the Old State House.*

10 Old State House

The lion and unicorn symbolize the connection with the Mother Country, a link which James Otis demanded be cut as early as 1761. Five years later, the hated Stamp Act was debated here and, on July 18, 1776, Colonel Thomas Crafts stepped on to the balcony to read the Declaration of Independence. Two hundred years later, Queen Elizabeth II stood on the same spot and spoke in celebration of the American bicentennial. Note

the ring of cobblestones outside the seat of the Massachusetts Assembly, recording the Boston Massacre of 1770, when five Bostonians were shot by British soldiers (see page 8).

▶ *Cross Congress Street diagonally.*

11 Faneuil Hall

In Boston, Faneuil rhymes with Daniel, and the name recalls the French merchant who funded the construction of Boston's marketplace in 1742. In the meeting hall above, freedom of speech was a prerogative. Locals congregated in 1764 to object to the Sugar Act. In the following years, their topics of protest were taxation and English troop movements. Samuel Adams' rebellious speech in 1772, stirring up anti-British feelings, was particularly provocative. But debate did not stop with Independence.

Over the centuries, Bostonians have spoken their minds here on issues such as slavery, alcohol, the Vietnam War, and women's rights. Like the Old State House, there is a reminder of England: the grasshopper that tops the building is thought to be a copy of the weathervane on the Royal Exchange in London.

Boston's oldest public building, the 1713 Old State House

▶ *Turn right into Haymarket.*

14 Haymarket

Stall-holders still set out their produce here on Fridays and Saturdays as countless others have done for 300 years. Massive road building and the construction of a tunnel under the city is disrupting much of the downtown area, so Mags Harries' clever sculpture, usually set flat in the street, has been removed temporarily. Called *Asaroton*, the Greek for rubbish, it is a bronze version of market-day leftovers.

▶ *Follow the red line through the construction to Hanover Street. Turn right on Richmond Street, then left on North Street to North Square.*

15 Paul Revere's House

Revere's talent as a silversmith, bell-maker, engraver, and even false teeth-maker fade away in the light of his fame as messenger. He rode to Lexington and Concord on the night of April 18, 1775 to warn that "the British are coming!" (see page 11).

His tiny wooden home, at No. 19, is the oldest in Boston (1680) and is as plain and simple inside as Revere left it.

▶ *Leave North Square on Prince Street, turn right on Hanover*

▶ *Follow the red line across North Street to Union Street, and No. 41.*

12 Union Oyster House

This place enjoys the title of the "oldest continuously operated restaurant in America." It started life as a shop, but became a place to eat in 1826. Orator and lawyer Daniel Webster used to sit at the mahogany bar, consuming up to six glasses of brandy and three dozen oysters at a single sitting.

▶ *Turn onto Marshall Street for the Boston Stone.*

13 Boston Stone

Myth insists that this millstone marked the true center of Boston, and that all distances were measured from here. This is a tribute to the public relations skills of a tavern owner who set the stone up as a publicity stunt back in 1737. The stone itself was used originally for grinding pigment by Thomas Child, a painter from London.

FOR HISTORY BUFFS

Among the pages of history devoted to the men of the Massachusetts Bay Colony, Ann Hutchinson is only a footnote. Yet this woman dared to discuss her own views of what was, then, the "official" religion. The punishment for such a challenge to the Puritan hierarchy was exile. In 1638, she left home and, with her followers, moved south. They founded the second settlement in New England in what is now the state of Rhode Island.

Paul Revere's House, restored to its original appearance, now operates as a small museum

Street, then left on Paul Revere Mall to the Old North Church.

16 Old North Church

Sexton Robert Newman had to flash lanterns ("One if by land, and two if by sea") to fellow patriots across the Charles River to warn them of British troop movements. He hung up two from the 191-foot (58m) steeple that is still visible in many parts of the city. Supposedly, one John Childs *flew* from the steeple in 1757, though contemporary reports do not explain how. Officially named Christ Church, it is the oldest in Boston (1723), and remains a place of worship. Boston Harbor Tea is sold here to boost funds, and a sign by the collection box suggests that "if it weren't for the Old North Church, you might be making donations in pounds."

▶ *Go uphill on Hull Street.*

17 Copp's Hill Burying Ground

This is not a resting place of famous historic figures, though Sexton Newman is buried here,

as is early black community leader, Prince Hall. Nonetheless, the old headstones are worth a look, particularly that of Daniel Malcolm. Used for target practice by the British soldiers who camped here, the scars are still clear to see.

▶ *Continue downhill on Hull Street; turn left on Commercial Street, then right across Charlestown Bridge on the right-hand sidewalk. At the north end of the bridge, follow the red line down the steps and along Water Street.*

18 USS *Constitution*

Like HMS *Victory* in England, this is still a commissioned ship and an icon for the navy. A magnificent example of a

wooden warship, her greatest glory came in the war of 1812 against the British, who were then masters of the sea. She destroyed four enemy frigates and sloops and earned the nickname, "Old Ironsides," when, as cannonballs bounced off her hull, a seaman shouted "Huzzah! Her sides are made of iron!" In fact, the ship is made of live oak, a particularly tough wood from southeastern U.S.A.

▶ *From the Navy Yard follow the trail to the Bunker Hill Monument.*

19 Bunker Hill Monument

A 221-foot (67m) obelisk commemorates the first major battle of the Revolutionary War, which was fought on this hill on June 17, 1775. Facing a mighty British force, the ill-equipped colonists stood their ground, mindful of the now legendary order, "Don't fire until you see the whites of their eyes!" Though the colonists were eventually routed, they reduced the British army's numbers considerably and the battle was significant in their ultimate victory. There is an exhibition on the site, and musket firing takes place in summer.

FULL DAY

Boston
Old & New

Boston's development started by the water, then moved inland to Beacon Hill where the wealthy lived. Later, it included Back Bay, which was reclaimed land. Allow a full day for this tour, which traces highlights of that growth, from narrow streets to grand boulevards, with Georgian houses and modern skyscrapers.

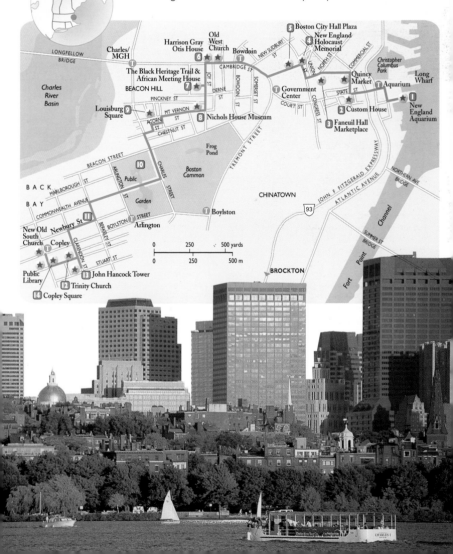

SCENIC ROUTES

For an unusual view of Boston, hop aboard one of the Boston Duck Tours' amphibious vehicles. Designed for the Allied landings on the Normandy beaches during World War II, they lumber over land and surge through water. During the 80-minute ride, a conDUCKtor describes the 40 points of interest en route. Best of all is splashing down into the Charles River for excellent views of Boston and Beacon Hill. The tours start in front of the Aquarium.

i 147 Tremont Street; 15 State Street

▶ Start at the Aquarium MBTA stop. Walk to the New England Aquarium on Central Wharf.

❶ New England Aquarium

By 1960, Boston's waterfront was an area of vacant warehouses and unused wharves. The decay was reversed in the 1970s by a renewal program that re-established and emphasized the city's age-old role as a port. One of the first projects was the New England Aquarium, at the end of Central Wharf (1817). At low tide, the smell of the sea and the tidal flats permeates the outdoor plaza in front of the Aquarium, where seals swim in the open-air pool and the *Discovery*, an auxiliary boat, hosts shows by trained sea lions.

Indoors, the centerpiece of the aquarium is a huge three-story-high glass salt-water tank (187,000 gallons/41,555 litres), one of the largest in the world, where sharks and eels prowl up and down past Myrtle, a 500-pound (227kg) green sea turtle who likes to have her back scratched by the aquarium's divers.

Whale-watching cruises leave daily from Long Wharf (April to October).

▶ Return to the Aquarium MBTA Stop. Cross under the expressway to State Street. At the corner of India Street is the Custom House.

❷ Custom House

This massive 1847 granite building was described as "one of the noblest pieces of commercial architecture in the world" by 19th-century poet Walt Whitman. Certainly it is one of the biggest Greek Revival structures in the country and took ten years to build, with 3,000 pilings each weighing over 40 tons (36,363kg) being driven into the soggy soil.

In 1915, the 495-foot (148.5m) high tower was added. This shattered the city's height limit and won it the title of the "tallest building in New England." The four clock faces are notorious for showing different times.

▶ Turn right on Commercial Street and continue into Quincy Market.

❸ Faneuil Hall Marketplace

The well-traveled visitor may see nothing remarkable about this array of shops and restaurants in restored 19th-century buildings. Yet this 1976 urban redevelopment was the first of its kind, and its success has been copied all over the world ever since.

In Colonial days, when sailing ships tied up at Long Wharf, the Marketplace was used by vendors of fruits, vegetables, and other commodities. By 1825, Faneuil Hall was too small, so Mayor Josiah Quincy authorized the construction of the Quincy Market and its two offspring, the North and South markets. Today, restaurants, pubs, and fast-food counters satisfy the hunger of over 14 million visitors a year. (See also page 42.)

▶ Go through the Market, then cross North Street to Congress Street. Turn right and continue to the Holocaust Memorial.

Quincy Market, a lively collection of eating places and shops

❹ New England Holocaust Memorial

This memorial, both dramatic and intimate, is located on a busy traffic island between City Hall Plaza and the 18th-century Blackstone Block, the six glass towers are lit from within at night. Each is six stories high and etched with six million random numbers, symbolizing the victims of the concentration camps. On the base of each tower are quotes from survivors, which tell of love, hope, and despair. One, from Gerda Weissman Klein, recalls a 13-year-old's gift to her best friend in the camp: "Imagine a world in which your entire possession is one raspberry, and you gave it to your friend."

FOR CHILDREN

Under 10s have their own special Museum in Boston's Congress Street. The Children's Museum has a wonderful array of things to do, things to climb on, things to build and things to look at that are so much fun, they don't realize how much they are learning. Special events draw on popular icons, such as Sesame Street and Arthur's World.

▶ Cross Congress Street and continue up the steps to the City Hall Plaza.

❺ Boston City Hall Plaza

The area around City Hall was once the red-light district, with its attendant slums, burlesque theaters, and boarded-up shops. Known officially as Scollay Square, it once deserved its "Combat Zone" nickname. In the 1960s, the run-down buildings were demolished and replaced by the John F. Kennedy federal office buildings and a new City Hall, a pyramid standing on its head, designed by I. M. Pei. In winter the plaza

looks barren, but in summer it becomes a lively meeting-place, with pushcart vendors, office workers, and free evening concerts on the stage behind City Hall.

▶ *Continue through the Plaza to Cambridge Street; turn right.*

SPECIAL TO...

Beacon Hill looks like a film-set for a costume drama, with brick sidewalks, gaslights, and handsome houses with shutters and window boxes. Acorn Street, one of the last remaining cobbled thoroughfares in the city, is the narrowest on the hill, yet wide enough to comply with building regulations of the period, which insisted that two cows must be able to pass by one another. Note the odd purple panes of glass. Back in 1818, a batch of window glass shipped over from Hamburg was tainted with manganese oxide which gradually turned purple after exposure to light.

---

6 Harrison Gray Otis House

Beacon Hill, with some of the most elegant homes in Boston, dates back to just after the Revolution, when Harrison Gray Otis started to build houses here. This lawyer, mayor of Boston, and U.S. senator was also a property developer, so he could afford to have Charles Bulfinch, the noted architect of the day, design his home at 141 Cambridge Street. Often called the First Otis House, its perfectly proportioned, if rather dull brick exterior hides a sophisticated and surprisingly colorful interior. At the top of a handsome staircase, the grand drawing-room looks much as it did 200 years ago. Today this is the headquarters of the SPNEA, the Society for the Preservation of New England Antiquities, with an architectural museum in the basement.

▶ *Cross Cambridge Street and go up Joy Street.*

7 The Black Heritage Trail

At this point the itinerary and Boston's Black Heritage Trail meet. Celebrating the history of the city's black community, the Trail encompasses 14 significant sites, two of which are on this route. The Abiel Smith School in Joy Street has recently reopened after extensive renovation, and contains displays relating to the long struggle for equal education for African American children in the city, which started in 1787 and ended when segregation was finally abolished in 1855. Established with an endowment from white businessman, Abiel Smith, the school eductaed black children for some 20 years of that interim period.

Just off Joy Street, in Smith Court, is the African Meeting House, which is the starting point of the Trail. It was built by black Americans in 1805 as a place where they could worship without being relegated to the gallery, as was the case in white churches. The meeting house became the home of the New England Anti-Slavery Society – such a force in the Abolitionist Movement that the building became known as the Black Faneuil Hall. Today it houses the Museum of Afro-American History, which traces the civil rights movement.

▶ *Continue up Joy Street and turn right on Mount Vernon Street. At No. 55 is Nichols House.*

8 Nichols House Museum

Red-brick houses line Mount Vernon Street, one of the loveliest streets in Boston. The museum is a time-warp, where nothing has been changed since the owner, Rose Standish Nichols, died in 1960. Her will ensured that "people from around the world without a letter of introduction could see the inside of a fine house." From a wealthy Boston family,

she is remembered as a landscape gardener and a fervent worker for international peace. Her needlework and paintings lend a personal touch to the 1804 mansion, which also has bronzes by her uncle, the sculptor Augustus Saint-Gaudens.

▶ *Continue west along Mount Vernon Street to Louisburg Square.*

9 Louisburg Square

The name of this square recalls the struggle between France and Britain for supremacy in North America. Even though local troops had fought successfully for the Crown against the French at Fort Louisburg, Nova Scotia, back in 1745, this elegant square, named after their victory, was built a century later. Much like a London square, the grassy quadrangle is a private park for owners of the surrounding posh homes. Residents included celebrities such as writer Louisa May Alcott (No. 10), who spent her last two years here. Opera singer Jenny Lind, the "Swedish Nightingale," was married at No. 20.

▶ *Retrace your steps on Mount Vernon Street and turn right*

SPECIAL TO...

The early 19th-century equivalent of smoking a joint after dinner was sniffing ether. Dr. William Morton, a dentist, noticed that participants in these "ether frolics" felt no pain if they bumped into the furniture. He experimented with ether, using it on patients before extracting a tooth. On October 16, 1846, in Boston's Massachusetts General Hospital, he supervized an operation that successfully removed a tumor from a patient, using ether as an anaesthetic. This major breakthrough for surgery is commemorated with the statue *The Good Samaritan* in the Public Garden.

---

on Willow Street, then zigzag right onto Acorn Street, go left on West Cedar Street, then right on Chestnut Street and, finally, left on Charles Street. Across Beacon Street is the Public Garden.

🔟 Public Garden

Boston can thank a group of public-spirited green thumbs for America's first botanical garden. From 1837 until their success over 20 years later, they battled to protect the city's green heart from developers. Today, their triumph provides a retreat for locals and visitors alike. In spring and summer, flowers bloom by the paths, while the swish of fountains masks the noise of the traffic. Children plead for rides on the slow, stately, foot-pedaled swan boats, introduced

in 1877, and peer at the fountain sculpture of Bagheera, the panther immortalized in Kipling's *Jungle Books*. A home-grown favorite is the sculpture of Mrs. Mallard and her six duck-lings, at the corner of Charles and Beacon streets. Robert McCloskey's *Make Way for Ducklings* is a much-loved chil-dren's tale of a mother duck stopping Boston traffic as she shepherds her brood from the Charles River to the pond in the Boston Public Garden. A chil-dren's parade each spring retraces the route of the duck-lings.

▶ *Cross the Garden using the suspension bridge and exit through the Arlington Street gate onto Commonwealth Avenue. Walk one block, then*

turn left on Berkeley Street, then right on Newbury Street.

🔟 Newbury Street

Water covered this area of Boston until the second half of the 19th century when Back Bay was filled in and transformed into a residential district. The back-bone is Commonwealth Avenue, a Parisian-style boulevard, lined with fine trees and grand statues of long-forgotten worthies. Running parallel to "Comm Ave" is Newbury Street, known for its up-market and trendy art galleries, boutiques and cafés. Yet, the apartments on and around the street create a neigh-borhood atmosphere. Old build-ings have new uses: between Berkeley and Clarendon streets, the Church of the Covenant (1867), renowned for its stained-glass windows, is now an art gallery; Boston's former Museum of Natural History is full of expensive menswear; and the

Boston's Public Garden was the first botanical garden in the country Inset: Robert McCloskey's *Make Way for Ducklings*

many of the original glass panels off the 62-story skyscraper. The difficulty was rectified and now the glass acts as a mirror, reflecting Trinity Church. From the viewing gallery of the John Hancock Observatory, 740 feet (225m) up, you'll be rewarded by a panorama stretching for 100 miles (160km) on a clear day.

▶ *Copley Square is a huge city block, bounded by the Boston Public Library, Trinity Church, New Old South Church, the Copley Plaza Hotel and the John Hancock Tower.*

⒕ Copley Square
Copley Square (1883) was described by one observer as a "desert of dirt, dust, mud, and wind." Now it is a pleasant place of fountains, benches ... and zooming skateboarders. The Boston Public Library, the first in America to lend books for free, is Charles McKim's adaptation of an Italian Renaissance palazzo. Constructed with a quarryful of yellow Siena marble, the 1895 building was decorated with works by then-contemporary artists and sculptors such as John Singer Sargent and Daniel Chester French.

▶ *There is an MBTA stop at Copley Square to return to the Aquarium, or travel elsewhere in the city.*

Trinity Church reflected in the John Hancock Tower

▶ *Across Stuart Street is the John Hancock Tower.*

severe face of the New England Insurance Company fronts a trendy fashion shop.

▶ *After one block, turn left on Clarendon Street and continue to Boylston Street. Turn right, left and into Copley Square.*

⒓ Trinity Church
Two of America's finest architects, Charles McKim and Henry Richardson, worked on Trinity Church in the late 19th century. Richardson's design was inspired by medieval Europe, while the interior coloring was a tribute to William Morris's pre-Raphaelite movement. On the Boylston Street side of the church, the statue of the Rev. Phillips Brooks commemorates the passionate preacher who used to ride his horse at breakneck speed. He also wrote *O Little Town of Bethlehem*.

⒔ John Hancock Tower
Once the tallest building in New England, the headquarters of the John Hancock Life Insurance Company has had its problems. Architect I. M. Pei's unusual rhomboid shape was beset by air currents that sucked

SATURDAY, NOV. 13
5:00-7:00 PM
BAKED BEAN SUPPER
ADULTS $5 CHILDREN $2
CHRIST CHURCH, UNITED METHODIST

HALF A DAY

Cambridge &
Harvard University

Established as Newtowne back in 1630, this was the first capital of the colony. Two years after Harvard College was founded in 1636, the town changed its name to Cambridge, to give it the same kudos, no doubt, as the English university city. Today, the mixture of grand museums, historic houses, wealthy residents, and student *joie de vivre* make it one of the most vibrant and attractive places in New England.

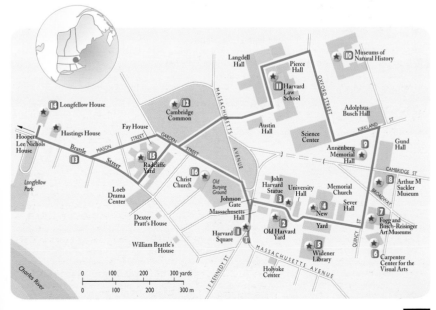

ⓘ Cambridge Discovery Inc,
Harvard Square

▶ Start at the Harvard Square
MBTA stop.

❶ Harvard Square

All around the traffic island is the bustle and noise of "the square." Here you can buy international newspapers at the kiosk, eat international cuisine at the numerous restaurants, then buy all-American sportswear at the Harvard Cooperative, the large department store, known as "the Coop" (rhymes with hoop).

▶ Walk up Massachusetts
Avenue and turn right through
Johnson Gate, the entrance to
Old Harvard Yard.

❷ Old Harvard Yard

Harvard is not only the oldest university in America, but also one of the most influential. From its earliest days, it has symbolized the independent attitude of the Colonists and, significantly, America's first printing press was set up here in 1640. Harvard Yard, the center of the campus for over 350 years, is really two vast, open quadrangles, totalling 22 acres (8.8 hectares). The first yard is the

FOR HISTORY BUFFS

America's oldest university is also one of its most prestigious. One of the seven so-called Ivy League schools (so old that ivy grows on their hallowed walls), Harvard emphasizes academic excellence, shunning the sports scholarships, and razzmatazz of the country's younger universities. The 7,000 undergraduates now include the women of Radcliffe (see page 55), but there is also an impressive graduate program ranging from the prestigious Harvard Law and Medical Schools, to newer disciplines, such as Business Administration and Government.

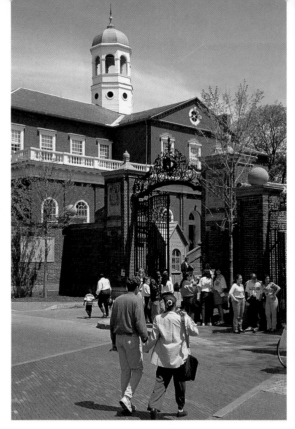

home of the Freshmen (first-year students) who live in the red-brick dormitories. On the right is Massachusetts Hall, the university's oldest surviving building. Established as a laboratory and dormitory in 1720, it housed American troops at the start of the Revolution.

ⓘ Harvard University, 26 Oxford
Street

❸ John Harvard Statue

Directly across the yard, in front of the granite University Hall (1815), this seated statue is labelled "John Harvard, founder 1638." The sculpture is wittily referred to as the "Statue of the Three Lies." Harvard was a benefactor rather than a founder, the foundation year was 1636, and the statue is actually of Sherman Hoar, a Harvard student who modelled for 19th-century sculptor Daniel Chester French.

▶ Continue past University Hall
and enter New Yard.

Lowell House, typical of Harvard's elegant Georgian buildings

❹ New Yard

The second, larger portion of the Yard is also called Tercentenary Theater because it was here that the 300th graduation ceremonies were held in 1936. Criss-crossed by walking paths, a figurative bridge links the spiritual and intellectual centers of the university. To the left is Memorial Church, "Mem Church." It was completed in 1932 as a tribute by Harvard alumni to classmates killed in World War I, and has been updated for victims of World War II and, later, the Korean and Vietnam conflicts.

▶ To the right is the Widener
Library, the world's largest
university library.

❺ Widener Library

In this temple to the written word, information spans the centuries, from a first folio of Shakespeare and a Gutenberg

Bible, to microfilm files and computer screens. Built between 1913 and 1915, the library was given in memory of Harry Elkins Widener, a wealthy graduate who drowned on the *Titanic*. The library is not open to the public.

▶ *Straight ahead is Quincy Street.*

❻ Carpenter Center for the Visual Arts

This glass and concrete block at No. 24 Quincy Street is the only example in America of a building by the 20th-century Swiss architect Le Corbusier. Its film archives are famous for their variety and depth. Film shows of unusual or historic movies are often held here.

❼ Fogg and Busch-Reisinger Art Museums

Many institutions of higher learning have their own museums. Harvard has eight on campus, of which the Fogg, Busch-Reisinger and the Arthur M. Sackler have world-class reputations.

The Fogg, which opened in 1895, is the oldest of the three. Behind the neo-Georgian façade on Quincy Street is a courtyard modeled after a 15th-century Italian palazzo. The collection concentrates on European art from the Middle Ages to the present, with a strong line-up of Italian Renaissance paintings, as well as a self-portrait by Van Gogh, and *Red Boats* by Claude Monet.

Directly behind the Fogg is the Busch-Reisinger Museum, in the Otto Werner Hall. Here, the main focus is works by the Expressionists, Europeans such as Franz Marc, Paul Klee, Wassily Kandinsky, and Emile Nolde.

▶ *Go north on Quincy Street, cross Broadway, and the Arthur M. Sackler Museum is on the right.*

❽ Arthur M. Sackler Museum

This is the university's third art museum, in British architect James Sterling's strikingly

contemporary building, opened in 1985. Famous for its exquisite collection of Chinese ceramics, bronzes, and jades, it specializes in Ancient Greek, Islamic, and Asian art, from Indian miniatures to Japanese prints. On the fourth floor, among the Greek art, are several large ceramic vases, dating from about 340 BC. There are also jade dragons, bronze ritual bells, and a large bronze wine container, over 3,000 years old, from China.

▶ *Continue along Quincy Street, crossing Cambridge Street. Memorial Hall is on the left.*

❾ Annenberg Memorial Hall

Memorial Hall re-opened after a major restoration in 1996. Built in 1878 to honor the Harvard men who died in the Civil War, it epitomizes the Gothic Revival style, with a Great Hall soaring up to a jig-saw puzzle roof of

Well-displayed period furnishings complement the Fogg's paintings and sculptures

carved beams and timbers. Here, Winston Churchill was given an honorary degree in 1943. The stained-glass windows portray stories and heroes from the Bible, American history, and Greek mythology. In a controversial move, "Mem Hall" has been made into a dining room. Where nervous undergraduates once took exams, first-year students gossip at mealtimes under the chandeliers. To one side is Sanders Theater, an intimate auditorium finished in dark wood. It was the setting for Harvard graduations up until 1911, but is now used for the performing arts.

▶ *At the end of Quincy Street bear left across Kirkland Street, then turn right onto Oxford Street.*

10 Museums of Natural History

Don't be put off by the fusty-sounding names of the four museums: there is plenty to fascinate adults and children alike in this brick building. Highlights include the 22-pound (10kg) meteor which fell from the sky in 1992, and landed on a car in Peekskill, New York, and the life-size skeleton of a 42-foot long (12.5m) *Kronosaurus*. This gigantic crocodile lived 135 million years ago.

Best known of all is the unique Ware Collection of Glass Flowers, 3,000 scientifically accurate, life-size models of flowers and plants made out of blown glass.

▶ *From Oxford Street, go into Harvard Law School. Pass under the arch to the right of Pierce Hall, and bear left on the path along Langdell Hall.*

11 Harvard Law School

The Law School was started in 1817, with six students. Today, each new class of 540 students has been selected from over 7,000 applicants. Langdell Hall, on the right, has the largest law library in the world, and a public reading room on the fourth floor that stretches the length of two football fields.

Next is Austin Hall, a small brownstone building completed in 1881 by Henry Hobson Richardson. Each spring in the Ames Courtroom, on the second floor, finalists in the third-year competition argue their cases before a Justice of the U.S. Supreme Court. The sessions are open to the public, but seating is by ticket only.

▶ *Bear right upon leaving Austin Hall and follow the path between Hemenway Gymnasium and Gannett House. Cross Massachusetts Avenue at the traffic light and walk across Cambridge Common.*

Longfellow House: this clapboard building was abandoned by its Loyalist owner in 1774

12 Cambridge Common

This small green park is all that remains of the fields and pastures where the American army assembled after the 1775 battles of Lexington and Concord (April) and Bunker Hill (June). On July 3, George Washington took command of the American army here, and a plaque marks the location of the Washington Elm beneath which this event took place. At least, that is the story ...

▶ *On the far side of the Common, turn right on Garden Street, then left on Mason Street. Turn right on Brattle Street and continue to No. 101.*

13 Brattle Street

All along Brattle Street are fine houses, built before the American Revolution. Since most were then occupied by supporters of the crown, it was called "Tory Row." The owners left hastily, and all that remains are their names, recorded on blue plaques. Hastings House, No. 101, is a fine example, as are Nos. 113 and 115, which belonged to the daughters of Henry Wadsworth Longfellow, who lived at No. 105.

Built in 1685, the Hooper-Lee Nichols House at No. 159 is

now the headquarters of the Cambridge Historical Society, who also organize guided walks.

14 Longfellow House

The Tory, or British sympathizer, John Vassall lived in this yellow clapboard mansion. He built it in 1759, in anticipation of his marriage to Elizabeth, the sister of the last Royal Lieutenant Governor. In 1775, he was thrown out by the patriots, who moved in with the wounded from the Battle of Bunker Hill. Next, the hospital became George Washington's headquarters for nine months. Washington enlarged it to make room for guests.

In the following century, the celebrated American poet, Henry Wadsworth Longfellow rented a room here. Later, he received the house as a wedding present and lived here from 1837 to 1882. During that period he wrote *Hiawatha* (1855) and *The Village Blacksmith* (1839) here, and completed his translation of Dante, among other works. Here, also, he entertained Dickens, Emerson, Hawthorne, Twain, and Wilde. Longfellow was particularly fond of the view across to the Charles River, and it remains unspoiled, thanks to his children, who gave the land to the City of Cambridge in 1913.

A lengthy restoration project has installed environmentally controlled areas to preserve historic documents and artifacts, and renovated the gardens.

▶ *Retrace your steps on Brattle Street and turn left into Radcliffe College.*

15 Radcliffe Yard

Radcliffe College started out in 1879 with just 27 women students in a small two-story house. It was named in honor of Londoner Lady Anne Radcliffe, who gave £100 to Harvard back in the 17th century. Admissions to Radcliffe have always been highly competitive, and many "Cliffies" have become well known, including Helen Keller,

whose life was portrayed in the film *The Miracle Worker*. Nearly a century after its founding, Radcliffe merged with Harvard, and now students receive a Harvard degree embossed with the seals of both colleges. In Radcliffe Yard, the Federal-style Fay House was built in 1807 and was the first building acquired by the college. Today it is the site of the Admissions Office.

▶ *After crossing the Yard, exit onto Garden Street, and bear right to Christ Church.*

16 Christ Church and the Old Burying Ground

In the foyer, just inside the outer door of Christ Church, a plaque on the right marks a bullet hole made, so the story goes, when the British were marching to Lexington in April, 1775. Later

Christ Church, designed by Peter Hamson, the architect of King's Chapel in Boston

that year, George and Martha Washington attended services here, using the pew directly below the pulpit, on the left. Between the Christ Church and the First Church is Cambridge's oldest cemetery, God's Acre. The earliest existing grave is that of Anne Erinton, an early settler who passed away on December 24, 1635. Eight presidents of Harvard are also buried here.

▶ *Continue down Garden Street to Massachusetts Avenue and bear right to Harvard Square and the MBTA stop.*

SPECIAL TO...

Close by the sidewalk is a stone milestone, carved in 1734. Look carefully at the words: "Boston 8 miles." Today that distance is covered in 8 minutes on the MBTA.

CULTURAL CRADLE

America's culture, as well as its sense of history, started in New England. The 19th century, in particular, saw the development not just of American themes but of a distinctive American "voice" and viewpoint. What binds the most talented artists and writers together is their sense of New England, in print and on canvas, set to music or presented on stage. Names such as Robert Frost (poet), Nathaniel Hawthorne (novelist), Winslow Homer (painter), Norman Rockwell (illustrator), and Eugene O'Neill (playwright) conjure up bleak landscapes and clapboard houses, glistening seas and "salt-of-the-earth" families, while Charles Ives' music interprets the moods of the countryside.

Literature

The first New England writer to make an international name for himself was Henry Wadsworth Longfellow (1807–82), a poet who was also a professor at Harvard. Hugely popular, his narrative poems told home-grown tales, from *The Song of Hiawatha*, a story of Native Americans, to *The Midnight Ride of Paul Revere*, which encapsulates the start of the American Revolution. Nathaniel Hawthorne (1804–64) also took inspiration from New England history, though he explored the psychological effects of Puritanism in novels such as *The Scarlet Letter* and *The House of the Seven Gables*. His friend Herman Melville (1819–91) received little critical acclaim in his lifetime. A New Yorker who wrote at Arrowhead in Western Massachusetts, Melville's most famous novel was *Moby Dick*, an allegory of good and evil which drew on his experiences aboard a New England whaler as a young man.

While Hawthorne and Melville relied on the realism of history, two authors, Emerson and Thoreau, took a more spiritual path. Transcendentalism was a movement led by Ralph Waldo Emerson (1803–82), a charismatic speaker and writer whose philosophy is best summed up by his often quoted saying: "who so would be a man must be a non-conformist." He appealed to Americans to throw off the yoke of European tradition and to look at their individual experiences. His friend, Henry David Thoreau (1817–62) did just that, going "back to nature." The result of his simple life by Walden Pond, on the edge of Concord, was the idealistic book, *Walden: Or Life in the Woods* (1854).

Both men spent time in Concord, where Louisa May Alcott (1832–88) also lived and wrote *Little Women*, a huge best-seller, based on family life. Another woman writer, Harriet Beecher Stowe (1811–96), brought the issue of slavery to thousands of homes with *Uncle Tom's Cabin*. The book, which was originally published as a weekly serial, sold 300,000 copies. While Stowe wrote to further a cause, Emily Dickinson (1830–86) wrote for herself. A recluse whose poems were only discovered after her death, she lived her entire life not just in Amherst in Western Massachusetts, but also in the same brick Federal house where she had been born.

New England also attracted writers from elsewhere in the States. Samuel Longhorne Clemens, better known as Mark Twain (1835–1910), was born in

Left: Henry Wadsworth Longfellow
Below: Topsy, from Harriet Beecher Stowe's *Uncle Tom's Cabin*

(Mrs Keeley as Topsy. "Is drefful wicked.")
"SLAVE LIFE," OR "UNCLE TOM'S CABIN."

Missouri, but many of his best-loved stories, such as the antics of Huckleberry Finn and Tom Sawyer, were written in his Hartford home. His tales of the American West, written with humor and an easy style, brought him a wide audience. By contrast, high society was the subject of novelist Edith Wharton (1862–1937). The author of *The Age of Innocence* did much of her writing at The Mount, her retreat in Lenox, Massachusetts.

The quintessential New England poet was Robert Frost (1874–1963) who spent most of his life in New Hampshire and Vermont. So great was his stature that he was the first poet to participate in a presidential inauguration. In 1961, he read his poem *The Gift Outright* at President John F. Kennedy' swearing-in. His descriptions of a Vermont snowstorm and swinging on birch trees are easily remembered; his forthright expression of universal truths have a darker side.

Theater

New York was always the cradle of American theater, but America's first major playwright, Eugene O'Neill (1888–1953), learned his craft in New England. The New Yorker studied at the 47 Workshop of George Pierce Baker in Harvard before making an impact with the Provincetown Players on Cape Cod. Ten of his plays were produced from 1916 to 1920. A Nobel and Pulitzer prize winner, O'Neill is remembered at the theater bearing his name near New London, Connecticut. The cottage where he spent his boyhood summers was the setting for *Long Day's Journey into Night*.

Music

While Puritan influences restricted early New Englanders to music in churches, the region has been a powerhouse of classical music in the 20th century. The best known composer is the avant-garde Charles Ives (1874–1954), born in Danbury, Connecticut, the son of a bandmaster. Fiercely proud and inde-pendent, Ives bucked European tradition to draw on traditional American folk songs, hymns, and marches. The result was his *New England Symphony, Three Places in New England,* and *Sonata No. 2* for piano and flute. The last was nicknamed *Concord, Mass 1840–1860,* perhaps because of its dedication to the town's literary circle of Emerson, Thoreau, Hawthorne, and the Alcotts.

New Englander Colonel Henry Higginson enjoyed the Austrian attitude to music so much that he set up the legendary Boston Pops in 1885, based on the romance and fun of Viennese orchestras. In 1929, the Pops went outdoors to perform, as they still do to this day. The Boston Symphony, now one of the world's great orchestras, has extended its popularity and fame thanks to the summer season in Tanglewood, in western Massachusetts.

CONNECTICUT

Connecticut is rarely recognized as a vacation destination. Although popular with Manhattanites for weekends, many Americans and overseas visitors overlook it when planning a trip to New England. Yet it has a history dating back to 1635, a rich tapestry of villages and towns, countryside that looks softer than elsewhere in the northeast and miles of unspoiled shoreline. Contrasts are to be found everywhere. Although well over half the state is heavily forested, Connecticut is also heavily populated. Most residents live in the suburbs, on the southwest coast and alongside the Connecticut River that cuts through the middle of this rectangular state.

From the early days, the state has been the home of a host of inventors whose ideas still provide employment. Eli Whitney's cotton gin brought mass production techniques to the world. Sam Colt, inventor of the Colt 45 revolver, set up an arms and ammunition industry that survives today. Clocks and door locks, tires and the pay telephone were all developed here. Now, chemicals, jet engines, and insurance are major employers. One of the wealthiest states in the country, in 1988 it also boasted the highest per capita income.

Norfolk is one of the best preserved villages in the northeast

The affluent southwestern corner of Connecticut is virtually a suburb of New York City. Further north, the Litchfield Hills, idyllic for artists and craftsmen, are also a retreat for show business celebrities. Two hundred years ago, the same wooded hills were stripped to fuel the furnaces and forges that processed iron for the guns used during the Revolution.

The coast, especially the eastern strip, is the most popular with visitors. Mystic is an admirable re-creation of an early 19th-century seafaring village complete with sailing ships.

There is a rich cultural heritage, because of the influence of Yale University and writers such as Mark Twain, Harriet Beecher Stowe, and dictionary-writer Noah Webster. Painters and actors have also made their homes here, and antique shops and art galleries abound.

Tour 8

Hartford is known as the "Insurance Capital of America." The business began in 1794. It is also a city of "firsts" and "oldests." It claims the first municipal rose garden and development of the first American dictionary; the oldest newspaper, the *Hartford Courant*, and oldest state house. Two of America's most revered writers also lived here: Mark Twain and Harriet Beecher Stowe, who was Twain's neighbor. Twain's Victorian house is one of the most intriguing you'll see, deliberately designed to be unusual.

Tour 9

When it comes to universities, Yale and Harvard go together like Oxford and Cambridge, in England. Just as Harvard and Cambridge are in attractive towns, so Yale and Oxford are in industrial cities. Yale, with its ivy-covered buildings, is one of the finest academic institutions in the country, with impressive museums and art galleries. Countering all this culture, the Frisbee was supposedly invented here, along with two of America's most popular fast foods: the hamburger and the pizza.

Tour 10

Western Connecticut has bumpy, wooded hills dotted with villages that don't seem to have kept up with the 20th century. Although New York City is within commuting distance, urban frenzy is banned here. This is the countryside the way urban folk prefer it, with waterfalls and covered bridges, pleasant shops and small art galleries. As for history, Litchfield boasts the first American law school, which was set up in a tiny house over 200 years ago. The innocent-looking town of Lakeville turned out tons of arms to fuel the battle against Britain, winning itself the nickname of the "Arsenal of the Revolution."

Tour 11

Connecticut's coast was settled in the early 17th century by British emigrants who named the small towns after their homes: New London, Guilford, Essex and Old Lyme. The oldest stone house in New England, complete with fortifications, was built back in 1640. Later, locals turned their hand to building ships and submarines. The finest maritime museum in the States is at Mystic, where boats and docks re-create the romance, if not the reality, of life aboard the sailing ships of the 18th and 19th centuries.

Later, the seaside attracted artists and writers, while the Eugene O'Neill Theater Center outside New London gave actors such as Al Pacino and Meryl Streep their early opportunities. Despite the popularity of the bigger towns, there are still sleepy corners where visitors can sit and munch a sandwich in peace, overlooking tranquil Long Island Sound.

Mystic Seaport is a re-creation of a 19th-century seaport

Hartford

One of the oldest cities in the country, Hartford was founded in 1636 by a native of Hertford, England. There is an English flavor to the narrow streets and parks of Hartford, downtown is easily navigable, and skyscrapers rise high above the Connecticut River. In this state capital are well-preserved historic places, the nation's oldest public art museum, world-famous rose gardens, and the homes of two of America's best-known and best-loved writers, Harriet Beecher Stowe and Mark Twain.

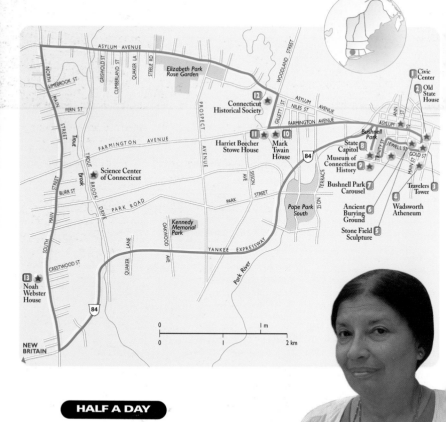

HALF A DAY

The Senate Chamber of the Old State House – the first state house in a newly independent United States

i I *Civic Center Plaza*

▶ *Park your car in the Civic Center garage, entrance on Asylum Street.*

❶ Civic Center

Under a circular dome in the heart of downtown Hartford, the Civic Center is a shopping center, restaurant and professional sports arena, all in one. Since the Hartford Whalers ice-hockey team left, a little of the glamor has gone, but the outstanding University of Connecticut basketball squad fills the arena, while the Hartford Wolf Pack, an affiliate of the New York Rangers ice-hockey team, now faces off here.

▶ *Leave the Civic Center and walk east on Asylum Street to Main Street. Cross and enter the Old State House.*

❷ Old State House

Painstaking restorations have revived the oldest state house, designed in 1792 and completed in 1796 by New England's star architect Charles Bulfinch. It stands on Meeting House Square, where the Colony was founded in 1636. There is no mistaking the daily opening time at 10am, since it is preceded by the ceremonial firing of a cannon by uniformed "Continental troops." Guides in full period dress give the facts and relate anecdotes about rooms, such as the Council and restored Senate Chambers. The highlight in these high-style, Victorian masterpieces is the original version of Gilbert Stuart's famous portrait of the first president of the US, George Washington. Also in the Old State House is Mr. Steward's Museum of Art and Curiosities, plus an interactive center of state history. The Museum Store specializes in state products, crafts and foods. Outside, a farmer's market follows in the Colonial tradition of setting up stalls by the meeting house.

▶ *Walk south one block to Travelers Tower, on the corner of Gold Street.*

SPECIAL TO...

The Connecticut Freedom Trail was established in 1995 to honor the history of the state's African American community, and covers a series of buildings and sites that represent the concept of freedom. Hartford's Old State House features in the trail for the part it played in the famous Amistad trials, a two-year legal battle that ultimately set free and repatriated to Sierra Leone a group of Africans who, in 1839, had taken control of the Spanish vessel carrying them to a life of slavery in Cuba. Reenactments of the trial feature in the Old State House's program of events.

---

3 Travelers Tower
Soaring 527 feet (160m) above street level, the "free Renaissance"-style, pink-granite Travelers Tower is capped by a prominent beacon light. From the observation deck atop the tower, visitors are rewarded with a breathtaking view of downtown Hartford, the Connecticut River and the entire Connecticut Valley from Mount Tom to Meriden Mountain in the south.

▶ *Across the street, on the corner of Main and Gold streets is the Wadsworth Atheneum.*

4 Wadsworth Atheneum
One of New England's leading "must-see" museums, "the Wad" was founded in 1842, so it takes the title "the nation's oldest public art museum." Housed in an impressive neo-Gothic building, it boasts masterpieces from the 16th through the 20th centuries, including classics by Picasso

(*Harlequin*) and Van Gogh (*Self Portrait*). The most intriguing painting is *House Fronting New Milford Green* by Ralph Earl, painted in 1796. The house still stands. Other home-grown talent includes members of the Hudson River School, the 19th-

The Gothic Revival Wadsworth Atheneum. Inset: statue of Nathan Hale, local schoolmaster and patriot

Travelers Tower was once the tallest building in New England

century group of landscape painters who achieved a definite American style. There is also a fine collection of African-American art, decorative arts, costumes and textiles.

▶ *Cross the street diagonally to the north side of Gold Street and proceed down Gold Street, stopping at the Stone Field Sculpture and the adjacent Ancient Burying Ground.*

5 Stone Field Sculpture

"$250,000 for a pile of rocks? That's ridiculous!" That was the reaction of many locals when the Hartford City Council voted to fund the sculpture created by Carl Andre in 1977. His work of art consists of 36 large stones laid out in rows to form an isosceles triangle. A similar furor erupted in England when London's Tate Gallery bought "a pile of bricks," a total of 120 bricks in two layers which the American sculptor entitled *Equivalent VIII*.

6 Ancient Burying Ground

Center Church, built in 1632, is Hartford's oldest church. Behind it, the Ancient Burying Ground is one of the city's few surviving historic sites from the 17th century. In the small, green, fenced-in graveyard, more than 400 brownstone markers stand at attention, marking the final resting places of Hartford's founding families. Epitaphs record lives that were only occasionally lengthy, more often short. Many

show dates of birth from the 1590s to the early 1600s, in Hertford, England.

▶ *Continue walking down Gold Street to Bushnell Park. Turn right along the border, Jewell Street. Opposite Ann Street, across from the YMCA, the Bushnell Park Carousel is in the park.*

7 Bushnell Park Carousel

The carousel is a Stein and Goldstein, hand-carved merry-go-round built in 1914, with 48 prancing horses and chariots rollicking to the tunes of a 1925 Wurlitzer band organ. At only 50 cents a ride, it is one of New England's bargains. Hot dogs and other snacks are available when the park is open.

▶ *Walk a few steps west to Trinity Street. Look right to the Sailors and Soldiers Memorial Arch, built in 1886 to honor the 4,000 Hartford citizens who served in the Civil War. Turn left and proceed up the hill half a block to the State Capitol. A statue of the French General Lafayette, ally of George Washington, sits on horseback in the middle of the street at the driveway entrance.*

8 State Capitol

Another refurbished landmark (built 1789), the Capitol is the home of the House of Representatives and Senate, Connecticut's legislature. Against a backdrop of white Connecticut marble are Gothic spires, a gleaming gold dome, statues, medallions, and bas-reliefs commemorating important people and events in state history. Gaudy to the point of being brash, architect Frank Lloyd Wright called it "The most ridiculous building I know of." Open to the public, the assemblies are in session from February to May in even years and February through June in odd years. More statues and historical relics decorate the interior.

TOUR

8

▶ *Cross Capitol Avenue to No. 231.*

🟈 Museum of Connecticut History

The State Library and Supreme Court sandwich this museum, which contains the Fundamental Orders of Connecticut and the Colt Firearms Collection. The latter showcases Samuel Colt's genius for the invention, making, and marketing of his patented revolvers and rifles. The museum also has a variety of political, industrial, and military artifacts, with an emphasis on the Civil War era.

▶ *Return to the Capitol. Walk through it (round it, if closed) to the rear exit and continue north down the hill and through the park to Asylum Street. Turn right and walk one block back to the Civic Center to retrieve your car. Leave downtown, driving west on Asylum Street under the railroad bridge. Bear left at the fork onto Farmington Avenue. After 1 mile (1.6km), on the left is the home of Mark Twain.*

🔟 Mark Twain House

The internationally known writer and wit Samuel Clemens, alias Mark Twain, lived in this spectacular orange and black brick Victorian mansion for 17 years. He commissioned this

Gothic eccentricity in 1871, when he settled in Hartford with his family. In 1881, he had the 19-room home completely refurbished by Louis Comfort Tiffany. The library is the epitome of Victorian opulence, with carved wood, patterned carpets, and lavishly decorated walls and ceilings. Guides describe the life of the writer, his soirées with guests such as English writer Rudyard Kipling, and the way he retired to the billiard room to write books such as *A Connecticut Yankee in King Arthur's Court* and *The Prince and the Pauper*, because his children had commandeered his study. One of the first private citizens in

The State Capitol; its exuberant design reflects Victorian pride

Hartford to have a telephone, Twain had so many problems with the new-fangled instrument that he kept a chart to record its inefficiencies. Symbols representing noise on the line range from "artillery can be heard" to "artillery and thunder can be heard."

▶ *Next door to the Twain house, at Forest Street, is the home of Harriet Beecher Stowe.*

🇽🇮 Harriet Beecher Stowe House

The "little lady who started the big war" (Civil War, 1865–70), was how President Abraham Lincoln referred to the author of *Uncle Tom's Cabin*. Published in 1852, the book was a blockbuster, selling over 300,000 copies in the first year alone. A stage version was even performed. The sentimental story of slaves in the south was unabashed, though successful, propaganda for the Anti-Slavery Movement. Nowadays, no-one remembers any of her other 30 books. Moreover, the term "Uncle Tom" has come to mean a black person who does not stand up for the rights of his race.

This house, in what was quiet farmland a century ago, was Stowe's home from 1873 until she died in 1896. Her home is

---

SPECIAL TO...

Samuel Colt (1814–62) was a self-taught and persistent inventor who revolutionized hand guns. Aged 21, he patented his Colt Paterson revolver and used the assembly-line techniques of fellow Connecticut inventor Eli Whitney to mass produce weapons. His 1848 Colt Dragoon was the first U.S. Army regulation revolver and years later, the American West was won with what was, ironically, called the Colt Peacemaker.

FOR HISTORY BUFFS

On the Mississippi River, when a boatman called out "*Mark Twain,*" the pilot knew that the depth was two fathoms. This was the pseudonym taken by Samuel Clemens, in 1862, when he became a newspaper reporter. Born in Missouri in 1835, Twain popularized life in the West with books such as *The Adventures of Tom Sawyer* (1876) and *The Adventures of Huckleberry Finn* (1884). Despite his folksy stories, he was no hayseed, but a well-traveled man, awarded an honorary degree by Oxford University in 1907.

now restored and paintings by her and her writing table, plus memorabilia of her career and her family lend a personal touch.

▶ Continue west on Farmington Avenue for half a block. Turn right on Woodland Street, then take the first left onto Asylum Avenue. Just before the first traffic light, the Connecticut Historical Society is on the left.

12 Connecticut Historical Society

Inside, the museum offers rotating exhibits on state history, plus permanent displays of furniture and the decorative arts from Connecticut craftsmen of the 17th, 18th and 19th centuries. Browse through the bookshop, with its extensive genealogy collection, enabling people to trace their roots back to England and other nations of origin.

Mark Twain's House, in the Nook Farm district of Hartford

▶ Back on Asylum Avenue, continue through the traffic light and take the right fork. After a mile (1.6km), having passed through two more traffic lights, the Elizabeth Park Rose Garden is on the left (see **Back to Nature** panel).

▶ Return to Asylum Avenue and drive for 1½ miles (2.2km), through two traffic lights. At the third light, turn left on North Main Street and go 2 miles (3km) through the West Hartford Center shopping district. North Main becomes South Main. Continue to No. 227, on the right.

13 Noah Webster House

Born in 1758, Noah Webster graduated from Yale and became a teacher. He soon saw the need to standardize spelling, so published his *Bluebacked Spellers*, which sold some 70 million copies and became the basis for elementary education

BACK TO NATURE

The Elizabeth Park Rose Garden was the first municipal rose garden in the nation and now boasts some 15,000 rose bushes in about 800 varieties, which bloom and perfume the air from late May until late October. There are also swaths of tulips, plus rock gardens, ornamental grasses, and unusual collector specimen trees and nature walks.

throughout the country. The "Schoolmaster of the Republic" did not stop there. He recognized that the language of America was evolving from the original English words, spelling and pronunciation, and spent 20 years compiling *An American Dictionary of the English Language*. Published in 1828, the two volumes contained some 70,000 words.

Inside the house are a first edition of his dictionary, his spellers and some 200 editions of his works. Guides in 200-year-old Colonial dress lead the way through the authentically furnished rooms. There are demonstrations of carding wool, weaving on the massive loom, cooking, bread baking, and butter churning.

▶ Continue south on South Main Street and turn left onto I–84 eastbound at exit 41 to return to downtown Hartford.

FOR CHILDREN

The Science Center of Connecticut on Trout Brook Drive (roughly parallel, and to the east of South Main Street), is a great place for children, with lots of hands-on exhibits and other fun things to do. There's Kids Factory, Mathmagical Toys, marine life touch tanks, a planetarium, computer laboratory, and much more.

New Haven &
Yale University

Founded in 1638 by a group of settlers, the town first depended on seafaring. In the 19th century, thanks to inventors such as Eli Whitney, assembly lines turned out clocks, carriages, and guns by the thousands. More recently, New Haven has had to face the urban problems of unattractive development and crime, though efforts to renew and restore civic pride are paying off. At the heart of the city is Yale, one of America's leading universities, adding an enviable cultural dimension to the city.

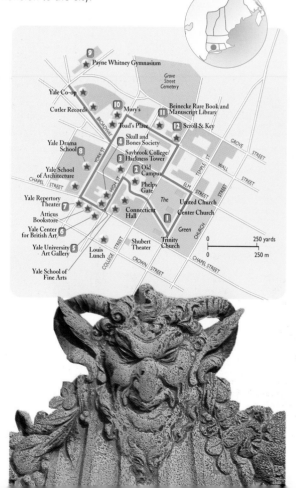

i *59 Elm Street; Yale University, 149 Elm Street*

▶ *Start on The Green on the corner of Temple and Elm streets.*

❶ The Green

New Haven has been called "the first planned city in the U.S.A." because of its original (1638) grid-like street design, visible from the 16-acre (6.4-hectare) Green. Here, residents came to gossip, to debate, and to pray at the trio of handsome churches, each with its different architecture, but all built in the early 1800s.

The United Church, often compared with London's St. Martin-in-the-Fields, has long held public meetings and debates on topics ranging from slavery in the 1800s to Civil Rights in the 1970s. It is also sometimes referred to as the North Church.

In the middle of The Green is Center Church, and ever since the mid-1600s, a meeting house or church has stood on this site. Cool and elegant within, handsome Tiffany stained glass fills the arched window above the altar. Trinity Church, the third, was the first Gothic Revival church in the country, and was constructed with materials

Neo-Gothic Harkness Tower, a New Haven landmark

SPECIAL TO...

Ever wondered who invented the hamburger? One of the strongest claims comes from Louis Lassen of New Haven who served them here at Louis Lunch. That was back in 1895, and the simple brick house with a communal table and two booths, probably looks much now as it did then. It stands in the middle of a parking lot at 263 Crown Street. The hamburgers, however, come as a surprise. Forget the griddle and the buns, these beef patties are cooked in front of diners on a vertical gas grill and served on toast.

allowed to pass through the British blockade of New Haven harbor during the War of 1812. Compared with the white cupola and steeple of its neighbors, the tower seems heavy and ponderous. Two impressive buildings, City Hall and the Post Office, overlook the Green.

▶ *Walk diagonally north across the Green towards the imposing battlements and towers of Yale University and enter the Old Campus through the Phelps Gate.*

Yale University is an architectural showpiece

② Old Campus

Phelps Gate, the front door to Yale, leads to the Old Campus, a typical university quadrangle. The oldest building here is also the oldest in town. Connecticut Hall, with its handsome windows and brick, was built between 1750 and 1753. Nathan Hale, Class of 1773, whose green patina statue sits outside, lived here during his student years. Three years later he was hanged in New York by the British who caught him spying. His last words: "I only regret that I have but one life to lose for my country" became a rallying cry. He was only 21. The right foot of Timothy Woolsey's statue is particularly shiny thanks to superstitious students giving it a rub before exams.

Off to the right, before leaving the quadrangle, is a rough-hewn granite bench. Here, A.

Bartlett Giamattei, a former president of the college would sit, philosophizing about life and comparing it to a baseball game. His best loved essay, *Green Fields of the Mind*, is baseball-oriented. So keen was he on baseball,

---

SPECIAL TO...

Among the contributions Yale students have made to the world, nothing is quite as much fun as the Frisbee. Since 1947, students supposedly have whizzed flat aluminium pie dishes at one another across the Old Campus. When Wham-O, inventors of the hula-hoop, bought the patent for a plastic flier, they called it a Frisbee, because those dishes came from Bridgeport's Frisbie Baking Company. Such major inventions are often in dispute: Middlebury College in Vermont (see page 117) also claims to be the home of the Frisbee.

FOR HISTORY BUFFS

Like its perennial rival Harvard, near Boston, Yale is one of America's Ivy League schools. Originally started by the Puritans in 1701, to train clergymen and administrators, the first Collegiate School moved to New Haven 15 years later, and changed its name to Yale in recognition of wealthy benefactor, Elihu Yale. Students were nicknamed the "Elis" in honor of the English merchant, whose donation of books was sold to finance the institution. The roll call of famous Yale students ranges from dictionary compiler Noah Webster and architect Eero Saarinen to film star Jodie Foster, Class of 1984. From the renowned graduate schools, especially the Law School, recent celebrities include President Bill Clinton and his wife Hillary, who first met here.

America's favorite summer game, that he gave up academia to become the Commissioner for Baseball and run the professional sport. Sadly, he died soon after taking up the appointment.

▶ *Cross the quadrangle and exit onto High Street.*

3 Saybrook College and the Harkness Tower

Above the elaborate wrought iron gate as one exits is an inscription: "For God, For Country and For Yale." The seal of the college has the Latin words *Lux et Veritas* (Light and Truth), but these jollier words are the last lines of Yale's student song, *Bright College Years*, composed in 1888.

Across the street are the twin buildings of Saybrook and Branford Colleges, reminders of the school's locations before it moved to New Haven. Yale consists of a dozen separate and self-governing colleges. Their buildings were funded by the Harkness family, commemorated by the tall, dark, Gothic Harkness Tower which soars *221 feet (67m)*, and houses a 54-bell carillon, one of the largest in the world. Its partner, the Wrexham Tower, is modelled on the church steeple in Wrexham, Wales, where Elihu Yale is buried.

▶ *Turn left and continue on High Street.*

4 Skull and Bones Society

Just before walking under the arch, the windowless and ominous-looking stone building on the right is the Skull and Bones Society. Founded in 1832, it is Yale's oldest secret society. Although the membership is never publicized, it supposedly included former president, George Bush. Among many "Bones" legends is one that the remains of the great Apache chief, Geronimo, are interred within its walls.

▶ *Pass under the arch linking the Yale School of Fine Arts (left)*

with the Yale University Art Gallery (right), whose entrance is at 1111 Chapel Street.

SPECIAL TO...

Call them secret societies or senior societies, only half a dozen of the most famous, such as Skull and Bones, are known. Each has only 15 members, all of them seniors who choose their successors from the junior class. Only members have keys to the unmarked windowless buildings where, rumor insists, Masonic-like rituals take place. Some clubhouses resemble grand English manor houses, others echo Greek mausoleums, giving rise to the nickname, "the tombs." All are totally independent of the university.

---

5 Yale University Art Gallery

The nation's oldest college art gallery dates back to 1832 and is one of several fine museums here, some of which offer free admission. A replica of the original gallery is named for John Trumbull (1756–1843), the founder, and exhibits his work. This artist depicted major moments of the Revolution, such as the Battle of Bunker Hill in Boston, and the signing of the Declaration of Independence. Today, the museum boasts an enormous international collection. From the past are Greek, Roman, Egyptian, and pre-Columbian antiquities. From 19th- and 20th-century Europe are paintings by Manet, Millet, Matisse, and Magritte. Of the museum's two buildings, the 1953 addition is the work of architect Louis Kahn. He also designed the Yale Center for British Art, across Chapel Street.

▶ *Cross Chapel Street.*

6 Yale Center for British Art

The center's enormous collection, the gift of Paul Mellon in 1966, traces the development of

---

SPECIAL TO...

America's second-favorite fast-food is the pizza, and that, too, belongs to New Haven. In 1925, Italian immigrant Frank Pepe started selling his special "tomato pies" from a horse-drawn cart. As their popularity grew, he opened Pepe Pizzeria on Worcester Street in New Haven's Little Italy. His trademark *focaccio*-like crust is still cooked in a brick oven, after almost 60 years.

SPECIAL TO...

"Bulldog, Bulldog, Bow wow wow. Eli Yale!" goes the chant. For over a century, the bulldog has been the mascot of Yale's sports teams. Some say an English student introduced the dog; others credit Professor Andrew Graves, whose pooch accompanied him everywhere. The dog was so clever, the story goes, that he barked whenever Yale scored in a football game. Since 1933, there has been a succession of bulldog mascots, all called "Handsome Dan." The 1996 version, Handsome Dan the 14th, is known to his friends as Whizzer.

British art over the centuries and includes a roll call of the great: van Dyck, Gainsborough, Reynolds, and Turner. For more specialist tastes are the works of visionary William Blake and animal painter, George Stubbs (*A Lion Attacking a Horse*).

▶ *Continue on Chapel Street, passing the Atticus Bookstore. Here browsers and buyers are joined by sippers of exotic teas and coffees served in the small café. Walk to the corner of Chapel and York streets.*

7 Yale Repertory Theatre

Since 1966, a small professional company, boosted by students from the graduate school, has

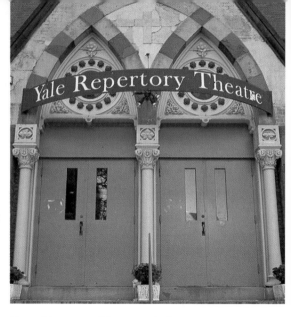

Home of the renowned Yale Repertory Company

presented avant-garde, cutting-edge work in this 500-seat converted Victorian gothic church.

▶ *Diagonally across from the theater on York Street is the Yale School of Architecture. What looks like nine stories on the outside actually hides 36 floors, and caused much discussion when it was put up in the 1960s. Turn right on York Street.*

8 Yale Drama School

This is one of Yale's many illustrious graduate schools; students who have attended a three-year course here include Paul Newman and Meryl Streep. Contrary to popular myth, Jodie Foster did not attend the Drama School: she was a liberal arts undergraduate.

▶ *Continue on York Street to Elm Street. Turn left, then veer right onto Broadway. Look up to the right.*

9 Payne Whitney Gymnasium

Dominating the skyline is the tower of what looks like a Gothic cathedral. Inside, however, are neither pillars nor pews but "Yalies" in sweat pants and sneakers. The Trophy Room contains memorabilia dating back to 1842. Although the university does not award athlet-

FOR HISTORY BUFFS

Eli Whitney, the Yale graduate who became "father of mass production," made his name by inventing the cotton gin, which separated cotton fibers from the seeds. Although he patented the design in 1794, it was much-copied, so he did not make his deserved fortune.

Next, his analytical brain turned to the making of guns. By standardizing components, he produced guns faster and cheaper in his factory than craftsmen could by traditional methods.

ics scholarships, sports facilities are as good as anywhere in the country, and "The Game," the annual football game against Harvard, is both a passionate match and a social occasion.

▶ *Return to York Street and turn left. Halfway down the block, at No. 300, is Toad's Place, well known to rock music fans. Next door is Mory's, one of the best-known spots in town.*

10 Mory's

Today, Mory's is a private club for eating and drinking, but it started out as a bar and inspired a famous ballad, the Whiffen-poof song:

*"To the tables down at Mory's
To the place where Louis dwells ... "*

Louis Linder was the club's proprietor back in 1909 when four students, members of the Yale Glee Club singers, formed the barbershop-style Varsity Quartet. They took the name of the Whiffenpoof, a mythical half-bird, half-dragon that was a character in a contemporary Broadway show. Now, the 14-strong Whiffenpoofs are the oldest a cappella choir in the country, giving 150 concerts a year. They still meet at Mory's every week.

▶ *Turn right on Wall Street and walk to the corner of Wall and High streets.*

11 Beinecke Rare Book and Manuscript Library

This three-star building alone is worth the journey to New Haven: the exterior, the most memorable of the university's modern buildings, looks like an unbroken cube of white Vermont marble supported at four corners by the lightest of steel pads. Even more memorable is the interior, glowing with bronze-hued light filtering through the translucent marble. The central stack is a six-story glass tower of rare books. On the mezzanine level are two large cases: one holds a rare 1455 Gutenberg Bible, one of only 22 known, the other a complete edition of *Birds of America* by naturalist John James Audubon (1785–1851).

▶ *Continue on Wall Street, to the corner of College Street.*

12 Scroll & Key

Enigmatic and bearing no name or sign, this stone building, with minarets and mystical carved figures, is home to another of the private secret societies.

▶ *Turn right on College Street, left on Elm Street, and return to the Green.*

TOUR
10

The Housatonic
Valley

1 DAY • 151½ MILES • 245KM

The rolling Litchfield Hills and the Housatonic River give a special char-

acter to the scattered villages that dot the peaceful northwest corner of

Connecticut, among the thick woods.

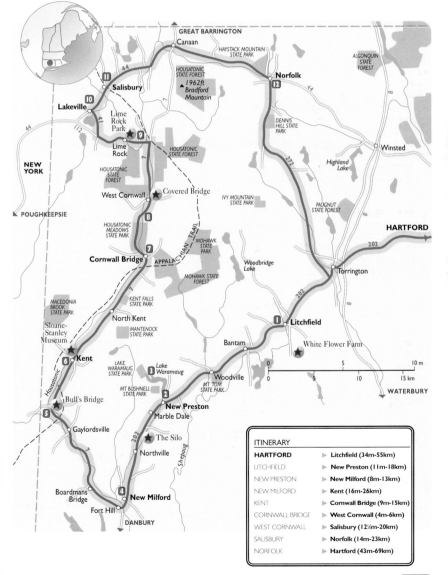

ITINERARY

HARTFORD	▶	Litchfield (34m-55km)
LITCHFIELD	▶	**New Preston (11m-18km)**
NEW PRESTON	▶	**New Milford (8m-13km)**
NEW MILFORD	▶	Kent (16m-26km)
KENT	▶	**Cornwall Bridge (9m-15km)**
CORNWALL BRIDGE	▶	**West Cornwall (4m-6km)**
WEST CORNWALL	▶	Salisbury (12½m-20km)
SALISBURY	▶	**Norfolk (14m-23km)**
NORFOLK	▶	Hartford (43m-69km)

Litchfield, a classic example of the perfect New England town

$\boxed{i}$ *Hartford Civic Center*

▶ *Leave Hartford on Route 44 west. After 16 miles (26km), Route 202 branches off to Torrington. Continue through Torrington and drive 6 miles (10km) to Litchfield.*

❶ Litchfield

Rather as a judge surveys his court, so Litchfield dominates the local landscape. Appropriately, the Tapping Reeve House on South Street was owned by Judge Tapping Reeve, who had America's first law school built in the grounds. Opened in 1773, it produced judges by the score, as well as three justices of the U.S. Supreme Court, 17 senators, and two vice-presidents. Exhibits here relate the importance of the school and its students to the new nation. During that era, Litchfield was also famous for its leather goods, mills, and factories. Townspeople have deliberately redesigned their homes and the common to re-create the

The Housatonic River valley

classic New England village seen today.

The First Congregational Church, with its white columns, has a stately position at the head of the Green with North, South,

East and West streets reaching out in their appropriate compass headings. North Street, often labelled one of the country's most beautiful, boasts textbook examples of late 1700s Georgian and Federal architecture, such as the Sheldon Tavern. The sturdy

restaurants. The West Street Grill is known for its celebrity customers, from politicians to movie stars.

ⓘ *Information booth, The Green*

▶ *Drive west for 11 miles (18km) on Route 202.*

❷ New Preston

The road climbs abruptly to New Preston, alongside the tumbling waterfalls of the Aspetuck River, which give a clue to the town's industrial background. In the early 1800s, no less than 21 water-driven mills operated between New Preston and Marble Dale, barely a mile away. The mills did not survive the transition to steam power, but New Preston thrives on a new economy centered on its chic antique shops.

▶ *Continue through New Preston for ½ mile (1km) to Lake Waramaug.*

❸ Lake Waramaug

To the Indians, Lake Waramaug was the "place of good fishing." Today, most visitors just come to catch the view, and to visit the Hopkins Vineyard, where the red-painted Yankee barn houses the winery and shop.

SPECIAL TO...

Skitch Henderson, Broadway veteran and director of the New York Pops Orchestra, lives in a typical New England country home called The Silo, located halfway between New Preston and New Milford. It is also home to a school of cookery, an art gallery, and a gourmet store of limitless variety, and attracts friends of the Hendersons and neighboring celebrities such as Bill Blass, Whoopi Goldberg, and Tom Brokaw.

▶ *Return to New Preston and take Route 202 south for 8 miles (19km) to New Milford.*

❹ New Milford

The Town Hall on the Green stands on the site of Roger Sherman's birthplace. He is the only native of Connecticut whose signature appears on all the significant documents concerning America's independence. Near the bandstand is a tank whose small scale and Victorian styling make it an unusually decorative armed forces memorial.

▶ *Drive through New Milford on Routes 202 and 67 southwest, cross the Housatonic River bridge, turn right at the traffic lights onto Route 7 north and continue through peaceful countryside to Bull's Bridge.*

❺ Bull's Bridge

Bull's Bridge, one of just two covered bridges in the state which still see daily use, is barely longer than a large car. Beneath, the Housatonic River rushes through a particularly rugged gorge. Raging waters and winter ice jams destroyed four successive bridges until the present one, which has lasted since 1842. Back in 1781, a horse in George Washington's party fell into this gorge while making the crossing. Washington's own financial accounts record "getting a horse out of Bull's Bridge falls, $215.00." The high price suggests that the horse was probably the general's.

▶ *Continue on Route 7 to Kent.*

SCENIC ROUTES

From New Milford north to Canaan is one of Connecticut's prettiest drives. Running parallel to the Housatonic River the entire way, Route 7 is bordered by the Litchfield Hills to the east and the Taconic Mountains to the west. Housatonic is an Indian word meaning "place beyond the mountains," and it offers tempting photo opportunities.

SPECIAL TO...

White Flower Farm, 3½ miles (5.6km) out of Litchfield via South Street, is an emporium of flower gardening. Its *Garden Book*, a weighty catalog published twice a year, offers a wealth of horticultural information. Visitors from mid-June through August are treated to the technicolor extravaganza of the begonia displays, a high point in the season.

red-brick building at the corner of North and West streets was the Litchfield County Jail. Built in 1812, it was in use until the 1990s.

Also on North Street is the red saltbox house that was the home of two 19th-century personalities: the charismatic preacher Rev. Henry Beecher and his sister and author, Harriet Beecher Stowe. The Litchfield Historical Society on the Green has a fine collection of early paintings, decorative arts, and furniture, and the Green is lined with trendy shops, galleries, and

6 Kent

Just as Litchfield was once industrial, so Kent was known for its iron foundries. Where pig iron was smelted in the early 1800s, the Sloane-Stanley Museum and Kent Furnace now stands. A dedicated historian and fine artist, Sloane chronicled all aspects of early American life, from the building of barns to his favorite subject, the making and using of tools. The museum, housed in a big barn, includes a dog-powered butter churn, an authentic frontier cabin, and a re-creation of his art studio, right down to his paint-splattered telephone. Ruins of the furnace stand on the grounds, recalling a vanished local industry. Next door is the Connecticut Antique Machinery Association Museum, with its large collection of steam engines and tractors, and a working narrow-gauge railroad.

▶ Stay on **Route 7** north for 5 miles (8km) to Kent Falls State Park. Continue to Cornwall Bridge.

RECOMMENDED WALKS

Kent Falls State Park is one of a dozen or so state parks and forests in this corner of Connecticut. All are popular spots for picnics and hiking. Here, the special attraction is a broad view over Connecticut's wild terrain.
For a grand view, climb the steep 200-foot (60m) path beside the falls, which are often used for advertisements and feature in the TV soap opera, *The Guiding Light*.

---

7 Cornwall Bridge

From here north, the valley narrows and the hills steepen. Hardly more than an intersection and the bridge, the hub of this little community is Baird's General Store, a well-known stopping point for Appalachian Trail hikers. The "world's longest continuous footpath" stretches 2,050 miles (3,280km) from Georgia to northeast Maine. It crosses Route 7 only a few steps from the front porch where weary walkers stack their backpacks.

SPECIAL TO...

You can visit the workshop of the Cornwall Bridge Pottery, south of Cornwall Bridge, to see the craftspeople at work and view the huge wood-fired kiln in which their stylish pots are fired. Seconds are on sale here; the main shop is in West Cornwall.

▶ Cross the Housatonic again; bear right after the bridge and continue north to West Cornwall on **Route 7**.

SPECIAL TO...

The only covered bridges for cars in the state are here: at West Cornwall and Bulls Bridge, Kent

---

Water tumbles down a 200-foot (60m) flight of natural steps in Kent Falls State Park

the left. Although U.S. Olympic teams make this their home base, Clarke's also outfits day trips for recreational paddlers and provides a shuttle service to and from the entry/exit points. The favorite "playground" for the kayakers is beneath the covered bridge at West Cornwall, built in 1837.

▶ *Stay on* **Route 7** *north for 4¹/₂ miles (7km), bearing left on* **Route 112** *for ¾ mile (1km) to Lime Rock Park.*

9 Lime Rock Park

Deep in the rural idyll, the self-styled "Road Racing Center of the East" comes as a surprise. The deceptively simple 1¹/₂-mile (2.4km) track has tested the best from every category of motor-sport. Drivers from Formula 1 to NASCAR and sports car racing have all taken the wheel here. Among celebrity competitors often seen here are the actors Paul Newman and Tom Cruise.

▶ *Continue west for 3³/₄ miles (6km) on* **Route 112**. *Climbing out of the Housatonic Valley, grand views open up of magnificent farms. To the north and west, the Berkshire Hills continue and blend into the Catskill Mountains of New York and the Green Mountains of Vermont. Turn north onto* **Route 41** *and drive for 1¹/₂ miles (2.4km) to Lakeville.*

10 Lakeville

Two fascinating museums lie opposite each other at the heart of the Lakeville Historic District. The first is Holley House Museum, where costumed guides portray the everyday life of a late 19th-century family and the social issues of the times. You can squeeze into a lace-up corset, view a seven-holer outhouse and learn about topics as diverse as pre-electric refrigeration and women's suffrage. Across the street, the Salisbury Cannon Museum is where weapons were

8 Cornwall Bridge to West Cornwall

This is one of the prettiest stretches of the Housatonic, known as a fly-fisherman's paradise. Throughout the summer, anglers practice the elegant art of casting and placing the fly delicately on the water.

Somewhat rougher are the sports of white-water canoeing and kayaking. Paddlers meet at Clarke's Outdoors, a log cabin on

made during the Revolutionary War. Here the portrayal of the working lives of seven individuals employed at the factory adds a personal touch to the business of making cannons – and the reason they were required.

▶ *Continue north on* **Routes 41** *and* **44** *for 2 miles (3km) to Salisbury.*

11 Salisbury

Salisbury has unofficially become the "Tea Capital" of Connecticut thanks to Chaiwalla, a specialty tea room, and Harney & Sons, master tea blenders and manufacturers found on Main Street. Nearby is the venerable Salisbury Ski Jump, where the annual winter festival in February brings competitors from as far as Norway and Finland.

i Chamber of Commerce, Main Street

▶ *Follow* **Route 44** *for 7 miles (11km) to Canaan and on for another 7 miles (11km) to Norfolk.*

12 Norfolk

Connecticut's highest town, tucked away in the northwestern corner, has an elevation of 1,770 feet (540m). Here, the Battell Chapel, with its Tiffany glass windows, faces the central Green which sits atop the hill. Each summer, the Norfolk Chamber Music Festival, with the Yale Summer School of Music, attracts music fans as it has for almost a century. Rachmaninov, Caruso, and Paderewski are among the legends who have performed during the season. Many of the street signs, painted by hand, have been brightened up with pictures of animals.

▶ *From the Green take the tranquil country drive back to Torrington on* **Route 272**. *This is a peaceful stretch of hilly evergreen and oak forest, dotted with lovely homes and farms. Return to Hartford.*

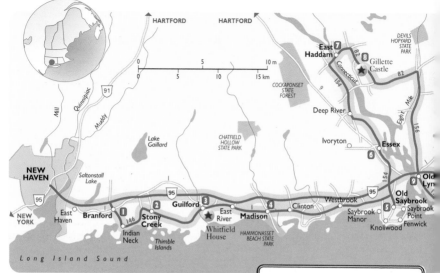

The Connecticut Shore

2 DAYS • 158 MILES • 254KM

New Haven is a mixture of industry and academia. Some areas are grimy survivors of the Industrial Revolution that had its roots here; other areas are a delight, thanks to the ivied walls and grassy quadrangles of Yale University. East of New Haven, the Connecticut shore is dotted with some surprisingly sleepy villages, sheltered from traffic by I–95, the interstate highway that speeds traffic on its way and diverts it from the coast.

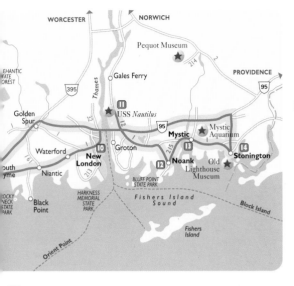

Tom's Cabin, stayed in Guilford on her grandmother's farm where she got to know the black servants.

▶ *Continue on Route 146 and turn onto Route 1 east.*

4 Madison

On the Green at the entrance to the town is the late 17th-century Deacon John Grave House. It has been a school, infirmary, arsenal, tavern, and courtroom in its time but has recently been restored.

Madison also has one of the few beaches on this shore that is open to all. Located in the enormous Hammonasset Beach State Park, the area also includes a nature reserve.

▶ *Continue on Route 1 east, then turn right to Old Saybrook.*

5 Old Saybrook

Though busy and commercially developed, Saybrook still has many fine Colonial homes, including the General William Hart House (1767), with its corner fireplaces and herb garden. Saybrook's most famous son is David Bushnell (1742–1824), credited with building the first "sub-marine" (see below).

▶ *Return north on Route 154 and drive for 5 miles (8km) to Essex.*

ⓘ *One Long Wharf Drive*

▶ *Start in New Haven on Route 95 east. Take exit 53 and at the rotary take Route 146 east to Branford (7 miles/11km).*

1 Branford

The pleasant town of Branford has an old-fashioned green with an unusually opulent library, church, and school nearby. The only historic mansion open to the public is the Nathaniel Harrison House on South Main Street, a restored 1724 "saltbox" with beautiful period furnishings and flower and herb gardens.

▶ *Stay on Route 146 for 6 miles (10km), following the shoreline through Indian Neck to Stony Creek.*

2 Stony Creek

Millions of Americans and foreigners have seen the pink granite produced from the local quarry: it was used in Grand Central Station and for the pedestal of the Statue of Liberty. Just off shore, the water is speckled by the tiny Thimble Islands. Called the "Hundred Islands" by the Colonists, there are actually over 300 of them scattered throughout Long Island Sound. Some are barely big enough to

accommodate the cottages built on them, often on stilts. With names like Treasure Island and Money Island, it is no surprise that the pirate Captain Kidd supposedly hid out here. Small boats are ready at Stony Creek harbor to give tours.

▶ *Continue on Route 146 for 4 miles (6km) to Guilford.*

3 Guilford

There is a particularly English feeling about this town, founded in 1639 and built around an unusually large green. Luckily, it escaped serious damage during the War of Independence, and around 80 pre-Revolutionary houses still stand.

The oldest, the 1639 Henry Whitfield State Museum, is also the oldest stone building in New England. Sitting on a slight rise in the middle of a large lot, this originally looked more like a fortified manor house, but the steeply-pitched roof and small, leaded, lattice windows reflect its remarkable age.

Other homes with history include the 1660 red saltbox Hyland House, and the 1774 Thomas Griswold House, occupied by Griswold descendants until 1958. Harriet Beecher Stowe, who later wrote *Uncle*

FOR HISTORY BUFFS

In the 1770s, Yale student David Bushnell was fascinated by explosives. Tests of his limpet mine, in Otter Cove near Old Saybrook, impressed George Washington and renowned inventor Benjamin Franklin. But Bushnell's pride and joy was his *American Turtle*. Reconstructed at the Connecticut River Museum in Essex, this self-propelled underwater capsule is considered the first "sub-marine." It was lost in battle against the British.

6 Essex

In a 1996 book called *The 100 Best Small Towns in America*, Essex came out number one. Founded in 1648, it became quite wealthy due to the skill of its carpenters and shipwrights. The splendid Colonial, Georgian, and Federal homes on Main Street were built by their bosses, the shipbuilders and sea captains. The town's social hub is the 200-year-old Griswold Inn. Here, collections of marine art and 19th-century firearms add to the atmosphere of "the 'Gris," a busy, though jolly, hotel-restaurant. At the end of the street, in an old warehouse on Steamboat Landing, is the Connecticut River Museum. This tells the story of Essex and of the Connecticut River, from its source in northeastern New Hampshire to the mouth. Star attraction is the reproduction of

Cruising on the Connecticut River near East Haddam

David Bushnell's remarkable underwater craft, *American Turtle*. A stone's-throw away, the keel was laid for the *Oliver Cromwell*, the colony's first custom-built warship, back in 1776. From then on, Essex was an important ship-building center. The tradition continues nearby at the Brewers Dauntless Shipyard, which produces sleek modern yachts. The 1732 Pratt

House is well-preserved in the style of 1800, with an herb garden.

▶ *Return to* **Route 154** *and drive north to* **Route 82** *east. Turn right and cross the Connecticut River on the turntable bridge to East Haddam.*

SCENIC ROUTES

The Essex Steam Train and Riverboat Ride is organized by the Valley Railroad Company, whose volunteers restore, maintain, and operate old steam engines and cars. They puff through the countryside for the hour-long trip up to Haddam, stopping at Deep River, and connect with a river boat for an hour-and-a-half long cruise.

SPECIAL TO...

No prizes for guessing how Ivoryton, 2 miles (3km) west of Essex, got its name. In the old days, ivory from Africa was unloaded in Essex and driven here in horse-drawn carts. It was then cut and polished into piano keys, buttons and combs. Although a factory nearby is now the world's largest producer of piano and organ keyboards, ivory is no longer used. The hamlet itself is tranquil, with huge beech trees on its main street, a general store, and a summer theater.

BECKY THATCHER

7 East Haddam

Just at the end of the bridge, high above the river, stands the Goodspeed Opera House. This six-story, white "wedding cake" is a grand reminder of the late 19th century, when East Haddam was a resort town, used by Mr. William Goodspeed's very own steam ships. Restored in the 1960s, the house's specialty is musical comedies. It hosted pre-Broadway runs for brand-new shows such as *Man of La Mancha*, in 1966, and *Annie*, in 1977. Now, new musicals are presented in a second theater in Chester, while this house concentrates on revivals. Land for East Haddam's original 17th-century settlement was sold to the English by local Indians in exchange for 30 coats. The one-room schoolhouse, where hero Nathan Hale once taught, is preserved next to the church.

▶ *Continue on* **Route 82** *south to Gillette Castle.*

Typical two-story New England Colonial house, Old Lyme

8 Gillette Castle

At the turn of the century, actor William Gillette (1853–1937) had superstar status, drawing huge audiences to see his 1,300 performances portraying Sherlock Holmes. By 1919, he had poured a million dollars into this extraordinary fake medieval stone castle. An amateur inventor with an odd sense of humor, he made many of the "puzzle locks" on its doors and designed a system of mirrors to be able to see who was visiting. Now owned by the state, the 122-acre (49-hectare) grounds make a fine picnic spot, high on the bank overlooking the river, and there are hiking trails and horse-drawn carriage rides.

▶ *Continue on* **Route 82** *for 5 miles (8km) to* **Route 156** *south. Drive a further 9 miles (14km) to Old Lyme.*

9 Old Lyme

Old Lyme, one of America's first art colonies, is the unofficial home of American Impressionism, thanks to Florence Griswold. At the turn of the century, "Miss Florence" decided to take in boarders; first one, then more artists moved into her fine, Greek Revival home, drawn by the light and the serenity of the surrounding beaches and marshes. Instead of signing the visitors book, guests

such as Willard Metcalf, Childe Hassam, and William Chadwick painted scenes on their land-lady's doors and wall panels. The dining room is profusely decorated. This 1817 house, in the heart of the Old Lyme Historic District, is now a museum with a fine collection of the *plein air* movement. Next door, the Lyme Academy of Fine Arts is one of America's leading art schools.

▶ *Leave town and follow* **Route 156** *east, crossing Niantic Bay, with a view of the Millstone Energy Center, a nuclear power plant. After 16 miles (26km), arrive in New London.*

SPECIAL TO...

Called the "Fresh River" by Dutch explorer Adriaen Block and the "Great River" by English settlers, the waterway for which the state of Connecticut is named was always the Quinnetukut to the Indians. The name means "the long river whose waters are driven by wind and tide." It starts in the three Connecticut lakes, way up in the northeastern corner of New Hampshire, near the Canadian border.

THE MARITIME TRADITION

The Atlantic Ocean has had a profound affect on the development of New England. Five of the six states in the region are adjacent to the coastline, and the Europeans who first arrived all had to cross the stormy North Atlantic. Once they arrived, ships maintained the umbilical cord linking them with the Mother Countries, and permanent communities grew up around safe harbors. The abundance of fish offshore made fishing an easy and reliable means of finding food, and it became so vital to the early settlers that fishermen were exempt from military service.

Above: humpback whales can reach 40 to 50 feet

Once the Colonies were established, shipping became an important part of the economy, though strict laws from London insisted that all manufactured goods had to be imported from England, alone. Enforcement was another matter, and not only were "illegal" cargoes landed, customs duties were, on occasion, evaded.

Ships were a necessity for England, and the navy increasingly relied on timber from Maine. Soon, the boats themselves were being constructed in the Colonies, since shipbuilding costs were from 20 to 50 percent less than in the Mother Country. Shipbuilding thrived and by 1760, one-third of the total British merchant tonnage was produced in the American Colonies.

By this time, the patterns of triangular trade routes were established. Merchant ships sailed from New England with grain, timber, and fish for the West Indies. These were traded for fruit, sugar, and molasses, which were taken on to England. There, the holds were loaded up with manufactured goods to be transported back home. Similar routes connected New England with Africa and the Mediterranean.

After years of lax enforcement, Britain decided to toughen up its policing of the trade laws in order to raise more revenue from the Colonies. Not only did this

hurt the New England economy, but it fostered anti-London feelings. The major ports of Boston and Portland, along with New York to the south, were targets before and during the Revolution.

Shipping again became a contentious issue during the Napoleonic Wars in Europe. Although the U.S. remained neutral, Britain interfered with American shipping, hoping to deprive the French of supplies. In addition, seamen were taken off captured ships and forced to sail for Britain. Eventually, these grievances led to the War of 1812.

From their early days, Colonists learned from the Indians how to catch whales when the mammals swam near shore, and towns such as New London and Mystic in Connecticut, and New Bedford and Provincetown in Massachusetts thrived at the expense of the whale. In 1774, 360 whaling ships sailed from Nantucket. Rhode Island developed a huge candle-making industry based on whale products. The oil was used to light streets and homes in Europe, while bones and baleen were used to make anything from umbrella spokes to corset stays. Only the discovery of oil (made into kerosene) in Pennsylvania, in 1859, ended the bloody trade. The business of whaling was epitomized in Herman Melville's novel, *Moby Dick*, based on his own experiences

aboard ship. Today, museums such as Nantucket's Whaling Museum, housed in a former whale oil refinery, record the exploits of American sailors who roamed the oceans in the early 19th century.

Apart from their heavy involvement in the slave trade, "Yankee traders" sailed round South America to do business with China and the Pacific islands, bringing back huge wealth to towns such as Boston, Salem, and Portsmouth. Along the Maine coast, at Kennebunkport and Kittery, Bath, Camden, and Belfast, shipbuilders continued traditions begun as early as 1607, when the *Virginia* was the first ship built in the Colonies, near Bath.

Today, New England's nautical traditions concentrate on the pleasure industry, with yachting keeping the shipbuilders and sail-makers of the region at the forefront of technology. For the first half of the 20th century,

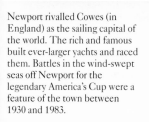

Tall ships at Mystic Seaport

Newport rivalled Cowes (in England) as the sailing capital of the world. The rich and famous built ever-larger yachts and raced them. Battles in the wind-swept seas off Newport for the legendary America's Cup were a feature of the town between 1930 and 1983.

In Bristol, Rhode Island, the Herreshoff Marine Museum recalls the Herreshoff Company's contribution to sailing. Between 1893 and 1934, eight consecutive winners in the America's Cup competition were built on the site, as well as the first torpedo boats for the U.S. Navy. In Newport, the Naval War College Museum emphasizes America's rise to power as a world force on the high seas. Out at Fort Adams State Park, at the Museum of Yachting, is the breathtaking *Shamrock V*, Sir Thomas Lighton's 1930 challenger for the America's Cup.

"Windjammers," old sailing ships, are now a popular way of spending a vacation, afloat along the coast. In Maine, Rockland and Camden are the best-known centers, while summer festivals such as Windjammer Days in the Boothbays and the finish of the Great Schooner Race, at the Rockland Breakwater, celebrate the nautical tradition.

Nowhere records New England's tradition better than Mystic Seaport on the Mystic River in Connecticut. An American whaler, the *Charles W. Morgan*, built of wood in 1841, is one of several sailing vessels ready for visitors to explore.

RHODE ISLAND

Rhode Island, "Little Rhody," is the smallest state, yet it also boasts the longest name: officially, it is The State of Rhode Island and Providence Plantations. This densely populated and heavily industrialized state received its title back in 1644, when two colonies were combined. A mere 48 miles by 37 miles (77km by 59km), it is nicknamed the "Ocean State" because of its 400 miles (640km) of shoreline, which includes some 100 beaches with public access. Not all the coast runs along the Atlantic Ocean; it also borders Narragansett Bay, which bites into the southeast corner of the state and stretches 28 miles (45km) inland, to the capital city of Providence.

Although the Vikings may have visited North America in the 11th century, Giovanni da Verrazano, the Italian explorer, is on record for sailing past what is now Block Island in 1524. He named it after the Island of Rhodes in Greece. When Roger Williams and a band of followers fled the intolerance of the Puritan colony in Massachusetts in 1636, they settled in what is now Providence. Two years later, Anne Hutchinson was similarly banished, and led another group to Aquidneck Island, now better known for the town of Newport. Both communities believed in religious freedom, for Christians as well as non-Christians. The first synagogue in the U.S. was built in Newport, while the first Baptist church was founded in Providence.

Sailboats reflecting in Newport's harbor

Rhode Island has been a holiday destination for almost two centuries. In the early 1800s, the seashore attracted wealthy Southerners, keen to escape the summer heat of the plantations. Families such as the Astors and Vanderbilts spent the summer social season in their "cottages," whose magnificence rivalled European palaces. Tennis, then the sport of the rich, made its American debut at the casino in Newport, and the International Tennis Hall of Fame now has its home here.

But it is sailing, rather than tennis, that is most associated with Newport. For some 50 years, the town hosted the America's Cup challenges, until 1983 when Australia broke the home team's winning streak and took the Cup "down under." Nevertheless, Newport remains the sailing capital of the East Coast.

Tour 12

Providence, the capital of Rhode Island, is a gem of a city, all too often overlooked by visitors to New England. The riverfront and downtown area have been successfully restored and revitalized, while the historic district around Benefit Street is full of 18th- and 19th-century houses, now used for offices and museums, classrooms and private homes. Nearby is Brown University, the seventh oldest in the country, founded in 1764, and the Rhode Island School of Design, one of the country's leading art schools. Not surprisingly, this area is known as College Hill. Across the river is Federal Hill, where Little Italy is full of delicatessens and cafés. With its ethnic mix and large student population, Providence is a lively city, with a thriving music scene, art galleries, and numerous restaurants. The *haute cuisine* is a by-product of Johnson and Wales University, which specializes in the culinary arts and hospitality business.

Tour 13

Newport is situated at the southern tip of an island, with a harbor on one side and beaches stretching along the other. This town of contrasts has its share of plain pre-Revolutionary houses as well as opulent summer homes, such as Château-sur-Mer and The Breakers. A century ago, entrance was only for the privileged few; today, visitors are welcome to see the priceless art and grandiose architecture.

Marble House, Newport, was modeled on the Grand and Petit Trianon at Versailles

Sailing has long been popular here, with the most famous race of all, the America's Cup, a long tradition. Even though the Cup has been lost to Australians and, most recently, New Zealanders, Narragansett Bay still brings in the sailing crowd. Newport also attracts tennis fans, who visit the Hall of Fame. In summer, you can see one of the few professional tournaments outside the British Isles that is still played on grass. The town also draws music lovers. Since the first Newport Jazz Festival in 1954, the outdoor summer concerts have become important fixtures on the U.S. music calendar.

Providence

Providence, the third largest city in New England, is only now getting the credit and attention it deserves as one of New England's most approachable destinations. Compact and walkable, with fine examples of pre- and post-Revolutionary architecture, it has a lively and artistic student body as well as high-quality restaurants, thanks to the influence of one of America's leading culinary schools.

HALF A DAY

Native American monument, Narragansett

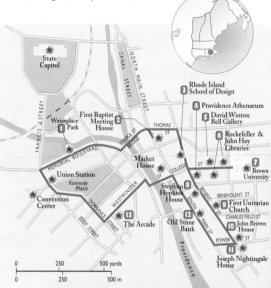

ⓘ *Waterplace Park*

▶ *Start at the Convention Center (park the car here, or in one of the public parking lots nearby). Walk to Memorial Boulevard.*

❶ Waterplace Park

This gem of design is the focal point of Providence's extensive riverfront redevelopment. Cobbled walks, brick paths, planted terraces, amphitheaters, gleaming wrought ironwork, and graceful bridges make the Providence River area a model of downtown urban beauty. This is the perfect place to view the State Capitol, sitting imperially on the hill. Built in 1904 of Georgia marble, its dome is second in size only to St. Peter's in Rome. On top, the gilded statue *Independent Man* symbolizes the free-thinking founders of Rhode Island. Inside hangs one of the most famous paintings in the country: the full-length portrait of George Washington, which appears on dollar bills, painted by Rhode Islander Gilbert Stuart.

▶ *Continue along Memorial Boulevard, cross the Providence River on Steeple Street Bridge; follow Steeple Street up the hill to No. 75 North Main Street.*

❷ First Baptist Meeting House

Although Roger Williams founded the Baptist congregation in 1638, the first church was not built for 50 years. This house of worship dates from 1775. A plan for St. Martin-in-the-Fields in London provided the inspiration for architect Joseph Brown, but the ability of the 185-foot steeple (56m) to withstand storms was due to the carpenters' extensive shipbuilding experience.

▶ *Turn up Thomas Street to Benefit Street. Turn right to No. 224 Benefit Street.*

❸ Rhode Island School of Design

Rhode Island School of Design, always abbreviated to "Ris-dee," is one of America's leading art schools. The modern entrance to the school's museum is in the Daphne Farago Wing where the focus is *Mantled Figure*, Howard Ben Tre's sculpture in solid cast glass. Works by Monet and Picasso, an Egyptian mummy, and a 9-foot (2.7m) tall Buddha, dating back ten centuries, are among the rich and varied 65,000-piece collection.

▶ *Continue along Benefit Street to College Street, then turn left and walk up the hill to No. 251.*

❹ Providence Athenaeum

In the old days, a club for learned men was often called an "athenaeum," in honor of Athena, the goddess of wisdom. This Greek Revival building was finished in 1838, and its stern exterior contrasts with the warm intimacy of the main reading room, with its tiers of books. Here, poet Edgar Allen Poe met and wooed local widow Sarah Whitman, who accepted, then rejected him (she is thought to have inspired his poem *Annabel Lee*). Today, anyone in need of inspiration needs only to look up to busts of the Greek historian, Homer, the English authors Milton and Keats, and the American statesman, Daniel Webster. Among the fine bindings and rare editions is an original portfolio of illustrations of American birds by the 19th-century naturalist, John James Audubon.

▶ *Continue up College Street. On the left is the List Art Center and the David Winton Bell Gallery.*

Providence has undergone massive renewal and revitalization in recent years

5 David Winton Bell Gallery

A distinctive modernistic building on College Street houses the List Art Center and the David Winton Bell Gallery. The gallery has a permanent collecion of over 4,000 works, from Rembrandt prints to contemporary pieces, and also stages a varied program of exhibitions.

▶ *Continue to the corner of College and Prospect streets.*

6 Libraries

This could be called "library corner." On the right is "the Rock," the bustling J. D. Rockefeller Library, open only to Brown students. Opposite is the "Hay," the hushed John Hay Library, where the public may explore the vast book collection and the small gallery in the lobby.

John Hay graduated from the university in 1858. A poet and

The famous *Brown Bear* statue at Brown University

historian, he was also the U.S. Secretary of State at the turn of the century.

▶ *Cross Prospect Street and enter the campus of Brown University.*

FOR HISTORY BUFFS

Roger Williams founded Providence, but the city's success in the late 18th and early 19th centuries followed the fortunes of the four Brown brothers.
John was a merchant. Joseph, the architect, designed the Market House, First Baptist Church, and a mansion for brother John. Moses founded the Providence Bank and financed the mill at Pawtucket, which started the Industrial Revolution in New England. Nicholas gave land and money to Rhode Island College, which was to be later renamed Brown University in 1804.

---

7 Brown University

The Van Wickle Gates, leading to the quadrangle, open just twice a year: to let new students in and graduates out. Founded in 1764, Brown is the seventh-oldest university in the country, and became co-ed in 1971. The main quadrangle boasts a variety of architecture, with the oldest building, University Hall (1771), being used as a barracks by French and American troops during the Revolution. The larger-than-life bronze *Brown Bear* statue rearing up, with its rather kindly expression, supposedly stands on a slate from the rock where Roger Williams first set foot on his arrival from Massachusetts in 1636. At the upper end of the college's grounds is the Carrie Tower, built by Paul Bajnotti of Turin in memory of his wife. It is inscribed: "Love is as strong as death."

▶ *Return down the hill on College Street and turn left on Benefit Street.*

FOR HISTORY BUFFS

Which Civil War general gave his name to a fashion trend? General Ambrose Burnside, whose statue stands in City Hall Park. So well-known were his side whiskers that the style became known as "sideburns." He went on to be governor and senator for Rhode Island, and lived at No. 314 Benefit Street.

---

8 Benefit Street

Originally known as Back Street, because it ran behind the houses facing the main street, Benefit Street was transformed from a path into a proper road in 1758 "for the common benefit of all." Now it is known as the "Mile of History," with its many 18th- and 19th-century houses: note details such as the old-fashioned street lights and boot scrapers.

At No. 43 Benefit Street, on the corner of Hopkins Street, stands the clapboard Governor

GIVEN BY ALVMNI AND VNDERGRADVATES
TO BROWN VNIVERSITY

Stephen Hopkins House. This delightful example of early 1700s architecture was the home of the ten-time Governor of the state and signatory of the Declaration of Independence.

▶ *Continue along Benefit Street.*

9 First Unitarian Church
John Holden Greene, the architect, rated this 1816 church his finest achievement. High in its steeple hangs the largest ever bell cast by the Paul Revere Foundry. Better known now as the messenger who rode from Boston to Lexington in 1775 to warn the Colonists that the British were approaching, Revere was a silversmith and bell-maker.

▶ *Continue on Benefit to the corner of Power Street.*

10 John Brown House
John Brown was a successful merchant who opened up trade with China after the American Revolution. His brother, Joseph, designed this imposing brick house, whose entrance is at No. 52 Power Street. President John Quincy Adams once called it "the most magnificent and elegant mansion that I have ever seen on this continent." Filled with fine examples of Rhode Island's furniture-making tradi-

tion, it exemplifies the gracious living of the 18th century.

▶ *Continue a few steps further along Benefit Street to No. 357.*

11 Joseph Nightingale House
Supposedly the country's largest wood-frame house, this 200-year-old ochre and cream merchant's home has been restored so completely, it could have been built yesterday.

▶ *Return to Power Street and walk down the hill. Turn right on South Main Street and walk 1½ blocks to the Old Stone Bank.*

12 Old Stone Bank
After the geometric simplicity of most of the buildings on this walk, the art nouveau-style gilt and green dome seems extravagant. Originally acquired by Brown University to be the new home of the Haffenreffer Museum of Anthropology, the future of the building is now under review, since the announcement that the new Haffenreffer will be on campus.

▶ *Continue to Westminster Street, then cross the river to The Arcade.*

Brown University's first building, University Hall, is now a National Historic Landmark

13 The Arcade
Shopaholics in the early 19th century had their own indoor shopping malls. This was the U.S.A.'s first, built back in 1828. The stores and goods may have changed, but it is still popular with visitors as well as locals. The cantilevered stairways and ironwork are still remarkable today.

▶ *Continue on Westminster Street to Dorrance Street. Turn right, heading towards the restored Union Station. At Exchange Street, turn left and return to the Convention Center.*

SPECIAL TO...

Quahogs, often pronounced *ko-hogs* in Rhode Island, are the local clams. The shells were once used as *wampum*, or currency, by the Native Americans. Nowadays, big shells are often saved for a dish or ashtray. Baby quahogs, called cherrystones or littlenecks, are eaten raw, on the half shell, while mature quahogs are used in chowder.

Newport

The original settlement of Newport was founded on the principles of religious tolerance, attracting Jews, Quakers, Baptists, and followers of the established Church of England. With its safe, deep-water harbor, it rivalled Boston and Philadelphia by the middle of the 18th century. The city tour route starts with a walk through the Newport of the early days, and finishes with a drive past the grand mansions of the late 19th century, referred to as the "Gilded Age." As well as fine museums, Newport offers wide, flat beaches, making this an appealing destination for families. **HALF A DAY**

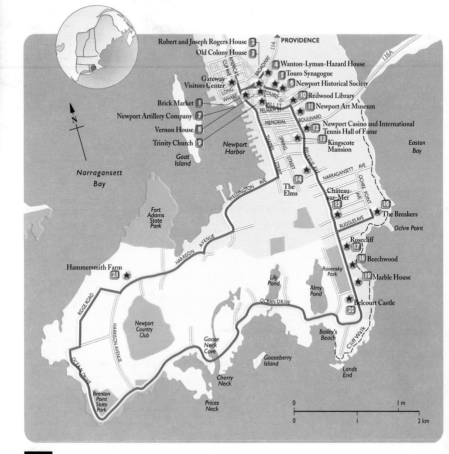

Robert and Joseph Rogers House [2]
Old Colony House [3]
Gateway Visitors Center
Brick Market [1]
Newport Artillery Company [7]
Vernon House [8]
Trinity Church [9]

PROVIDENCE
[4] Wanton-Lyman-Hazard House
[5] Touro Synagogue
[6] Newport Historical Society
[10] Redwood Library
[11] Newport Art Museum
[12] Newport Casino and International Tennis Hall of Fame
[13] Kingscote Mansion
[14] The Elms
[15] Château-sur-Mer
[16] The Breakers
[17] Rosecliff
[18] Beechwood
[19] Marble House
[20] Belcourt Castle
[21] Hammersmith Farm

Newport Harbor
Goat Island
Narragansett Bay
Fort Adams State Park
Easton Bay
Ochre Point
Ravensky Park
Lily Pond
Almy Pond
OCEAN DRIVE
Bailey's Beach
Lands End
Newport Country Club
Goose Neck Cove
Gooseberry Island
Cherry Neck
Brenton Point State Park
Prices Neck

0   1 m
0   1   2 km

ℹ️ *Gateway Visitors Center, 23 America's Cup Avenue*

▶ *Park in the parking lot behind the Visitors Center. Walk south along the avenue for one block to Long Wharf. Cross the avenue and proceed through Brick Market Place, a tree-lined mall of small shops, to the Brick Market Building.*

❶ Brick Market Building

This handsome three-story building, built in the late 1770s, was the commercial hub of Colonial Newport. Its arches and columns were radical features in their day, marking a move away from the strictly geometric Georgian style. Now it is the Museum of Newport History, with furniture, tools, interactive computer displays, and a fine model of the side-wheel steamer *Bristol* on display.

In the triangular Washington Square, the statue of Oliver Hazard Perry is a reminder of the naval hero who grew up in Newport. Aged 28, he defeated the British on Lake Erie in what was an important battle during the War of 1812. "We have met the enemy and they are ours," was his victory message.

▶ *Walk up the hill to the Robert and Joseph Rogers House.*

❷ Robert and Joseph Rogers House

Nearly 300 years old and still standing, this house displays the swells and bulges resulting from the settling of its foundations. The once rectangular windows have shifted into a curious variety of rhomboids and trapezoids. Closed to the public as it is now used for offices, this is one of only a handful of Federal-style houses in Newport.

▶ *Continue up the square to Old Colony House.*

❸ Old Colony House

In a town constructed primarily of wood, this brick building would have looked even more imposing in the 18th century. The oldest capitol building in the country, it was the headquarters of government from 1739 until 1900, when the new State House was opened in Providence. Important announcements read from the central second-floor balcony range from the coronation of King George III in 1760, to the results of elections for Rhode Island governors.

FOR HISTORY BUFFS

"...Whereas George the Third ... forgetting his dignity ... instead of protecting is endeavoring to destroy the good people of this colony ..." Those words, read to a crowd waiting outside the Old Colony House, announced the repudiation of English authority in the colony of Rhode Island. The date was May 4, 1776. Two months later, on July 4, came the Declaration of Independence of all 13 colonies.

▶ *From the Old Colony House turn right and walk along*

Newport is an attractive little town set dramatically against Narragansett Bay

▶ *Broadway to No. 17, the Wanton-Lyman-Hazard House.*

❹ Wanton-Lyman-Hazard House

When this house was built around 1675, it was one of more than 260 in a thriving village. Notice that the chimney stack is in the middle of the steep roof, but the front door is off-center; this style was typical of the area and is known as the "Rhode Island floor plan." A century later, Tory-enthusiast Martin Howard lived here, but was forced to flee from an angry mob who were protesting against the Stamp Act.

▶ *Return to the square and turn left on Touro Street at No. 85.*

❺ Touro Synagogue

"Erected 5603". That inscription celebrated the opening in 1763 of the first synagogue in the States, the oldest Jewish place of worship in the Americas, founded by Rabbi Touro. A community of Sephardic Jews had been in Newport since 1658, when 15 families arrived from Holland. Like the Quakers, the Jews were important in building Newport's trading links and wealth. Architect Peter Harrison, who also designed the Brick Market and the Redwood Library, included 12 pillars to represent the 12 tribes of Israel in an interior that looks much like a classic New England meeting house.

TOUR

13 Newport

▶ *Continue to the building nextdoor.*

6 Newport Historical Society

The Newport Historical Society, a driving force behind the preservation of Newport's historic buildings, was established in 1853, though it evolved from an even earlier club. The Seventh Day Adventist Meeting House, built in 1729, was moved here in 1887.

▶ *Return to Washington Square and turn left on Clarke Street. Walk halfway down this street of colorfully painted houses to No. 23–25, the Armory of the Newport Artillery Company.*

The moon rises over white-steepled Trinity Church

7 Newport Artillery Company

Uniforms worn by Field Marshall Montgomery, Prince Philip, and President Anwar Sadat of Egypt are among the uniforms, flags, regalia and other artifacts in the museum

contained in this 1836 stone building. The "1741" over the door refers to the date of the Artillery's charter, making this the oldest military organization in the country.

▶ *Walk to the corner of Clarke and Mary streets.*

8 Vernon House

In 1781, General Washington met with French Generals Lafayette and Rochambeau to decide tactics for the next stage of the war. Rochambeau, commander of the French troops quartered in Newport, lived in this house. If you look closely you will see that what appears to be weathered stone block is actually wood.

▶ *Continue up Mary Street, turn right on Spring Street and proceed to Trinity Church.*

9 Trinity Church

Since 1726, the tall white spire has been a landmark on the hill above the harbor. In the vestibule is the church's original bell, "probably the first bell that rang over a New England church." The church's organ, made by Richard Bridge, came from London in 1733 and may have been played by composer Friedrich Handel himself. On the main floor stand box pews, which are privately owned and can be bought and sold. Note the individually chosen cushions and elaborate needlepoint covers for the kneelers. The inscriptions on Pew 81 commemorate the most famous worshippers, from George Washington to Queen Elizabeth II and Archbishop Desmond Tutu of South Africa. Stained-glass windows by Tiffany stand out against a background of white walls and green-gray woodwork. They were paid for by wealthy summer residents such as Cornelius Vanderbilt.

▶ *The next left is Mill Street. Turn left, and walk up the hill past Touro Park and the mysterious Stone Tower. Legend says that it*

was erected by Vikings in the 11th century. More probably, it was a look-out for Governor Benedict Arnold (grandfather of the Revolutionary traitor) who owned much of the land. Continue up to Bellevue Avenue and cross the street to No. 50.

10 Redwood Library

A £500 donation in 1746 bought the first books for what is the oldest continuously used library in the country. The benefactor was Abraham Redwood, a rich trader from the West Indies. The building is typical of the pre-Revolutionary era, with wood painted to look like stone. As well as books, there is a sculpture of Benjamin Franklin

by Jean-Antoine Houdin and paintings by Gilbert Stuart.

▶ *Walk next door.*

11 Newport Art Museum

Clipped gables, airy verandas, scroll-sawed trim and ornamental timbers, or "sticks," epitomize the "stick style" of 19th-century architecture.

Dating from 1862, this is the first of many buildings in Newport designed by Richard Morris Hunt, but it is vastly different from the extravaganzas that made him the defining architect of the later "Gilded Age."

▶ *Cross Bellevue to Touro Park and walk down Pelham Street to the harbor area. Along the way, you pass the tiny Arnold Burying Ground, where the stones date back to 1677. At the bottom, turn right and return to the Visitor's Information Center. The rest of the route is followed by car. Drive up Memorial Boulevard and turn right on Bellevue Avenue and head for No. 194.*

for "little house." The first major commission for Stanford White and the McKim, Mead and White architectural firm, its "shingle" style was another popular Victorian trend. It spreads over almost a full city block; there are shops on the ground floor, with the ever-expanding Tennis Hall of Fame above. Outside are the world's oldest continuously-used grass tennis courts, dating from 1881. (The All-England Club is older, but moved to its present Wimbledon site in 1922.) The annual professional tournament here is played each July, immediately after Wimbledon.

On entering the main gate to the Hall of Fame, there is the

players volleying. If you feel so inclined, book time on one of the 13 courts and play where the U.S. Open Tennis Championships were born.

▶ *From here, drive along Bellevue Avenue. A combination ticket provides entry to eight of the Preservation Society properties.*

ⓑ Kingscote Mansion

In 1841, the Bellevue Avenue area was only starting to develop as a residential neighborhood, and Kingscote Mansion looks positively simple compared to the grandiose designs of the 1890s. Typical of the Gothic

The Redwood Library, designed to look like a Roman temple

ⓒ Newport Casino and the International Tennis Hall of Fame

The Casino, not a gambling casino but a gentlemen's club, was founded in 1880 as a rival to the Newport Reading Room. It takes its name from the Italian

distant roar of cheering tennis fans and the voice of an announcer calling a famous match from the past. The all-encompassing collection of tennis memorabilia ranges from an 1876 tennis racquet-bending machine right up to a Monica Seles' ensemble, while state-of-the-art computer displays provide a net judge's view of two

Revival style are the elaborate barge-boards, lancet arch casement window, and sawn cornice trim. Designed by Richard Upjohn and built for George Noble Jones, some say that the expression "Keeping up with the Joneses" originated here.

▶ *Continue on Bellevue Avenue.*

14 The Elms

When Pennsylvania coal baron Edward Berwind went to France, he was so impressed by the 18th-century Château d'Asnières, near Paris, that he made it the model for this house. The Elms, built in 1901, has furnishings that span the Louis XIV and XV styles, while the formal gardens have spacious terraces and lawns. At the top of the house, a hidden third story contains the servants' quarters.

▶ *Continue on Bellevue Avenue.*

15 Château-sur-Mer

In 1857, William Wetmore invited 2,500 guests to a party in his five-year-old home. He paid for those festivities, and for this lavishly-decorated mansion, with profits from trading with China. The grounds have some fine old trees, a Chinese moon gate and a Colonial Revival pavilion.

▶ *Proceed another block on Bellevue, then turn left at Ruggles Avenue and follow the signs to The Breakers.*

16 The Breakers

This is the ultimate in extravagance and the most famous summer "cottage" of all. Two decades after Richard Morris

---

SPECIAL TO...

Newport's wealthy loved racing huge yachts. Their money and patronage stimulated interest in the America's Cup, the world's oldest international sporting challenge. The first race was held in England, round the Isle of Wight, in 1851, but from 1920 onwards, Newport was the host. The American winning streak finally ended in 1983, when Australia took the cup. In recent decades, the port has also acted as the finish line for single-handed transatlantic races. The full story is told in the Museum of Yachting at Fort Adams State Park, which also has fishing, sailing, and swimming exhibits.

Hunt renovated Château-sur-Mer, he created this mock 16th-century Italian palace for the railroad tycoon, Cornelius Vanderbilt II. Hundreds of craftsmen were employed, many brought over from Europe, but the grand salon was actually

---

FOR HISTORY BUFFS

Just over a century ago, Newport was the hub of the New York social set, perhaps the wealthiest group of friends in the world. Each summer would be spent in what were called "summer cottages." Built along Bellevue Avenue, Ocean Drive and Harrison Avenue, these deliberately rivalled Europe's palaces in size and splendor, as families such as the Vanderbilts and Astors vied to be America's royalty. In the two-month season, one lavish party followed another, with no expense spared.

---

built in France, disassembled, shipped across the Atlantic, and reassembled by the same French craftsmen. In the dining room, a painted ceiling is two stories above the life-sized figures and gigantic marble columns. Although the kitchen is the size of an average house, it looks surprisingly simple and functional, hung with yard after yard of copper cooking pots and pans. The stables house a display of family items, including historic coaches.

▶ *Return to Bellevue Avenue and continue.*

17 Rosecliff

The Grand Trianon of Versailles was the inspiration for the summer home of Mrs. Hermann Oerlich. Soft-white tiles cover the outside; inside, the 80-foot (24m) long ballroom is all cream and gold. Elegant and refined, Rosecliff sits near the ocean and was used for shooting the 1974 film, *The Great Gatsby* and, more recently, *True Lies* with Arnold Schwarzenegger.

▶ *Continue along Bellevue Avenue.*

18 Beechwood

At the end of the 19th century, Caroline Astor was the reigning queen of American society. To be invited to her parties meant social acceptance. Her famous list of "The Top 400" people supposedly reflected the capacity of the ballroom in her New York City residence. Today, costumed guides play the parts of the Astors, their guests and their servants, bringing to life the heyday of the country house party.

▶ *Next door is Marble House.*

19 Marble House

Marble House is another Richard Morris Hunt creation, built in 1892 by William Vanderbilt, the brother of Cornelius. The overpowering entrance is covered in Italian marble, while the dining room boasts one-of-a-kind bronze Louis XIV chairs weighing 60 pounds (27kg) each. Most

Cornelius Vanderbilt's Breakers, Newport's most splendid estate
Inset: the Newport coastline

wedding reception of Jacqueline Bouvier to John F. Kennedy. From 1961 to 1963 it was also the "Summer White House" for President Kennedy, who often vacationed here. It is still a working farm.

SCENIC ROUTES

The 3½-mile (5.6km) Cliff Walk, starting at Cliff Walk Manor on Memorial Boulevard and ending at Bailey's Beach, is an excellent way to see the splendors of the mansions from a different angle. You will also enjoy the many varied coastal views.

amazing of all is the ballroom, where "all that glisters" really is gold, or gilded. When Alva Vanderbilt divorced her husband, she took the house, then married Perry Belmont (see below).

▶ *Proceed to Belcourt Castle.*

20 Belcourt Castle

Alva Vanderbilt did not move far after she divorced William K. Vanderbilt and married his good friend, Perry Belmont. Where Vanderbilt was keen on yachts, Belmont followed horse-racing and helped build the Belmont Track in New York.

▶ *Ocean Drive starts here, following a scenic stretch of broken and rocky shoreline, dotted by breathtaking private homes, many of which rival the splendor of Bellevue Avenue. Bailey's Beach, the first on the left, was the beach favored by the "400." Some 5 miles (8km) farther, also on the left, is Hammersmith Farm.*

21 Hammersmith Farm

This shingled 1888 beach house on the Auchinloss estate gained worldwide prominence in the 1950s as the location for the

▶ *Bearing left at the next intersection will take you back to the Newport Harbor area, via Harrison Avenue, Halidon Avenue, Wellington Avenue and Thames Street.*

VERMONT

Vermont has been called "every American's second state" because of the small farms with red barns, and villages with white churches that make up the traditional image of "old-fashioned America." The most rural of all states, it has only one major town, Burlington, with 40,000 inhabitants. The remainder of the half million or so Vermonters are scattered throughout the rolling hills and valleys stretching north–south between Canada and the Massachusetts border.

Although Lake Champlain lies on its western flank and the Connecticut River forms the eastern border, Vermont is the only New England state with no access to the sea. What it does have is mountains. French explorer Samuel de Champlain first remarked on the *verts monts*, the green mountains, back in the 17th century. While still a colony, Vermonters argued over land ownership with neighboring New York; the Vermonters won. When the colonies threw off the yoke of the English crown, Vermont went its own way; from 1777 to 1791 it was a republic, minting its own coins and printing its own stamps.

Vermont's gentle rolling landscape

The population has always been small. The roller-coaster landscape is difficult to farm, winters are bitter and summers are short. Despite that, Vermont has had its moments of affluence. Early in the 19th century, its wool was in demand world-wide. When that trade was lost, dairy farming took over. Although forests now cover acres of land once cleared for pasture, cattle remain a significant revenue earner. The sharp flavor of Vermont cheddar cheese is rated by gourmets, while a more recent dairy-related success is Ben and Jerry's Ice Cream. Other natural resources such as marble and granite provide a base to the economy, matched by furniture-making, paper production, and computers. Most important of all, however, is tourism.

Each autumn, "leaf peepers" by the thousands invade the state, drawn by the natural phenomenon of the maple leaves turning to brilliant shades of red and gold. Since the first ski tow was set up in Woodstock in 1934, the winter season has attracted both downhill and cross-country skiers.

Tour 14

The southern Vermont town of Bennington rarely rates more than a few lines in the history books, yet it played its part in the Revolution, and a 306-foot (93m) high stone needle commemorates the 1777 battle. Nearby is the grave of one of the country's favorite poets, the 20th-century writer Robert Frost. Bennington's museum displays a fine collection of naive paintings by Grandma Moses. These, along with handsome old houses and business buildings, add up to a town that is worth exploring.

Tour 15

Southern Vermont looks softer than points further north and is known for its photogenic farms and villages. Weston, set on a hilltop, preserves the atmosphere of a typical 19th-century Vermont village. Ludlow offers its own ski mountain; while the center of Grafton, known for its cheese, has been preserved, scrubbed clean, painted white, and seems suspended in time. The only crowded place is Manchester, full of shoppers hunting for bargains at the numerous factory outlet stores.

Tour 16

This part of Vermont is best known for the world-class ski resort of Killington. Apart from that, it is also another peaceful area where artists and craftspeople create minor masterpieces in small villages tucked away in the Green Mountains. Former U.S. President Calvin Coolidge is a local hero, his birthplace and homestead have become minor shrines. A few villages, such as Woodstock, have been deliberately "prettied up," but overall, the natural, unhustled pace of life will reward those looking for a relaxed vacation. Take time to bike the back roads.

Tour 17

Compared with the quieter regions to the south, the northern section is a bustling part of the state. Celebrities range from Ben and Jerry, whose ice creams have taken the world by storm, to the Trapp Family of *Sound of Music* fame, who run an inn near Stowe. Teddy bears and Icelandic horses, a house with secret passages, and the Robert Frost Trail are some of the offbeat attractions. The Shelburne Museum is an outstanding collection of American folk art, housed in buildings that were moved here lock, stock and barrel from locations all over New England. The elongated Lake Champlain is fine for a ferry ride, water sports, or for those merely in search of quiet contemplation.

The first pumpkins of the season: they must be picked before the frosts arrive

Bennington

Outside the state, Bennington is best known for Ethan Allen and his Green Mountain Boys. This group of feisty Vermonters not only had a grievance against the British, but also against the neighboring, land-greedy "Yorkers" (New Yorkers) in the state next door. The historic district and its college make this an attractive small town.

Lake Paran

12 Old Train Station

Park-McCullough House **11**

NORTH BENNINGTON

Powers Market

Paran Creek Mill Complex

10 Bennington College

Covered Bridges

◄ RUTLAND

0 ————— 1 m
0 ————— 1 km

Walloomsac

Bennington Battle Monument **4**

Historic Bennington Railroad Station **6**

3 Catamount Tavern

Walloomsac Inn

Holden Leonard Mill **7**

Hawkins House

Potters' Yard **8**

Old First Church **2**

Bennington Museum **1**

Hemming's Sunoco Station **5**

Pennysaver Building **9**

WILLIAMSTOWN

BRATTLEBORO

[i] *Veterans Memorial Drive*

▶ *Park at the Bennington Museum to start the tour.*

❶ Bennington Museum
"Grandma" Moses (1860–1961) was known as much for her longevity as for her "primitive" portrayals of rural life. This farmer's wife only started to paint when she turned 70, recording countryside activities such as haymaking and maple sugaring. Critical acclaim led to an exhibition at New York's Museum of Modern Art. Although she lived just across the state line, in Eagle Bridge, New York, this Vermont museum has the largest collection of her work, with 28 paintings shown in a special gallery. A favorite picture, often used on greetings cards, is *Over the River*, which depicts the trip to Grandmother's house for Thanksgiving. Memorabilia are found in the old schoolhouse where she, her grandchildren, and her great-grandchildren all

studied. The museum also houses the 1777 Battle of Bennington flag, thought to be the oldest "Stars and Stripes" in existence. Watch for the Bennington pottery and glass collection from the 19th century and the Bennington Wasp (1920s), the only automobile ever to be manufactured in Vermont.

▶ *Walk up the hill to the small green in the center of Old Bennington. Look to your left.*

The grave of Robert Frost, a simple memorial to the poet, lies in Bennington cemetery

❷ Old First Church
"*And were an epitaph to be my story
I'd have a short one ready for my own.
I would have written of me on my stone:
I had a lover's quarrel with the world.*"
The final line of Robert Frost's 1942 poem, *The Lesson for Today*, is engraved on the plain stone marking his grave in the cemetery. One of the best-loved poets of his time (1874–1963), he captured the essential sights, smells, and character of New England.

Also buried here are five Vermont governors and many patriots who fell in the Battle of Bennington. The original 1763

meeting house was replaced in 1805 by this handsome church, whose stylish belfry contrasts with the usual spiked steeple.

Across the street is the old Walloomsac Inn. Here, refreshments were first served in 1766, so it claims to being the "longest-running tavern in America." It is now a private home.

▶ *Turn right on Monument Avenue and head towards the obelisk. Just on the right is a statue.*

The observation platform on top of Bennington's Battle Monument gives excellent views over the city

❸ Catamount Tavern

Looking ready to pounce on unwary passers-by, this big bronze wild cat commemorates the site of the Catamount Tavern, built in 1767. It was the meeting place of Ethan Allen and the Green Mountain Boys. The catamount, or catamountain, is the state mascot of Vermont. It is also called a puma, cougar, and lynx.

▶ *Walk to the top of Monument Avenue.*

❹ Bennington Battle Monument

Confusingly, the Battle of Bennington took place in New York. In 1777, the British were running low on food and arms, so General Burgoyne sent troops to capture the American stores which were stashed in a depot in Bennington. Before the Redcoats could reach the town, they were intercepted and overpowered by the patriots led by General Stark and Colonel Seth Warner. This was a significant victory in a regional campaign that ended with the surrender of Burgoyne at Saratoga a few months later.

The statue of local hero, Colonel Seth Warner, stands before the simple monument on the site of the supply depot. Over a century old, the statue, built of locally quarried lime-

stone, ranks as the tallest man-made structure in Vermont, soaring 306 feet (91.8m). Take the elevator to the observation levels for spectacular views of three states – New York, Massachusetts and Vermont. Each year, the victory is celebrated in style on Bennington Battle Day Weekend, in mid-August.

▶ *Return down Monument Avenue, noting the fine examples of Federal and Georgian houses on either side. Turn left on West Main Street and head down the hill into town. On the left is a service station.*

❺ Hemming's Sunoco Station

You could be forgiven for thinking this is a museum of classic vehicles. Although it is a functioning Sunoco station, the owners are the Hemmings family, the publishers of *Motor*

News. The store is full of car books, models, toys and artwork, as well as Vermont products. Unusual models of restored tractors, wreckers, steamrollers, and panel trucks from the 1920s to the 1940s are often on display outside.

▶ *Walk on for a block, then turn left on Depot Street. Continue to the junction with River Street.*

❻ Historic Bennington Railroad Station

The Bennington and Rutland Railroad was successful a century ago, when this temple of limestone and blue marble was built. However, passenger trains have not stopped here since 1933, although freight trundled through up to the 1950s. The handsome building survives as Bennington Station Restaurant, with evocative photographs of old steam engines on the walls.

▶ *Turn left on River Street and then right onto Benmont Avenue.*

7 Holden Leonard Mill

Back in the 19th century, Bennington was a manufacturing town, using the river to power grist and paper mills such as the Holden Leonard Mill. This massive building, with a central tower rising four stories high, has been converted to offices, but stands as a legacy to the industrial past.

▶ *Turn right on County Street. At the corner of North Street is the Hawkins House with its contemporary crafts. Cross North Street and continue to No. 324 County Street.*

8 Potters' Yard

In the 19th century, the town was known for its pottery, as the 4,000-piece collection in the museum shows. Today, around 40 potters still work in what was an old grist mill on County Street. This arts and crafts center, with small shops and a restaurant, is owned by David Gil, who has been designing his popular, colorful splatterware since 1948. As well as the jugs, pitchers, and vases, his dinner services are in great demand, both in restaurants and homes.

▶ *Return to North Street and turn left. This becomes South Street after the intersection with Main Street.*

9 Pennysaver Building

The houses and churches of 19th-century New England are familiar from postcards and calendars, but the commercial architecture can be just as fascinating. The former Putnam Hotel block curving round from South to Main and the Pennysaver Building at 107 South Street are typical. The *Pennysaver*, a free newpaper, still

occupies the premises. The huge, globular lights outside were originally gaslit.

▶ *Return to Main Street and turn back west, returning to the car. Now drive to the main intersection and go north on* **Route 7A**, *then left on to Northside Drive (which becomes* **Route 67A**). *After 3 miles (5km) reach Bennington College.*

10 Bennington College

Founded in 1925 to offer further education to women, Bennington College is now co-ed. It was once the most expensive private college in America, and former students include Broadway actress Carol Channing and film star Alan Arkin, as well as a host of artists. Known for its programs of fine arts, the campus is an attractive blend of mock colonial and modern buildings in a rural setting.

▶ *Continue on* **Route 67A** *to North Bennington (2 miles/ 3km). Three covered bridges cross the river on the left: the Silk Road, Papermill Village, and the Bert Henry Bridge on Murphy Road. On the right, entering the town, is a fine complex of water-driven mills on Paran Creek. This is a convenient place to park. Cross Main Street and bear left up West Street. At the corner of Park Street is the Park-McCullough House.*

11 Park-McCullough House

With its handsome curving veranda, this early example of an American Second Empire-style mansion (1875) gives an idea of how the wealthy lived in the latter half of the 19th century. The name combines that of lawyer Trenor Park, who built the house, and his son-in-law, John McCullough, one of the two Vermont governors who lived here. The 35-room house has a collection of early photographs by Carlton Watkins, who recorded life in the Wild West. Out in the stables are old sleighs and carriages. Open to the public, there is a small replica of the mansion on the front lawn.

▶ *Return to Main Street and turn left up the hill, past the imposing Greek columns of Powers Market. It is no more than a country store inside, but at the top of the hill is the station.*

12 Old Train Station

This delightful Victorian railroad station, decorated in shades of green and barn-red trim, dates back to 1880. Today, it is a popular dining venue.

▶ *Return to the car at the bottom of the hill.*

Taking a quiet moment in Bennington, once a center of Revolutionary action

While most of the world experiences a dull, even sad end to the year, New England's landscape goes out in a blaze of glory. Due to a combination of soil and trees, sun and rain, the hillsides change from green to a tapestry of scarlet and gold, purple and orange. This is the "foliage season." Rudyard Kipling, who lived for a while in Vermont, felt almost powerless to depict the transformation. "No pen can describe the turning of the leaves – the insurrection of the tree people against the waning year. A little maple began it, flaming blood-ed of a sudden where he stood against the dark green of a pine-belt. Next morning there was an answering signal from the swamp where the sumacs grow. Three days later, the hill-sides as far as the eye could range were afire, and the roads paved with crimson and gold." (*Leaves from a Winter Notebook*, 1900.)

in Vermont and New Hampshire. The Columbus Day holiday (second weekend of October) is the most crowded of the year in those tiny states. Hotels and inns tend to have "foliage season rates" that start in mid-September and carry on through mid-October. Of course, there is no promise from Mother Nature that she'll get her paint-brushes out at this time: a dry summer and the leaves could change earlier; a wet summer and the "foliage" could be delayed. To avoid the inevitable

Photographs cannot prepare you for your first sight of New England in September and October. Millions of visitors, "leaf peepers," visit the region every year, with cameras at the ready. Most go by car or on bus tours, but hot-air balloons and river cruise boats also provide a spectacular experience.

Science

Scientists have a clinical explanation for the changes. They say that sunny days, allied with chilly nights, stop the production of chlorophyll, the chemical that turns leaves green. This, in turn, allows other pigments such as anthocyanin (red) or carotenoids (orange, yellow) to show through in the leaves. The Native American explanation is far more entertaining: the Great Bear (in the sky) was killed in a hunt, and its blood dripped down onto the leaves. As for the yellow, that was attributed to the fat of the bear splashing out of the cooking pot.

The time

The leaves change color in a tide that sweeps down from north to south, usually starting in late September in Maine, northern Vermont and New Hampshire and reaching Connecticut in the south, around the middle of October. The most intense period is, by tradition, the first two weeks in October, especially

The dazzling colors of fall

crowds, a few visitors gamble and go north to Maine, where the weather might not be so gentle, but the roads are almost certainly quiet. Otherwise, the trick is stay off the main roads, and drift along the twisting country lanes which often have poor or even no signs at all. Take warm clothing; leaf watching is warm in the sun, but can turn chilly by the end of the day.

The trees
The dark green is usually provided by fir and spruce.
Scarlet and crimson: dogwood, red (or swamp) maple, sassafras and red oak.
Gold and yellow: poplar, elm, birch and gingko.
Orange: hickory, mountain maple and mountain ash.
Brown: oak.
Purple: sumac.

Hotlines
The New England states have special telephone numbers with up-to-date information on the progression of the color, and where to find it.

Connecticut (tel: 806/270–8080 or 800/CT–BOUND)
Maine (tel: 207/582–9300 or 1–800/932–3419)
Massachusetts (tel: 617/727–3201 or 800/227–MASS)
New Hampshire (tel: 603/271–2666 or 800/258–3608)
Rhode Island (tel: 401/277–2601 or 800/556–2484)
Vermont (tel: 802/828–3239).

2 DAYS • 151 MILES • 244KM

Southern
Vermont

"The Switzerland of North America" was a British ambassador's description of Vermont, yet the southern part is softer than the rest of this rugged state, with hamlets and houses scattered across the landscape. Almost every village has a green, a white steepled church, and an inn, and roadside stands selling maple syrup.

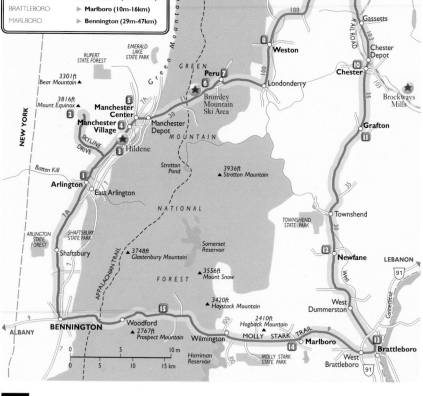

[i] *Veterans Memorial Drive*

▶ *Start in Bennington and drive north on **Route 7A**, passing through the town of Shaftsbury and the Vermont Pipe Shop before reaching Arlington.*

❶ Arlington
Illustrator Norman Rockwell, famous for his *Saturday Evening Post* magazine covers, spent the middle part of his life here, from 1939 to 1953, using local people as models for his countless views of everyday life. Some of them still live in the village today. Although the most complete record of his work is further south in Stockbridge, Massachusetts, a church here in Arlington also has a permanent record, though these are all reproductions. The country doctor who appeared in a Rockwell picture popular in many waiting rooms was one Dr. Russell, whose vast collection of Vermontiana is housed behind the library. Vermont's first grist mill was built here in 1764 by the splendidly named Remember Baker. Only a plaque remains to mark the site.

▶ *Proceed north on **Route 7A** for 4 miles (6km) to the foot of Mount Equinox.*

❷ Mount Equinox
The Carthusian order has a monastery here on the 3,835-foot (1,163m) Big Equinox peak, the highest point in the Taconic Range. The 5-mile (8km) Skyline Drive toll road climbs steeply to the Equinox

SPECIAL TO...

Running parallel to Route 7A is the Batten Kill River, one of the world's great fly-fishing streams, with 150 years of tradition. Equally famous, the Orvis Fishing Company started making bamboo rods in 1886, in a small plant not far from their current location. As well as exhibiting some 25,000 fishing flies, the American Museum of Fly Fishing nearby has rods belonging to celebrities such as Bing Crosby, baseball star Babe Ruth, and ex-President Bush.

Covered bridges are now recognized as historic landmarks. This example is at West Arlington

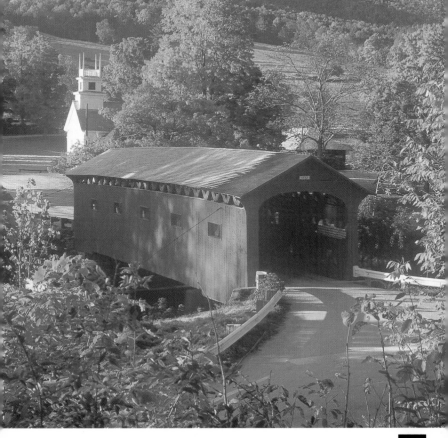

Mountain Inn with memorable views across to Quebec, New York, New Hampshire, and Massachusetts. Cars are warned to have good "brakes, radiators and transmissions" before attempting the drive. Cyclists and sports-car racers frequently test themselves on "hill climbs." The record ascent is just over 8 minutes by racing car.

SPECIAL TO...

Roadside stands and stores all sell maple syrup, a product synonymous with Vermont, even though the sticky, sweet liquid from the maple tree is made all over New England. Today, the traditional buckets and wooden sugar-houses of yesteryear have been replaced by plastic tubes inserted directly into the trees. Once the warm sun and cold nights of late winter/early spring cause the colorless liquid to rise, the sap is siphoned off. A good tree produces about eight gallons (36 litres) per season. The sap is then boiled down to make the caramel-colored sweetener. Anything from 30 to 50 gallons of sap is needed to make one single gallon (4.5 litres) of syrup. Grade A, the most delicately colored and flavored, costs the most, while Grade D would do for baking.

*Continue on **Route 7A** to Hildene.*

3 Hildene

Robert Todd Lincoln was the son of President Abraham Lincoln. As a child, he visited the Equinox Hotel with his mother, just before his father was assassinated, but only returned to the area many years later. Hildene, Lincoln's summer home, was built in 1904, and it was here that he died in 1926. Lincoln descendants lived here until 1975; the house is filled with authentic memorabilia of the Civil War leader, including Abe's "stovepipe" hat. The stately 24-room Georgian Revival home boasts a huge pipe organ and magnificent grounds. Polo matches are played on summer Sundays and, in winter, the former carriage house is a base for visitors who cross-country ski the 13 miles (21km) of trails. Candlelight tours of the interior are particularly evocative.

Continue for 2 miles (3km) to Manchester Village.

4 Manchester Village

There are three Manchesters: Center, Depot, and the oldest and highest, the Village. This is where the rich and powerful summered, either in their own luxury mansions, or at the legendary resort hotel, the Equinox. Dating back to 1769, this splendid Victorian hotel has been expanded and renovated over the years and today has 163 rooms and the renowned par-71 Gleneagles golf course.

Drive a further ½ mile (800m) into Manchester Center.

5 Manchester Center

Amid this rural bliss, outlet shopping comes as a shock to some visitors. Despite the out-of-place presence of Armani, Burberry, and Calvin Klein, some small-town charm remains. Down-home favorites such as the Quality Restaurant have served up genuine Vermont cooking for years.

*Drive 2 miles (3km) and turn onto **Route 11** east.*

6 Bromley Mountain Ski Area

The road climbs steadily for 8 miles (13km) to Bromley Ski resort, a pioneer among resorts since 1937. Visitors also come in summer to try out the mile-long alpine slide, the longest concrete slide of its kind in the U.S.

*Continue on **Route 11** east, then turn off to Peru.*

7 Peru

Peru, one of the state's little-known hamlets, was featured in the 1987 film *Baby Boom*, with Diane Keaton. A small woodworking shop shares the street with a church, an antique shop and several lovely homes.

*Return to **Route 11**, east, and drive to Londonderry. Turn left onto **Route 100**, north for Weston.*

8 Weston

Weston is well known, not only for its prettiness, but also for the two rival stores across the street from one another. The Vermont

The Old Tavern Inn, in the pristine village of Grafton

pleasant shops, and a narrow green. The only business of note is the National Survey, a map-making company and shop which has everything to do with cartography.

Chester Depot, the site of the old railway station, is now home to the *Green Mountain Flyer*, a summer tourist train with nice old carriages. The *Flyer* runs up to Bellows Falls through the Brockway Mills Gorge.

[i] *The Green (seasonal)*

▶ Take **Route 35** *south for 7 miles (11km) to Grafton.*

⑪ Grafton

In a state of many lovely villages, Grafton is probably the most photogenic of them all. It was once an affluent town on the Boston to Albany post road, with soapstone quarries and a thriving woolen industry, but after the Civil War, its economy collapsed. There was a revival in 1801, when the handsome Old Tavern was built with a California gold miner's money, but by the middle of the century, the village had all but died yet again. Help was at hand, however. In her will, Pauline Fisk instructed her nephews to use her fortune for a good cause of their choice. They came up with the idea of reviving Grafton.

In 1963, the Windham Foundation began the restoration of Grafton's historic charm that draws admiring visitors. For some, the houses are almost too pretty, too perfect for such a rural setting. The village has also revived a former industry: a nutty cheddar-style cheese, made by the Grafton Village Cheese Company. The tiny Village Store also has locally made preserves and hand-knits, and there is a working black-smith's shop. Two covered bridges complete the scene. On Sunday evenings in summer, the cornet band plays on the green, a tradition dating back to 1867.

Country Store and the Weston Village Store both do everything but bottle the nostalgia, and both offer an incredible variety of "country" and "Vermont" items that will bring visitors and their wallets to their knees. The circular town green, with its bandstand, inn, and brick church on the hill above, is extremely photogenic. The Weston Playhouse is one of New England's oldest and most popular summer theaters.

Just north of the village is the Benedictine monks' religious community of Weston Priory, a tranquil place where visitors are welcome to join in services and walk in the grounds.

▶ *Continue to Ludlow.*

⑨ Ludlow

In contrast to Weston, Ludlow may seem somber at first sight, but there is a gritty charm to this former mill town, on the banks of the Black River. Here, wool was recycled into inexpensive cloth called "shoddy," which has become a pejorative description

for anything cheap. The mill on Main Street is now an inn and the area has been revitalized. The successful Okemo Mountain resort, with its 3,343-foot (1,000m) hill, is widely acknowledged as having the best snow-making and grooming facilities in Vermont.

▶ Take **Route 103** *south for 13 miles (21km) to Chester.*

⑩ Chester

Hidden away in the woods on the way to Chester was the home of Russian Nobel Prize-winner, Alexander Solzhenitsyn. He lived here in isolation in Chester during his exile from the Soviet Union. The Stone Village on North Street, has, unusually for Vermont, some 30 cottages built of local stone. Dating from before the Civil War, these had hiding places for slaves escaping from the southern states on the so-called Underground Railroad to Canada.

The heart of Chester is the broad main street, with the comfortable Fullerton Inn,

▶ *Leave Grafton on **Route 35** south, which turns briefly into a dirt road after 6 miles (10km). At Townsend, take **Route 30** south for 5 miles (8km) to Newfane.*

🔢 **Newfane**

In summer, Newfane shows off its classic white Courthouse, church, and inns, all of which have gleaming Greek Revival columns. The long-established air of the place is deceptive. Two hundred years ago, the buildings stood 2 miles (3km) away, on Newfane Hill. In 1825, the residents moved the town, using the slippery snow and ice of winter to slide the beams and boards to today's site. Jail accommodations were so comfortable and the food so palatable that paying guests were allowed in to enjoy "good pies and oyster soup" along with the inmates. Excellent fare is still a tradition, with both of the town's inns renowned for their cuisine. On summer Sundays, the flea market on the green is one of Vermont's biggest and best.

The local museum is easy to spot, with its early 19th-century bell standing outside. Inside are simple memorabilia from the area – Victorian dresses, old maps, and a variety of household items.

Beyond town, Route 30 runs parallel to the West River, where rafters and paddlers take up the challenge of high water in spring. A local map of the river, produced by the eighth-grade class at the junior high school, shows all the rapids, covered bridges, dams and swimming-holes ... even the ones where "skinny-dipping" or nude swimming, is common.

▶ *Continue on **Route 30** to Brattleboro.*

🔢 **Brattleboro**

Fort Dummer, the first site in the state to be settled by Europeans, has now been covered by the waters of the nearby dam. Originally, this was the western frontier of the Bay Colony, used in defense against the French and the Indians.

Brattleboro is situated just down the road. In recent years, there has been a clean-up of the town's industrial infrastructure, centered about the main thoroughfare, Elliott Street. The former Union Railroad Station is now the Museum and Art Center, with five galleries. One is devoted to the history of the Estey Organ Co., the local firm that cheered up Victorian parlors across the nation.

Just north of the town at Dummerston, in a house called Naulakha, author Rudyard Kipling lived and worked from 1892 to 1896, after marrying a local girl, Carrie Balestier. Books such as *Captains Courageous*, the *Jungle Books* and the *Just So Stories* were all written here. One celebrity who never left town was the notorious 19th-century swindler, Jubilee Jim Fisk. "Jubilee Jim," who once cornered the New York gold market, is buried in the cemetery, with a monument by local sculptor Larken Mead. Mead gained true recognition for his memorial honoring a more reputable man: he carved the statue that graces Abraham

Lincoln's tomb in Springfield, Illinois.

▶ *Take **Route 9** west and start climbing into the hills. Pass Whetstone Valley Farm, known for maple sugaring in early spring, to Marlboro (10 miles/16km).*

🄔 Marlboro

The countryside looks attractive today, but back in 1763 it must have been daunting for the European settlers. Two families are credited with founding Marlboro, but neither pioneer family knew the other was nearby for over a year. The focus of town is Marlboro College, with its music school founded by pianist Rudolf Serkin. The six-week-long summer chamber music festival is a well established highlight, due to the long residency and efforts of cellist Pablo Casals in its early years.

▶ *Continue west on **Route 9**. After 15 miles (24km), there is a panoramic view from one of the highest points on the road. Continue to Wilmington.*

🄕 Wilmington and Woodford

The alpine-looking village of Wilmington is at the crossroads with Route 100, the north–south route that winds its way through the villages and ski resorts of the Green Mountains. Haystack Mountain and Mount Snow are just to the north.

Route 9 climbs on into the Green Mountain National Forest, passing through Woodford, Vermont's highest village. Prospect Mountain offers hiking opportunities.

▶ *Return to Bennington.*

Newfane's County Courthouse offers a touch of grandeur

Central
Vermont

The central part of the state gets busy in winter, due to the appeal of internationally known ski resorts such as Killington. In summer, attractions range from the Quechee Gorge, a sudden tear in the landscape, to Plymouth, the home of Calvin Coolidge. Rutland is nicknamed the "Marble City," because local quarries have provided floors and walls for many of America's grand civic buildings.

1 DAY • 109 MILES • 175KM

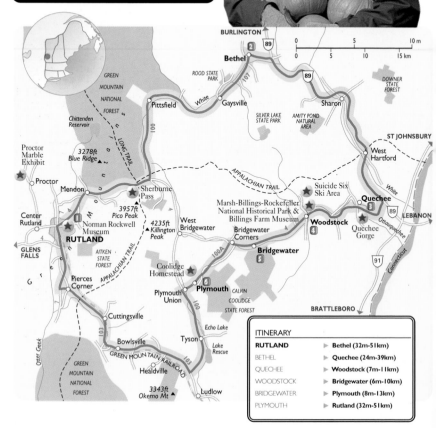

ITINERARY		
RUTLAND	▶	**Bethel (32m-51km)**
BETHEL	▶	**Quechee (24m-39km)**
QUECHEE	▶	**Woodstock (7m-11km)**
WOODSTOCK	▶	**Bridgewater (6m-10km)**
BRIDGEWATER	▶	**Plymouth (8m-13km)**
PLYMOUTH	▶	**Rutland (32m-51km)**

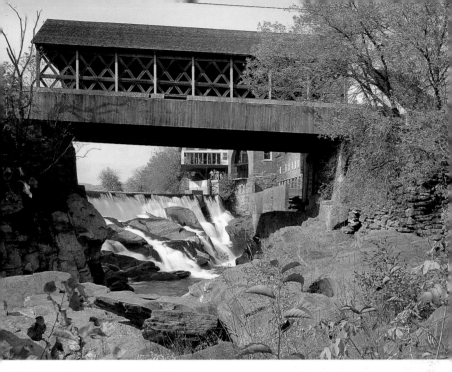

256 North Main Street

▶ *Leave Rutland on* **Route 4** *east. After 2 miles (3km) is the Norman Rockwell Museum on the right.*

❶ Norman Rockwell Museum

Better known collections of the popular illustrator's work can be found in Stockbridge (Massachusetts) and Arlington (Vermont), but you'll find 2,000 reproductions of well-loved covers from magazines such as *Saturday Evening Post, Life,* and *Literary Digest* here. There is enough to keep nostalgia hunters interested for an hour or more; some of his illustrations from children's books are also on display. After the Museum, the road starts its long climb into the Green Mountain National Forest. Pico Peak ski area is on the right. Near the summit, there is a sign for the Long Trail. In summer, the Pico Alpine Slide is a thrill for youngsters and brave adults.

▶ *Continue on* **Route 4** *over the Sherburne Pass, turn onto* **Route 100** *north, then take* **Route 107** *to Bethel.*

❷ Bethel

In the new showrooms of Vermont Castings are their popular wood-burning stoves, seemingly essential to any Vermont home. An exhibition at the White River National Fish Hatchery explains an ambitious project to bring back the Atlantic salmon to the Connecticut River. Abundant when the Colonists arrived, the fish have been virtually wiped out by dams, over-fishing, and pollution.

▶ *Follow* **Route 107** *and turn onto* **I-89** *south. After 18 miles (29km) take exit 1.* **Route 4** *leads to Quechee.*

❸ Quechee and Quechee Gorge

Quechee (Kwee-chy) Gorge is 162 feet (49m) deep. Jagged chunks of schist rock protrude from the walls. While the best view of Vermont's "Little Grand Canyon" is from the old railway bridge that spans the ravine, there is also a half-mile (800m) hike to the bottom. The Ottauquechee River that used to drive the woolen mills of Quechee now powers the converted Downer's Mill. It is

Quechee Falls, on the Ottauquechee River

here that Simon Pearce's well-known glass is made. Visitors can watch his craftsmen at work blowing glass. The Irishman opened his studios in 1981 and has since added a restaurant. All around the town are retirement communities.

RECOMMENDED WALKS

Two of the Northeast's most famous hiking trails part company near Pico Peak. The Long Trail runs the length of the state, some 260 miles (416km) from the Massachusetts line to Quebec. This "Footpath in the Wilderness," which touches some of the main peaks in the Green Mountains, opened in 1926. The southern part of it overlaps with the even longer Appalachian Trail, which runs from Maine down to Georgia. Be warned! These hikes are only for the hearty. They are administered by the Green Mountain Club, in Waterbury (tel: 802/244–7037) and have simple accommodations on the trails.

▶ *Continue on **Route 4** to Woodstock.*

FOR HISTORY BUFFS

Although Joseph Smith is always connected with Salt Lake City and Utah, the founder of the Mormons (Church of Jesus Christ of the Latter Day Saints) was actually born in 1805 on a farm near Sharon, 10 miles (16km) southeast of Bethel. His family left the state in 1816, but a huge granite monument at the top of a steep hill is a tribute to the prophet. Each foot of the 38½-foot-high (11.4m) obelisk represents a year of his life.

From Thanksgiving to Christmas, 85,000 lights brighten the visitor center. Brigham Young, the other great Mormon leader, was another Vermonter, born in Whitingham, near the Massachusetts border.

4 Woodstock

This is New England as most people imagine it: a covered bridge, bandstand on the green, shuttered Colonial homes, and an elegant inn. Regularly voted one of America's prettiest towns, Woodstock was one of the first in the state to develop as a two-season resort. In 1934 a Model T Ford car engine, set up at the bottom of a hill, was hooked up to a piece of cable on a wheel and Woodstock had the first ski tow in the U.S.A. The colorfully named Suicide Six Ski Area still tests even the most competent of skiers.

Woodstock has been a cultural center from its early days. One of the most intellectual of all its sons was George Marsh (1801–82), the lawyer, diplomat, and fervent conservationist. His friend, Frederick Billings, promoted modern farming techniques.

The Marsh-Billings-Rockefeller National Historical Park, which opened in 1998, is named in honor of the two, along with Laurence and Mary

SPECIAL TO...

The sentimental book and film *The Bridges of Madison County* revived interest in covered bridges everywhere in the early 1990s. Although the movie was set in Iowa, New England is renowned for its bridges. They are most often painted red, and there are three in and around Stockbridge, on the way to Bethel.

Rockefeller, who did so much to shape the landscape we see here today. Tours of the mansion show the countryside in art, with a fine collection of American works, while tours of the surrounding forests interpret the way in which the estate has been managed in order to balance the requirements of woodcrafts, recreation, education and ecology. A splendid new Visitor Center opened in 1999.

The park is in partnership

Everyday exhibits at the Billings Museum, Woodstock
Right: red barns and silos are a common sight in Vermont

with Billings Farm Museum, a working dairy farm where visitors can watch work in progress, including butter churning, cheese-making and maple sugaring. An excellent introduction to both the park and the farm can be seen in the museum theater, where the Academy Award-nominated film *A Place in the Land* is shown hourly.

Four bells cast by patriotic hero Paul Revere are at the Congregational Church.

▶ *Continue for 6 miles (10km) to Bridgewater.*

5 Bridgewater

Bridgewater and its namesakes further upstream, West Bridgewater and Bridgewater Corners, were all mill towns. In Bridgewater itself, one old mill has been turned into an outlet

One of the dozens of Victorian stained-glass windows in Wilson Castle, northwest of Rutland

SPECIAL TO...

Little more than a dot on the map, Healdville, just off Route 103 near Ludlow, is the home of one of Vermont's best cheeses. Nothing has changed in the rickety old wooden barn where the cheese makers begin their day at 7am, making Crowley cheese by the same methods the Crowley family used back in 1882. Around midday, the curds are cut and raked by hand to produce the sharp, tangy cheddar-like cheese that matures well.

center for designer clothes, with a crafts center.

The Long Trail Brewing Company has a pub-style visitor center here, where you can sample the brews and have a meal, either inside or on the deck overlooking the river.

▶ *Continue west on* **Route 4**. *After 2 miles (3km), turn left on* **Route 100A** *south for Plymouth.*

⑥ Plymouth

Calvin Coolidge (1872–1933), the 30th president of the United States, was born here, the only president born on the Fourth of July. The five-room Coolidge Birthplace, his father's general store next door, the Coolidge Homestead, and the Wilder House, his mother's childhood home, have been kept much as they would have been when Coolidge was a boy. The summer White House, used in 1924 by Coolidge, has been re-created nearby. He and many other Coolidges are buried in Plymouth cemetery. The President's father founded the Plymouth Cheese Company over a century ago; in 1960, a descendant revived the tradition which continues to make cheese on the site.

▶ *Continue on* **Route 100A**, *then turn left on* **Route 100** *towards Ludlow, passing the Green Mountain Sugar House. Set on the shore of Echo Lake, the Sugar House is a good place for maple-related products. Turn right on* **Route 103** *and return to Rutland.*

FOR HISTORY BUFFS

Vermont farms are built to cope with the extremely cold weather. The early settlers soon realized that the less they went outside in winter, the warmer they would stay. The farmhouses were often joined to the barn with a small hallway, an idea developed by the Dutch. In this way, the farmer could tend to his animals without having to go outside.

FOR HISTORY BUFFS

Despite the esteem with which he is held in his native state, Coolidge made his political career in Massachusetts, where he was Governor. Coolidge was visiting his father on the family farm in Plymouth when President Warren Harding died suddenly on August 3, 1923. At 2.47am, Col. John Coolidge took up the old family Bible and, in his role as a justice of the peace, administered the presidential oath to his son. Harding's administration had been tainted by corruption, so Coolidge's frugal New England virtues were welcomed. Famous for his quote that "the business of America is business," Coolidge believed that government should not interfere with industry.

Northern Vermont

In this sparsely-populated part of the state, there are a surprising number of attractions.

2 DAYS • 134 MILES • 215KM

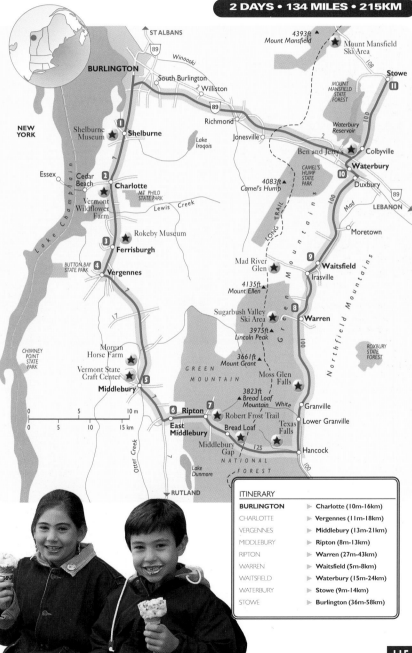

ST ALBANS

89

Winooski

BURLINGTON

South Burlington

2 Williston

89

Richmond

Lake Iroqois

Jonesville

NEW YORK

Shelburne Museum
1 **Shelburne**

Essex

Cedar Beach

2 **Charlotte**
MT PHILO STATE PARK

Vermont Wildflower Farm

Lewis Creek

Rokeby Museum
3 **Ferrisburgh**

BUTTON BAY STATE PARK
4 **Vergennes**

17

CHIMNEY POINT STATE PARK

Morgan Horse Farm

Vermont State Craft Center
5
Middlebury

4393ft
Mount Mansfield
Mount Mansfield Ski Area

108

MOUNT MANSFIELD STATE FOREST
Stowe
11

100

Waterbury Reservoir

Ben and Jerry's
Colbyville
Waterbury
10
Duxbury

89

LEBANON

2

CAMEL'S HUMP STATE PARK

4083ft
Camel's Hump

Mad
Moretown

LONG TRAIL

100

Mad River Glen
9 **Waitsfield**
Irasville

Green Mountains

4135ft
Mount Ellen

Sugarbush Valley Ski Area

8 **Warren**

3975ft
Lincoln Peak

100

Northfield Mountains

ROXBURY STATE FOREST

3661ft
Mount Grant

GREEN MOUNTAIN

3823ft
▲ Bread Loaf Mountain

Moss Glen Falls

White
Granville

Lower Granville

6 **Ripton** 7
Robert Frost Trail

East Middlebury
Bread Loaf

Texas Falls

Hancock

Middlebury Gap

NATIONAL FOREST

125

Lake Dunmore

100

0   5   10 m
0   5   10   15 km

Otter Creek

RUTLAND

Lake Champlain

ITINERARY

BURLINGTON	▶ **Charlotte** (10m-16km)
CHARLOTTE	▶ **Vergennes** (11m-18km)
VERGENNES	▶ **Middlebury** (13m-21km)
MIDDLEBURY	▶ **Ripton** (8m-13km)
RIPTON	▶ **Warren** (27m-43km)
WARREN	▶ **Waitsfield** (5m-8km)
WAITSFIELD	▶ **Waterbury** (15m-24km)
WATERBURY	▶ **Stowe** (9m-14km)
STOWE	▶ **Burlington** (36m-58km)

i **60 Main Street**

▶ *From Burlington, take **Route 7** south for 5 miles (8 km) and turn right for Shelburne Farms.*

❶ Shelburne

Most Vermont farms are humble affairs, with red barns, a white silo and a low-slung farmhouse. Shelburne Farms is the opposite, a millionaire's toy built in the 1880s and 1890s on a giant scale and using all the latest technical equipment available. After William Webb married Lila Vanderbilt, daughter of the rail-

Frederick Law Olmsted, the man who landscaped New York's Central Park, to map out their property. Like so many million-aires of the late last century, the Webb's "summer cottage" was extraordinary – a 110-room Queen Anne-style manor house. It is now the Inn at Shelburne Farms. The farm continues to be an experimental and working farm, where visitors can watch cheese-making, bread-baking, and furniture-making. Old-fash-ioned pleasures such as hay rides will entertain the small children.

When J. Watson Webb, the

Apothecary store, one of the exhibits at Shelburne Museum

road tycoon, they created a European-style estate.

The Webbs called upon

FOR CHILDREN

Children (and lots of adults) always love a boat trip, and there are plenty of opportuni-ties to cruise Lake Champlain. One of the most popular trips is from Burlington Boathouse aboard the *Spirit of Ethan Allen II*, a three-deck cruise ship with narration and on-board meals. Alternatively, you can go your own way. Waterfront Boat Rentals at Shelburne rent canoes, kayaks and motor boats.

SPECIAL TO...

Lake Champlain is shaped like a sausage, 120 miles (192km) long and anything from 400 yards (400m) to 12 miles (19km) wide. Samuel de Champlain, the 17th-century French explorer, recorded see-ing a 20-foot-long (6m) serpent with a head like a horse, and visitors have been trying to spot "Champ" ever since. Lake Champlain has four ferry ser-vices that cross from Vermont to the New York shores: from Grand Isle to Cumberland Head (12 minutes), from Burlington to Port Kent (an hour), from Charlotte to Essex (20 minutes) and from Larrabee's Point to Ticonderoga (6 minutes).

son of the Webbs of Shelburne Farms, married Electra Havemeyer, they began collect-ing art objects, large and small, and these now form the remark-able Shelburne Museum. The 37 buildings in which the quilts, paintings, toys, and farm equip-ment are displayed, are them-selves collector's items. These buildings, each a historical land-mark, have been rescued from all over New England and reassembled. You'll find a schoolhouse, railroad station, general store, barn, jailhouse, and inn, now serving as galleries. Most arresting of all is a boat – the 220-foot-long (66m) side-wheel steamer *Ticonderoga*. It was hauled for 2 miles (3km) from Lake Champlain to its final landlocked berth here on the farm. Although the folk art

Church Street market, Burlington

from Burlington to Troy. The old houses in the historic district remain, along with three covered bridges.

Slightly further along Route 7 is the Vermont Wildflower Farm with 6 acres (2.4 hectares) of woodland and flower fields. Self-guided trails explain the legends of wildflowers and how Native Americans used them for herbal remedies. Visitors can also buy seeds. This stretch of Route 7 has magnificent views across Lake Champlain to the Adirondack Mountains.

▶ *Continue to Ferrisburgh. On a hill to the left is the Rokeby Museum.*

3 Ferrisburgh
One of the state's underrated museums is the Rokeby, home of the Robinson family for generations. Beautifully furnished, the house is a tribute to their own artistic talents, with portraits and landscapes they have personally painted lining the walls. Rokeby was also one of the last stops on the Underground Railroad, the escape route for black slaves from the American South to Canada. It contains a secret passage and hiding room.

▶ *Continue south to Vergennes.*

4 Vergennes
Vergennes was named after France's foreign minister and a great supporter of the Americans in the Revolution. It claims to be the smallest city in the country, just one square mile (259 hectares) with 2,500 inhabitants. On Basin Harbor Road, in a 19th-century stone schoolhouse, you'll find Lake Champlain Maritime Museum. During both the Revolution and the War of 1812, American and British warships battled for supremacy on this elongated strip of water. Benedict Arnold (see page 80), later a notorious traitor, delayed the British in 1776 with a series of clever ploys, as explained in

the museum. A full-size replica of his gunboat, the *Philadelphia II*, is the highlight of the visit.

▶ *Continue on **Route 7** south to Middlebury.*

5 Middlebury
Middlebury is best known for its college, founded in 1800. Visitors who come to admire the old houses and museums such as the Sheldon and Painter Hall use it as a base. For more contemporary culture, the Vermont State Craft Center, in Frog Hollow, on Otter Creek Falls, is a modern showcase for the talents of some 230 artists and craftspeople from all over the state. Across the creek are the old marble works, filled with shops. The railway offers scenic rides up to Burlington and back.

Middlebury College claims to be the birthplace of the Frisbee in 1938. Yale students may dispute this (see page 68), but the Vermonters have a handsome statue of a dog leaping to catch a flying disk. It was unveiled in front of Monroe Hall on what they insist was the 50th anniversary of spinning pie dishes at one another.

[i] *2 Court Street*

▶ *Follow **Route 7** south, then turn onto **Route 125** for East Middlebury.*

6 East Middlebury
Two hundred years ago the hamlet of East Middlebury was

collection is justifiably high-lighted as one of the finest in the world, the Shelburne art collection is equally impressive. Pieces by American painters Andrew Wyeth and Winslow Homer are on display, as are European artists Rembrandt and Goya. You need a full day here to do justice to the museum.

The town of Shelburne has a more recent industry: the Vermont Teddy Bear Company, which exports its furry friends world-wide. Children can decorate and stuff "new born" bears.

▶ *Continue to Charlotte.*

2 Charlotte
Pronounced char-LOT, the town's heyday was in the early 19th century, when it was a stage-coach stop on the journey

---

RECOMMENDED WALKS

Split by the Mad River and the cascading Moss Glen Falls, Granville Gulf State Park borders the eastern boundary of the Green Mountain National Forest. There is a 6-mile (10km) scenic drive, as well as two hiking trails. The easy 1-mile (1.6km) loop on the east side of the road contrasts with the shorter, but tougher ½-mile (0.8km) hike to the west.

BACK TO NATURE

The Green Mountains, the backbone of Vermont, consist of more than one distinct range. The higher peaks are to the north, with Mount Mansfield (near Stowe), the highest in the state. About two-thirds of the mountains are protected by the Green Mountain National Forest, 340,000 acres (136,000 hectares) devoted to maintaining scenic beauty and providing recreational opportunities. Some 500 miles (800km) of trails criss-cross the forests. The headquarters of the Green Mountain National Forest is in Rutland.

little more than a spot for stage coaches to Boston to change horses. Then the television cameras arrived to film the hit TV comedy series *Newhart*, starring comedian Bob Newhart, at the Waybury Inn. Rooms in this quaint 1810 inn have been refurbished in period style.

▶ *Continue for 4 miles (6km) to Ripton on* ***Route 125****, the Robert Frost Memorial Drive.*

7 Ripton

The poet Robert Frost summered in the woods near Ripton for 23 years, and today the mountain to the north is named after him. Just after the hamlet of Ripton is a picnic area on the left, and a rough track leading to his cabin. On the other side of the road is the Robert Frost Interpretive Trail, a ¾-mile (1.2km) walk studded with plaques of quotes by the great man.

Seven miles (11km) after leaving Middlebury is the Bread Loaf Campus of Middlebury College. Once a hotel in the shadow of Bread Loaf Mountain, the campus is now well known for its summer writing schools and conferences. In winter it is a base for cross-country skiing.

▶ ***Route 125*** *climbs steadily, passing Bread Loaf and the Snow Bowl, a local but challenging ski area. Beyond the summit of Middlebury Gap the*

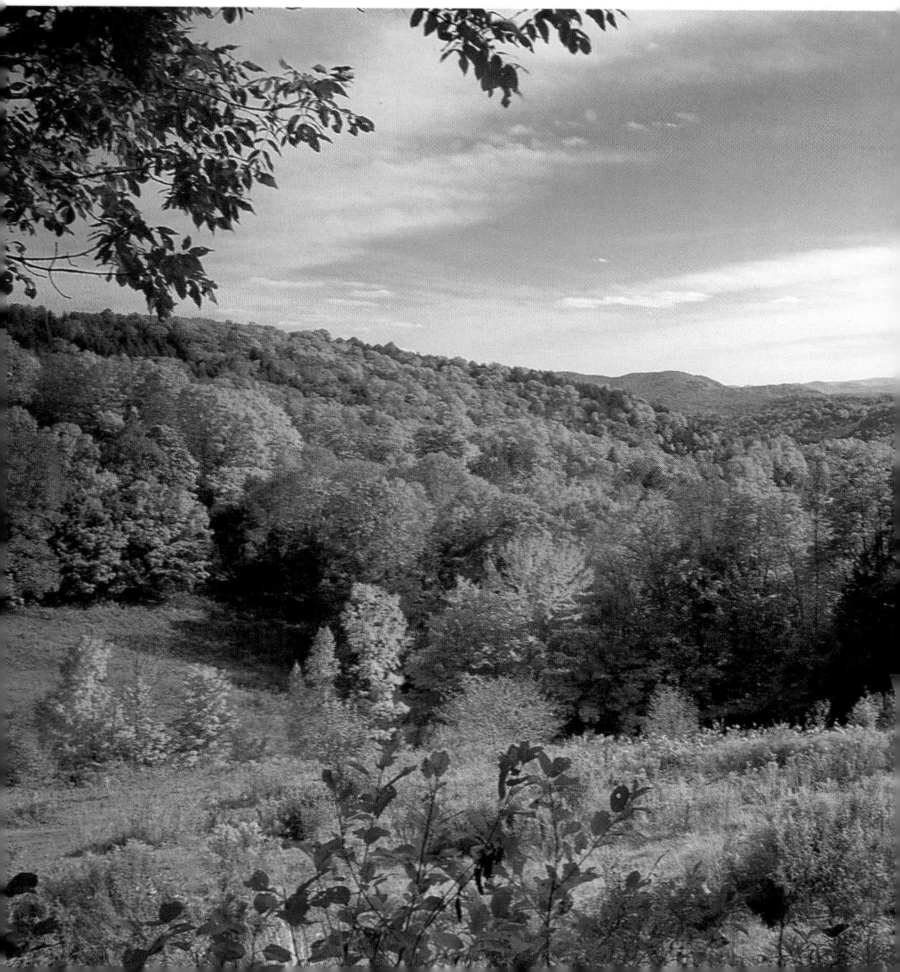

The densely wooded Green Mountains clothed in fall foliage

road drops down to Hancock, passing Texas Falls recreation area. At Hancock, turn left on *Route 100* north, alongside the White River. After 4 miles (6km) is Granville, and another 10 miles (16km) further turn right to Warren.

8 Warren

Despite the popularity of the neighboring Sugarbush Valley Ski Area, Warren has changed little. The simple exterior of the Warren Store belies a sophisticated little emporium of gourmet foods and fine wines for the city folk who visit. Simpler pleasures survive, with a wind chime artisan and glider rides from the little airport.

Just north of Warren is the left turn for Sugarbush, the heart of

one of Vermont's premier ski destinations. Opened in 1958, this affluent resort has expensive condominiums and a busy restaurant scene. Vermont's third highest peak, Mt. Ellen (4,135 feet/1,260m), and Lincoln Peak (3,975 feet/1,211m) are the two mountains that provide the ski thrills. In summer, golfers test themselves on the course designed by Robert Trent Jones, Sr. There are also tennis courts.

▷ *Continue to Waitsfield.*

9 Waitsfield

The Mad River Glen Ski Resort has boosted what was once a lumber and dairy town. It is smaller, older and less formal than the nearby Sugarbush resort, but offers more challeng-

ing runs for the advanced skier. It has given a boost to what was once a lumber and dairy town. Now arts, crafts, and chic shopping thrive. In contrast, the old covered bridge and the Mad River Canoe Company, the famous makers of recreational canoes, add a more down-to-earth element.

Nearby, the Vermont Icelandic Horse Farm is a treat for small children.

▷ *Take **Route 100** north to Waterbury (15miles/24km). Ben and Jerry's is 1 mile (1.6km) north of I–89.*

10 Waterbury

Waterbury means just one thing to ice cream aficionados: Ben and Jerry's. Ben Cohen and Jerry Greenfield's rags-to-riches story is the American dream, set deep in the Vermont countryside. In 1977, they started by producing home-made ice cream in Burlington, in a disused and dismantled service station. These days, the factory is in Waterbury, where tours with free tastings are a constant draw. In summer, old-fashioned ice cream machines and real cows, ready for milking, keep children entertained.

Waterbury has expanded to include other tasty attractions: the Green Mountain Chocolate Co., and the Cold Hollow Cider Mill, with its excellent pure pressed apple juices. The Green Mountain Club, half way to Stowe, administers the Long Trail and other outdoor activities.

▷ *Continue to Stowe, then follow **Route 108** to the Mount Mansfield Ski Area.*

11 Stowe

Near Stowe is Mount Mansfield Ski Area, one of New England's premier ski resorts, built on Mount Mansfield, Vermont's highest peak (4,393 feet/1,338m). In summer, a gravel toll road, the Stowe Auto Road, leads to the summit, a 4½-mile (7km) journey. This steep route,

Low mist over Stowe, the main skiing and recreation center for this popular area

with numerous steep, tight curves, is a test of both car and driver. For a more relaxed journey use the Stowe Gondola, a half-hour scenic swing over the forested slopes. With tennis courts, a golf course and an In-Line Skate Park, this is a summer destination for the active.

Another attraction is the Trapp Family Lodge in Stowe, built by the real-life family of *The Sound of Music* fame. A sign "invites you to share a little of Austria, a lot of Vermont." Actually, they offer quite a lot of everything since this resort has

grown substantially over the years. It is all very atmospheric and *gemütlich*, with staff in Austrian costume, though some find it a little overdone.

[i] *Main Street, Stowe*

▷ *Return on **Route 100** to I–89 and drive northwest to Burlington.*

RECOMMENDED WALKS

The Stowe Recreation Path is a 5-mile (8km) trail alongside a mountain stream. Undulating gently, and carefully cleared in winter, this trail is a tribute to the generosity of local residents, who have donated the right of way past meadows, swimming holes, woods, and cornfields for visitors to cross their land.

SPECIAL TO...

Justin Morgan was a Vermont teacher who created the country's first horse breed. A hardy colt called Figure was born in 1793, a mixture of Arabian and thoroughbred. The Morgan, as it became known, with its deep chest and powerful hind-quarters, stands some 14 to 15 hands (1.42–1.52m) high. Usually long-lived, mild-mannered, and bay in color, this multi-use equine was a boon to the army, who rode it and also used this hardy breed to pull guns and equipment. Now owned by the University of Vermont and open to the public, the Morgan Horse Farm is 2 miles (3km) north of Middlebury. The grounds are immaculate, with a slate-roofed 19th-century barn, lush meadows, and parade grounds, and is home to the 70 stallions, mares, and foals.

FOR CHILDREN

Stowe is a wonderful area for children with an adventurous spirit. They can hurtle 2,300 feet (700m) down Spruce Peal on the Alpine Slide, for instance, or speed around the Launch Zone Skate Park's ramps and street scenes on skates, skateboards or BMX bikes.
There are miles of mountain bike trails in the area, and younger children will love the public playground at the Stowe Elementary School. Local children raised the funds for it, including a donation from "Superman" (actor Christopher Reeve).

NEW HAMPSHIRE

New Hampshire's nickname is the "Granite State." Some say it refers to the rocky scenery, others maintain it describes the implacable nature of the residents. Certainly, the terrain is the very opposite of the English county that lent it its name. New Hampshire has only an 18-mile (29km) strip of Atlantic coastline, and a mere 80 miles (128km) away are the White Mountains, the tallest in New England. Hundreds of lakes, often bearing the Indian names given by earlier residents – Sunapee, Winnipesaukee and Squam – are scattered throughout the thick pine forests. Sixty covered bridges stretch across tumbling streams.

The early settlers were "economic refugees," who had left Europe to make a better life rather than to find religious freedom. The land and climate made the early days a struggle. Later, the Scots-Irish added their resolute character to the New Hampshire persona. Today, car license plates bear the state motto: "Live Free or Die." The rest of this Revolutionary rallying cry is "death is not the worst of evils." The fiery words are attributed to farmer-turned-general, John Stark, one of the New Hampshire men who formed the backbone of the American troops in the early days of the Revolution.

The Kancamagus Highway, in the White Mountains, is famous for its fall foliage

Today, the politics in New Hampshire are notably "grass-roots," with the 221 townships often regarded as "little republics." The state scorns income tax and sales tax, preferring to raise money by taxing liquor and betting. This tax – or lack of tax – structure has attracted businesses to move across the state line from Massachusetts. Shoppers also drive over the border from neighboring states to load up and save money. Since most of the one million inhabitants cluster near the Massachusetts border, the rest of the state seems sparsely populated. While agriculture has long been a mainstay of the economy, it has been the fast-flowing streams driving machinery that have benefited residents most. Towns like Manchester may not manufacture locomotives and fire engines any longer, but plastics, electronics, and paper products have successfully taken their place.

Tour 18

Portsmouth, New Hampshire's port, is wedged between Massachusetts and Maine. Forty years ago it was a rundown city, a place to escape rather than a tourist destination. However, the residents recognized the rich history beneath the dirt – instead of tearing down the old buildings, they started a major restoration project. Now the merchants' houses and warehouses, meeting houses and bankers' offices are the attractive heart of the city and a source of civic pride. Small parks and museums reflect Portsmouth's role as a ship-building center, others are filled with fine antique American furniture. Best known is Strawbery Banke, a collection of houses that show what everyday life was like over a period of four centuries.

Above: Strawbery Banke
Below: The Flume, a giant chasm where a mountain stream tumbles in a series of waterfalls

Tour 19

The White Mountains are a popular destination all year round. The focus is Mount Washington, first climbed by a European 350 years ago. It is now deluged by 250,000 enthusiastic tourists every summer. A cog railroad crawls its way up to the top. Those wanting to avoid the "madding crowds" can explore the numerous well-marked trails throughout the mountains, either for a day hike or a longer trek. In winter, "the Whites" attract both downhill and cross-country skiers. The spectacular scenery on this route includes "the Kanc," the Kancamagus Highway, one of America's prettiest drives.

Tour 20

Since 1981, Squam Lake has become a "must see" for fans of the film *On Golden Pond*. Nearby, larger Lake Winnipesaukee has long been a popular destination for summer visitors wishing to escape the heat and humidity of Boston. The western shore has become over-popular and built-up, but for the most part, this is a peaceful drive, with villages, craft shops, and museums en route. Anyone interested in top-quality crafts should plan to spend time in Center Sandwich, while Meredith is best known for its dolls.

Portsmouth

Portsmouth has one of New England's finest natural harbors and became wealthy on the timber trade, exporting lumber to Britain and the West Indies. Huge fortunes were made and spent on grandiose mansions, many of which still stand. A massive preservation program over recent decades has saved numerous fine buildings, making this a city for anyone interested in the architecture and craftsmanship of 18th- and 19th-century America.

HALF A DAY

Badgers Island

Seavey Island

MARKET ... CERES ST

BOW ST

St John's Church **14**

Moffatt-Ladd House **15**

Warner House **13**

Prescott Park

DEER STREET

HANOVER ST.

PENHALLOW ST.

CHAPEL ST.

DANIEL ST.

PLEASANT STREET

STATE STREET

STREET

Market Square **1**

Strawbery Banke **12**

Liberty Pole **11**

Peirce Island

CONGRESS STREET

South Church **2**

Ann Treadwell Mansion **6**

WASHINGTON ST.

HANCOCK ST.

MARCY STREET

MECHANIC ST.

Abraham Shaw House
Rockingham Hotel

John Paul Jones House **3**

COURT STREET

Governor Langdon House **7**

Thomas Thompson House **8**

GATE ST.

MANNING ST.

PLEASANT ST

9

Wentworth Gardner House **10**

MIDDLE STREET

John Peirce Mansion **4**

South Mill Pond

0   100   200 yards
0   100   200 m

Rundlet-May House **5**

BOSTON

i *500 Market Street*

▶ *Start at Market Square, the heart of the city.*

❶ Market Square

The lottery may seem a new idea but it has long been a means of raising money. Back in 1762, the militia's training ground was paved with funds from a public lottery. The Athenaeum, at No. 9, was originally the headquarters of a fire and marine insurance company, but became a private library in 1823. The classic pointed spire of North Church can be seen from anywhere in the downtown area, especially when it is illuminated at night. On the east side of the square stands the impressive wall of Bankers Row, the guardians of civic wealth for

The John Paul Jones House, where the Scots-born Navy officer lived

nearly 200 years. No. 24/26 is thought to be the oldest bank in America, and it was extensively rebuilt in 1904.

▶ *Leave Market Square, heading south on Pleasant Street. Turn right on State Street.*

❷ State Street

Contrasting with the elegant white spire of North Church is the squat tower of South Church, at No. 292. This solid-looking granite building dates from 1826 and is still used for worship by the Unitarian Universalists. Nearby was the starting point of the 1813 fire, which blazed towards the waterfront. Some houses survived, only to be lost to a 1950s urban planning project. Still standing is the Abraham Shaw House (1810) at No. 379. A few doors further on is the Rockingham Hotel (No. 401), whose lions

RECOMMENDED TRIP

Just off the coast are nine islands, the Isles of Shoals, partly in Maine, partly in New Hampshire. Take a picnic on the delightful one-hour boat ride. Visit Star, an island used as a church retreat which also has the Vaughan Cottage Memorial and Celia Turner Museum, or Appledore, once an artists' colony.

became the personal emblem of Frank Jones, a flamboyant brewer and entrepreneur whose bust is on the right. He turned the hotel into "the most elegant and superbly furnished establishment ... outside of Boston."

▶ *At the corner of State and Middle streets is Haymarket Square, with its enclave of elegant homes. At No. 43 Middle Street is the John Paul Jones House.*

❸ John Paul Jones House

Scottish-born John Paul Jones is known as the "father of the U.S. Navy." He did not own this handsome clapboard house, but rented rooms from Mrs. Sarah Purcell. The naval hero was in Portsmouth in 1777 to supervise the fitting out of the *Ranger*, and once again in 1781, for the building of the *America*. The house is now the headquarters of the local historical society.

▶ *Turn south on Middle Street. Cross the square to No. 18 Court Street.*

❹ John Peirce Mansion

"The best" of the city's 19th-century houses, according to some critics. No expense was spared when Peirce built this home in 1799. It was handed down through the family for generations until 1955, when the Baptist Church bought the property.

▶ *Two blocks further along Middle Street is No. 364.*

The White
Mountains

Weekend hikers and serious climbers come to test themselves against the mountains, of which Mount Washington is only one of 86 named peaks.

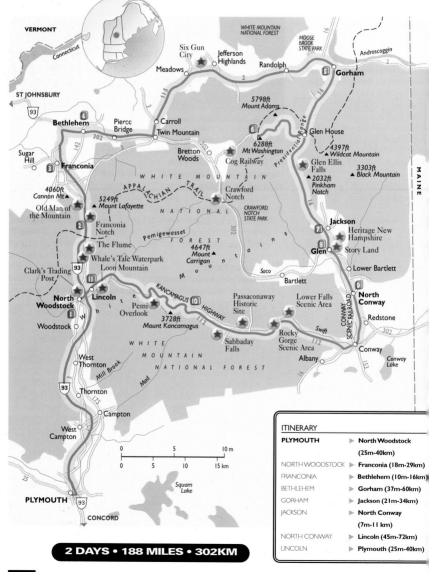

2 DAYS • 188 MILES • 302KM

The Old Man of the Mountain, the craggy, enduring symbol of New Hampshire, is as impressive now as it must have been in 1805 when first spotted by road builders. This rock formation inspired the clever Nathaniel Hawthorne short story, *The Great Stone Face*. When the glib New Hampshire senator Daniel Webster saw it, he reportedly said that "Men hang out their signs indicative of their respective trades; shoemakers hang out a gigantic shoe; jewelers a monster watch ... but up in the mountains of New Hampshire, God Almighty has hung out a sign to show that there He makes man." One family, the Nielsens, have made it their mission to preserve the face from crumbling. Three generations have worked on it since 1960.

ⓘ *Chamber of Commerce booth, exit 28, off I–83*

▶ *Starting in Plymouth, proceed north on I–93, noting the frequency of the "moose crossing" signs and warnings. After 25 miles (40km), exit 32 heads off for North Woodstock and Lincoln.*

❶ North Woodstock

With storefronts that look like film sets for Hollywood westerns, North Woodstock is not your typical New England village. The main attraction is Clark's Trading Post, a theme park from the days before theme parks were a "dime-a-dozen." Florence Clark took the unlikely title of "first woman to reach the summit of Mount Washington using a dog sled." The Clark family still runs the show after 70 years. The attraction, which began as a dog ranch now features performing bears, Merlin's Mystical Mansion, a garage from yesteryear, an old fire station, and other eccentric and eclectic Americana. Clark's

Trading Post also claims to have the world's last remaining Howetruss railroad bridge in the world, a covered, 120-foot (36m) long affair.

▶ *At this point I–93 becomes the Franconia Notch State Parkway. Continue north to The Flume and Franconia Notch Pass.*

❷ Franconia Notch

The Notch is the best-known high pass in New England. Ever since the first Europeans saw its towering granite walls 200 years ago, tourists have come to admire the gorge, formed by a massive prehistoric glacier. Preserved and protected in their own privately-funded State Park, these natural wonders are easily accessible and the Park is geared for those who wish to see the sights without much fight. The Flume Visitor Center has information on all the attractions in the Notch, as well as a shuttle bus to the Flume itself. Gravel paths and wooden walkways lead through a narrow gorge, 800 feet (240m) long. Its sheer walls stretch 90 feet (27m) straight up on both sides. Through the Notch, the Flume Brook bounces down the side of Mount Liberty and into the glacial pool.

Further along the road is the viewpoint for The Old Man of

Clark's Trading Post includes a reconstructed New England street

the Mountain, also called the Great Stone Face or Profile. Towering high above Profile Lake, and measuring 40 feet (12m) from forehead to chin, the five ledges of granite look like the silhouette of a man's face.

About a half-mile (800m) along is the Cannon Aerial Tramway II. Gondolas whisk 80 passengers at a time up to the top of Cannon Mountain (4,060feet/1,237m), climbing some 2,022 feet (616m) in just 7½ minutes. The view is well worth the fee, and there are plentiful, marked walks around the Summit Observatory Platform. Refreshments are available here.

Seats are limited on the Mount Washington Cog Railway, so advance booking is recommended

Next to the base of the tramway is the New England Ski Museum. Echo Lake, a little further on, is a natural mirror, reflecting Cannon Mountain and Mount Lafayette in its still waters. The energetic can cycle through the Notch on the 8-mile (13km) bike path which passes most of the attractions.

▶ Continue on Franconia Notch State Parkway, which becomes I–93 again. Take exit 38 for Franconia.

8 Franconia

Once a flourishing resort, Franconia has seemingly gone back to sleep. It has been overtaken by the more ambitious towns south of the Notch. Poetry lovers drop by the Robert Frost Place, the 150-year-old, white clapboard hillside farmhouse to which Frost returned in 1915, upon his homecoming from England. Aged 40 and still virtually unknown, he farmed the land, wrote three books of verse and won a Pulitzer prize, all in the next five years. Visitors can see his writing desk, signed first editions and a rare collection of his Christmas card

5 Gorham

Gorham is a useful stop for those who are keen on wildlife. At dawn and dusk, guides take visitors on a two-hour explanatory Moose Tour in search of these big beasts, which are abundant in the woods.

▶ *Leave town on **Route 16** south to Glen House, at the foot of Mount Washington.*

poems. In summer, there are readings by a poet in residence and a Festival of Poetry in late July and early August. A half-mile (800m) nature trail, highlighted with plaques along the way, presents 15 of Frost's favorite poems.

▶ *Return to **I–93** and drive 6 miles (10km) to exit 40 for Bethlehem. Turn on to **Route 302** east.*

4 Bethlehem

The little town of Bethlehem is more Victorian-looking than Colonial, reflecting its heyday as a vacation destination a century

Inset: a young moose

ago. Back then, thousands flocked here by train. The air was so clean and clear of pollution that the National Hay Fever Relief Association was started here in the 1920s. Now, apart from its antique shops, Bethlehem is a base for touring and hiking.

▶ *Stay on **Route 302** east for 8 miles (13km) to Twin Mountain. Turn left onto **Route 3**. At Carroll, take the **115** through Meadows, then join **Route 2** and head east to Gorham.*

1 DAY • 106 MILES • 169KM

Around Lake
Winnipesaukee

Lake Winnipesaukee is huge, the sixth largest body of water inside the country. The Native American name is "The Smile of the Great Spirit," though some experts prefer the more prosaic translation of "Beautiful Water in a High Place."

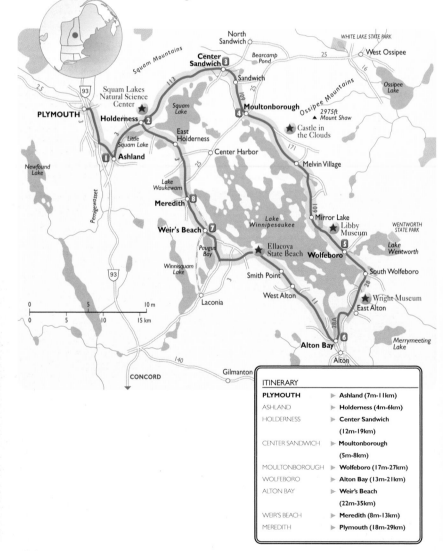

ITINERARY	
PLYMOUTH	▶ **Ashland** (7m-11km)
ASHLAND	▶ **Holderness** (4m-6km)
HOLDERNESS	▶ **Center Sandwich** (12m-19km)
CENTER SANDWICH	▶ **Moultonborough** (5m-8km)
MOULTONBOROUGH	▶ **Wolfeboro** (17m-27km)
WOLFEBORO	▶ **Alton Bay** (13m-21km)
ALTON BAY	▶ **Weir's Beach** (22m-35km)
WEIR'S BEACH	▶ **Meredith** (8m-13km)
MEREDITH	▶ **Plymouth** (18m-29km)

ⓘ *Chamber of Commerce booth, exit 28, off I-83*

▶ *Start in Plymouth and take I–93 south to exit 24 for Ashland.*

❶ Ashland

The small town of Ashland, once an important stop on the old Boston, Concord and Montreal Railroad line, retains the character of an old mill town. The Ashland Historical Society is based in the former home of Dr. George Whipple, the pathologist who won the Nobel prize for medicine in 1934. Next door, the Pauline Glidden Toy Museum has over 1,000 early toys. A local resident, the late Milton Graton, was one of New England's experts on the restoration and building of covered bridges. His last was built here in his home town, where his son Arnold continues the tradition.

▶ *Continue on **Route 3** to Holderness.*

❷ Holderness

Holderness sits on Little Squam Lake; to the east is the much larger Squam Lake. The Academy Award-winning 1981 film, *On Golden Pond*, starring Katherine Hepburn and Henry

Fonda, was filmed here, catapulting Squam Lake to fame, even though the film was supposedly set in Maine. Small boats cruise the peaceful lake and delight in showing visitors where the scenes were shot. It is a favorite nesting place for loons.

▶ *Follow **Route 113** for Center Sandwich (12 miles/19km). Pass Squam Lake.*

❸ Center Sandwich

Sitting between the Squam Mountains and Squam Lake, this is one of several Sandwich villages in the area. New England poet John Greenleaf Whittier (1807–92) spent time in Center Sandwich. This crusading Quaker championed the anti-slavery cause and used poetry in his emotional campaigns:

"What! mothers from their children riven!
What! God's own image bought and sold!
Americans to market driven,
And bartered as the brute for gold!"

Whittier wrote *Sunset* on the Bearcamp, the river which runs through Bearcamp Pond between Center Sandwich and North Sandwich. The Whittier covered bridge crosses the river in West Ossipee.

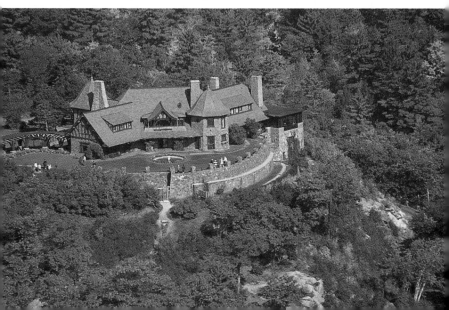

Aerial view of the turreted hilltop Castle in the Clouds

Above: near Lake Shore Park,
Lake Winnipesaukee
Inset: Weir's Beach

▶ *Drive south on* **Route 109**
*for 5 miles (8km) to
Moultonborough.*

❹ Moultonborough
This typical New England
village has the bonus of the lake
as a backdrop. Apart from its
idyllic setting, the big attraction
is "Castle in the Clouds," a
reminder of the astonishing
wealth garnered a century ago.
Set 750 feet (225m) up in the
Ossipee Mountains, this mock
castle and its extensive estate
offers spectacular views.
Millionaire Thomas Plant, who
made his money from shoes,
designed the $7 million house

himself, which explains the variety of architectural styles, from
Swiss chalet to Norman castle. A
touch of English Tudor is the
coup de grâce. It was built by
hundreds of craftsmen, including Italian stone masons brought
over from Europe. Water from a
spring on the grounds is bottled
commercially. The nearby Loon
Center and Markus Wildlife
Sanctuary specializes in New
Hampshire's ecology.

▶ *Continue south on* **Route 109**
*for 17 miles (27km) to
Wolfeboro. The route passes
through Melvin Village, known
for its antiques shops.*

*Continue along the shores of
Winnipesaukee, through
Mirror Lake.*

❺ Wolfeboro
Just before Wolfeboro, on the
edge of Mirror Lake, is the
Libby Museum which explains
the story of this hamlet and
America's oldest resort. Back in
1768, Massachusetts Governor
John Wentworth ordered a
summer house here. To reach
the house from Portsmouth, he
even had the "Governor's Road"
built. The retreat burned down
in 1820, and is now the site of an
archeological dig in Wentworth
State Park, 6 miles (10km) east
of town.

The Wright Museum, a new attraction in Wolfeboro, charts the story of America during World War II. As well as its collection of military vehicles, it reflects life on the home front, with room settings, costumes and other period items.

▶ Take **Routes 28 and 28A** *south for 13 miles (21km) to Alton Bay, right at the foot of Lake Winnipesaukee.*

6 Alton Bay

The little town of Alton Bay has much of the appearance it must have enjoyed in its summer heydays. There is a floating bandstand out in the bay, and the railroad station has been spruced up. Scenic lake cruises depart from the docks.

▶ Follow **Route 11** *northwest. This side of the lake is much more open, affording great views of the water and to the White Mountains in the north. Weir's Beach is 22 miles (35km) farther on via the Ellacoya State Beach, where you get a sense of how large Lake Winnipesaukee really is. Continue to Weir's Beach.*

7 Weir's Beach

Weir's Beach is the Coney Island of the region with amusement parks, crowded boardwalks, beaches, and a weekly fireworks display. One of New England's last drive-in movie theaters is here too. It is especially busy here when the motorbike races take place in nearby Loudon. Weir's Beach has two waterslide parks, but tamer rides are also available, such as on the scenic railroad that follows the lakeshore to Meredith. Another good way to beat the crowds is to take a cruise on the lake, either for its simple scenic value, or to appreciate the wildlife on a special nature cruise.

▶ Take **Route 3** *north to Meredith (8 miles/13km).*

8 Meredith

Quieter than Weir's Beach, with pretty docks and landings on the lake, Meredith is the home of the popular felt Annalee Dolls. Annalee Thorndike created these cutesy dolls in 1934 and now the factory is a major local employer. The dolls are bought by fans and collectors from all over the world. There is also a museum dedicated to them, which includes the first doll and some valuable pre-war models.

▶ Return to Plymouth via **Route 3** *through Holderness and I–93.*

MAINE

The Algonquin Indians called this region the "Land of the Frozen Ground" and the summer season is certainly the shortest here in New England, barely covering June through September. No-one knows how or why Maine received its present name. What is known is that it could swallow up the rest of the New England states. One single county, Aroostook, is bigger than the states of Connecticut and Rhode Island combined. Yet the population is only 1,200,000, mostly in the south and along the coast.

Residents and visitors alike come to Maine to enjoy the unspoiled natural beauty. Geographers estimate that the 230-mile (368km) long coastline would stretch to 3,500 miles (5,600km) if every cove and inlet were measured. Drive down the fingers of land that jut into the sea to find old fishing villages, quiet inlets, and rocky cliffs. Offshore lie around 2,000 islands, some linked to the mainland by ferry, the majority barely habitable, and all surrounded by treacherous rocks and ice-cold water.

View over Camden Harbor

The coast is the biggest draw and some parts, such as Oqunquit and Boothbay Harbor, become quite crowded in season. Getting away from it all, however, is easy since 90 percent of the state is wilderness and forest. Maine attracts hikers and canoeists into its hinterland with 32,000 miles (51,200km) of river and 6,000 ponds and lakes dotted around. There are few people, but thousands of moose.

Although many experts assume that the Vikings could have paid a visit a thousand years ago, it was the French and English who first settled here. In 1677, the territory was assigned to Massachusetts, but in the early 19th century, when that state began to struggle economically, it cut the ties and Maine became a state in its own right.

Maine's nickname, the "Pine Tree State," is appropriate. Not only is the coastline wooded, there are vast forests inland. The tall, strong pines once provided masts for the British Navy; now, they are made into paper and pulp. Shipbuilding started in 1607, in Bath, and continues there today.

Lighthouses stand as symbols of New England's maritime history
Left: L. L. Bean, Freeport

galleries. "Park and Shop," for example, allows visitors free parking in exchange for a stamp showing proof of purchase from local shops and restaurants. Much of the handsome brick and granite architecture post-dates the devastating fire of 1866, and some earlier buildings remain. Included among these is the home of the writer Henry Wadsworth Longfellow, dating back to 1785.

Tour 23

Getting away from it all is easy when you head for the lakes and mountains of Maine. This long drive explores the state's remote beauty, while also passing through some charming villages. The famous Shaker religious community lives in a village at Sabbathday Lake. Their pious faith still arouses admiration, even though only a handful of the sect survives. By contrast, the nearby Sunday River ski area is one of the liveliest in Maine. Winter temperatures will test a visitor's fortitude. Rangeley is not only the mid-point of this drive, but the town also boasts being precisely halfway between the North Pole and the Equator.

Tour 21

For many, the "real Maine" begins north of Portland. Here, the coastline breaks up into long skeletal fingers of granite, pointing out to form bays dotted with pine-covered islands. The sea has always been the focus of this region and the earliest Europeans who spent time here were transient fisher folk. Seafaring and boat-building are long traditions that have continued with the U.S. Navy in Brunswick, the huge shipyard in Bath, and numerous smaller boat-builders and museums. Although tourism is a major

industry, towns such as Camden, Wiscasset, and Damariscotta have been able to retain their charm.

Tour 22

Portland is often rated as one of the best cities in which to live: small enough to feel friendly, but with a lively cultural scene and innovative restaurants. In recent years, it has made a conscious and successful effort to brighten up its downtown and old harbor by recycling historic buildings and employing novel methods of attracting locals to the shops and

The Mid-Coast
of Maine

2 DAYS • 260 MILES • 418KM

Rocky bays, cliff-top lighthouses, and peaceful harbors
give the mid-coast of Maine its character. This route
leads to busy towns and quiet hamlets, past
historic houses and old forts. Artists and craftspeople
have long been attracted by the area, so there are
festivals and fine art galleries as well.

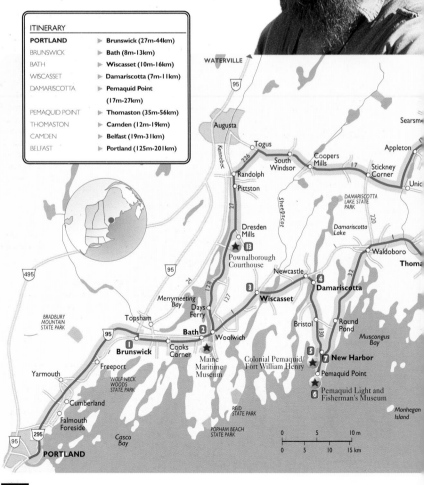

ITINERARY

PORTLAND	▶ Brunswick (27m-44km)
BRUNSWICK	▶ Bath (8m-13km)
BATH	▶ Wiscasset (10m-16km)
WISCASSET	▶ Damariscotta (7m-11km)
DAMARISCOTTA	▶ Pemaquid Point
	(17m-27km)
PEMAQUID POINT	▶ Thomaston (35m-56km)
THOMASTON	▶ Camden (12m-19km)
CAMDEN	▶ Belfast (19m-31km)
BELFAST	▶ Portland (125m-201km)

[i] *305 Commercial Street*

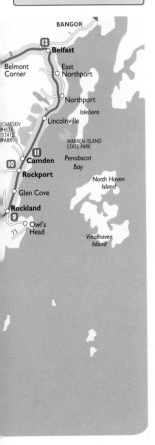

BANGOR

Belfast

Belmont
Corner

East
Northport

Northport

Isleboro

Lincolnville

CAMDEN
HILLS
STATE
PARK

WARREN ISLAND
STATE PARK

Camden

Penobscot
Bay

Rockport

North Haven
Island

Glen Cove

Rockland

Owl's
Head

Vinalhaven
Island

▶ *Leave Portland on I–295 north, which becomes I–95. Take exit 22 for **Coastal Route 1** to downtown Brunswick. Turn right on Maine Street, then left on **Route 24** to Brunswick.*

❶ Brunswick

Brunswick is an attractive town, centered on Bowdoin College. Originally founded in 1794 as a men's college, Bowdoin has admitted women since the 1960s. Famous graduates range from 19th-century authors Nathaniel Hawthorne and Henry Wadsworth Longfellow to explorers Robert Peary, the first man to reach the North Pole, in 1909, and his colleague, Donald MacMillan.

Memorabilia from their expeditions is the focus of the Peary-MacMillan Arctic Museum in Hubbard Hall, decorated with the only gargoyle in the whole of Maine (spot it on the left side of the building). The art museum, located in the imposing Walker Art Building, has a varied collection including Gilbert Stuart's familiar portrait of Thomas Jefferson, author of the Declaration of Independence, and third President of the United States.

[i] *59 Pleasant Street*

▶ *Leave the campus and turn right on **Route 24** north. Continue to Cooks Corner and rejoin **Route 1** north. Drive 5 miles (8km) to Bath.*

❷ Bath

The town may be 18 miles (29km) from the Atlantic Ocean, but boats have been launched on the deep Kennebec River since 1607. Bath's glory days were in the 19th century, when sailing ships made fortunes for the merchants, many of whose graceful homes still line Washington Street in the Historic District. Since 1891, the Bath Iron Works and Shipyard, the largest civilian employer in Maine, has built ships for the U.S. Navy. Right on the river, with the tallest crane (400 feet/120m) on the East Coast, it's impossible to miss.

Downriver from the shipyard is the Maine Maritime Museum, a collection of buildings with seafaring memorabilia and hands-on exhibitions. This is the place to learn the history of lobstering, understand how the many-masted schooners were constructed, and watch boats in the Apprenticeshop being built or restored. Warning: avoid going to or through Bath during the shipyard's rush hour, between 3:30 and 4:15pm.

[i] *45 Front Street*

▶ *Leave Bath on **Route 1** northeast and continue for 10 miles (16km) to Wiscasset.*

❸ Wiscasset

The Indian name means "coming out of the harbor but you don't see where." Today, "the Prettiest Village in Maine" is found easily by visitors, who flock to the antique shops, historic houses, and quirky museums. Wiscasset is the seat of Lincoln County, which once stretched to the Canadian border. Throughout the original colonies, towns pride themselves on the fact that "George Washington slept here." Here, the claim is that General Lafayette of France ate ice

SCENIC ROUTE

The Maine Coast Railroad from Wiscassett to Bath is an exciting trip through the tidal marshes of the coast, over trestles and causeways, passing some of the area's attractions. There is also a good chance of spotting such native wildlife as osprey, heron and moose. Refreshments are available on the train, and there is a program of special events.

cream at the apothecary shop that predated today's store, now called the Wizard of Odds and Ends. That was in 1824, long after Lafayette had helped the Americans during the Revolution.

On High Street is the Musical Wonder House. This is the private collection of Danilo Konvalinka, who calls it "the world's finest museum of restored international antique music boxes and mechanical instruments." The full tour is fascinating, though expensive; but it costs nothing to wander round the front hall and look at the 19th-century coin-operated music boxes, hurdy gurdies and perforated metal disc players.

At the end of High Street, in a commanding position above the harbor and Sheepscot River, stands Castle Tucker. Built in 1807, it was bought by Captain Tucker in 1858, after he retired from the sea and settled down to married life. From its free-standing switchback staircase to the dramatic southeast façade with its huge windows, the house is one of a kind, and remains much as Captain Tucker left it. The wallpaper is original, as are the furnishings. A descendant of the captain still lives here.

The Nickels-Sortwell House, on the corner of Route 1 and Federal Street, is another ship-captain's home. Built in the same year as Castle Tucker, it exemplifies the Federal period. Just along Federal Street is Lincoln County Museum and Old Jail. This large and foreboding granite building served as the county jail from 1811 to 1953. Below the tiny barred windows, the cold walls, 41 inches (105cm) thick in places, are covered with graffiti, such as the painstakingly detailed schooner under full sail.

▶ *Continue on* **Route 1** *northeast to Newcastle and turn right for Damariscotta.*

⁴ **Damariscotta**
This attractive yet unpretentious riverside community has plenty of old wood-frame and brick homes. The restored 1754 Chapman-Hall House on Main and Church streets is the oldest in the region. In summer, guides in period dress conduct you round the 18th-century kitchen and herb garden.

ⓘ *Damariscotta Region Information Bureau, Route 1*

Typical wood-frame house, near the township of Damariscotta

Pemaquid Point Lighthouse juts out on rocky ledges carved by ancient glaciers

FOR HISTORY BUFFS

"Damariscotta" means "the meeting place of alewives." This has nothing to do with women involved in brewing. It refers to a member of the herring family that was popular with Indians. The Indians also relished the local oysters and would congregate for "oyster festivals," leaving heaps of shells behind on the banks of the Damariscotta River. These "middens," an Old English word for "rubbish dumps," contain shells as large as plates. Ask at the Damariscotta Region Information Bureau for maps and permission to visit them.

▶ *Leave town on **Route 130** south for 11 miles (18km). Turn right on Huddle Road at signs for Historic Pemaquid and Pemaquid Point. Service stations are few and far between off the main highways, so be sure to fill up before heading down any of the numerous peninsulas.*

5 Colonial Pemaquid/Fort William Henry

The re-creation of Fort William Henry stands guard over the water, as did four earlier fortresses, and it now houses a museum of artifacts found on the site. Nearby, an on-going archeological dig has uncovered a 17th-century British settlement of houses plus a tavern, jail, burying ground, and customs house. It is thought to have been one of the first European settlements in the New World. Although fishing and trapping were productive in the area, raids by the French and their Indian allies, and long, hard winters took their toll.

▶ *Follow Snowball Hill Road to **Route 32** and drive south to Pemaquid Point.*

6 Pemaquid Light and Fisherman's Museum

There are 63 lighthouses in the state, but this is one of the most romantic and most photographed. The layers of rock show the geological formation of this distinctive coastline. When climbing upon the rocks near the ocean, be careful. The waters are dangerous; the undertow is strong, too.

▶ *Take **Route 130** north, then turn onto **Route 32** to New Harbor.*

7 New Harbor

New Harbor is a truly picturesque and unspoiled Maine fishing village. A memorial here honors Chief Samoset of the local Pemaquid tribe. The chief learned English from British fishermen, and had traveled south to explore the Massachusetts coast in March, 1621, where he discovered the Pilgrim community. Imagine their surprise when he greeted them with the words "Welcome Englishmen."

FOR HISTORY BUFFS

Just off Route 32 is Round Pond, another fishing harbor. This once supposedly hid the notorious Captain Kidd, who buried treasure under a huge boulder on a nearby island. Some say it was on Devil's Oven, others on Otter Island. The mystery remains.

RECOMMENDED TRIPS

From New Harbor, take a daytrip out to tiny Monhegan Island, only 1½ miles (2.5km) across at its widest, with the highest cliffs on the East Coast. The energetic can hike through a wildlife sanctuary with hundreds of species of wildflowers and birds, while the less energetic can visit the artists' studios. There are also cruises for watching seals and Atlantic puffins, now a protected species.

▶ Continue on **Route 32** north to Waldoboro (20 miles/ 32km). Turn onto **Route 1** northeast and drive 12 miles (19km) to Thomaston.

8 Thomaston

This is another ship captain and ship owners' town, although the most imposing house in Thomaston was built by a general, Henry Knox. He was an important figure in the Revolution and the country's first Secretary of War. He retired here in 1795 and built his mansion high on a hill overlooking the town. Still filled with its original furnishings, this building, with its white-painted façade and its two-story bay, looks remarkably like the south front of the White House in Washington D.C., designed in 1792.

Down on the waterfront, the Maine Watercraft Museum preserves a collection of vessels that represents the state's boat-building heritage, including a number of rare examples. Some of the boats can be rented by the hour; others are used for conducted sightseeing trips.

▶ Continue on **Route 1** to Rockland.

9 Rockland

The "Lobster Capital of the World" boasts a gem of a museum, the result of a 1935 legacy left by an eccentric 96-year-old. Lucy Farnsworth left money to the city for the upkeep of her family home and to found an art gallery in memory of her father. The William A. Farnsworth Art Museum specializes in American painters from the 18th, 19th, and 20th centuries.

The Wyeth Centre, which opened in 1998 in a historic church near the museum, houses the collection of Andrew and Betsy Wyeth. The Shore Village Museum has diverse collections, ranging from lighthouse equipment to dolls.

☐ Harbor Park

FOR CHILDREN

South of Rockland, in the state park off Route 73, is Owl's Head Light. The 52-step climb is worth it for the view over Penobscot Bay, but vertigo-sufferers should not peer over the 87-foot (26m) sheer cliff. Nearby is the Owl's Head Transportation Museum, a world-class collection of vintage cars, airplanes, motorcyles and carriages in working condition. Demonstrations are held throughout the summer, though the museum is open year round.

SPECIAL TO...

One of the most famous artistic images of Maine is Andrew Wyeth's *Christina's World*, portraying a crippled girl in a meadow looking towards her house. It was just one of his many depictions of members of the Olson family and their house outside Rockland. "I just couldn't stay away from there ... I'd always seem to gravitate back to the house ... It was Maine." The house is administered by the Farnsworth Art Museum and is open, in season, to the public.

▶ Follow **Route I** north to Rockport.

⑩ Rockport

The tiny village of Rockport has a tiny harbor with lots of cultural activities. The musically minded book into chamber music and jazz concerts at the opera house. Photographers head for the internationally known Maine Photographic Workshop, while the work of local artists and craftsmen is displayed in the many galleries. These include Maine Coast Artists, specializing in upcoming contemporary

Below: yachts in Camden Harbor
Right: lobsters at Boothbay Harbor

artists. In the little park down by the harbor is a statue of André the Seal. A children's book and film were based on the story of André, who lived here for 20 years.

▶ Leave Rockport on scenic Russell Avenue, going north, with sudden glimpses of the Camden Hills and Penobscot Bay. This becomes Chestnut Street in Camden.

⑪ Camden

*"All I could see from where I stood
Was three long mountains and a
    wood;
I turned and looked another way,
    and saw three islands in a bay."*

The panorama from the top of Mount Battie inspired Maine poet Edna St. Vincent Millay to compose this poem in 1917. The views today are still the same of the Camden Hills, Penobscot Bay, and, on a clear day, Monhegan Island. In the town, below the hill, Millay's statue stands by the harbor in what is, arguably, the state's most popular year-round resort. Conway Farm House, dating from 1770, is one of the oldest houses in the area. It is now a museum which includes the house, barn, smithy, maple sugar house and modern museum building.

[i] Public Landing

SPECIAL TO...

Lobsters, the specialty of Maine, are caught in the millions of traps set in the cold waters offshore. Traditionally, these box-like contraptions consist of an oak frame with cotton netting. Many visitors take them as souvenirs. However, don't be tempted to pick up any washed on to a beach by the tide: that counts as "molesting a trap" and carries a fine. Buy one from a road-side stand or, better still, stop at a fishing village, look for a pile on the dock or by a house, and make an offer to the owner.

▶ Follow **Route 1** north 6 miles (10km) to Lincolnville, then on 13 miles (21km) to Belfast.

🔢 Belfast

Belfast or Londonderry? A flip of a coin decided the name back in 1765. As usual in New England, a town's name pinpoints the home in the Old World. In this case, the Scots-Irish had come from what is now Northern Ireland. Over the centuries, Belfast has produced ships, axes, pantaloons, sarsaparilla, chickens, rum, and shoes. More useful, but less glamorous, was the invention of the flush tank for washing machines and toilets.

ℹ️ *Main Street*

▶ *The rest of this route is rural and scenic. Take **Route 3** west to Belmont Corner for 6 miles (10km), then **Route 131** south through scenic farmland, past stone walls and hilly vistas. Pass through Searsmont, Appleton and Union. Take **Route 17** west, then before Togus, turn onto **Route 226** south to Randolph. Follow **Route 126**, then turn on **Route 27** south. This passes a cluster of privately-owned white houses moved here from various parts of the state. Turn right on **Route 128**, an old Indian trail that follows the bay. Continue on **Route 128**.*

🔢 Pownalborough Courthouse

Now a museum, this is one of only a dozen surviving pre-Revolutionary courthouses in the country. Here, a judge could dispense justice in the court on the middle floor, walk downstairs to quaff ale in the tavern, and retire to his bed on the top floor.

▶ *Join **Route 127** south at the pretty village of Days Ferry (the original river crossing) and continue to **Route 1** southwest at Woolwich by the Bath bridge. Return to Portland.*

Portland Head Light, the oldest lighthouse in Maine

HALF A DAY

Portland

Portland aptly deserves its symbol, the phoenix, as well as its motto, *Resurgam*, "I shall rise again." In fact, the city has arisen nearly as often as the sun. Dating back to a settlement called Falmouth, it was virtually destroyed by Indian raids in 1676. After rebuilding, the community flourished until an English fleet bombarded the town in 1775, as punishment for supporting the independence movement.

Once again restored, and renamed Portland in 1786, the port buzzed with business and finance, until the Great Fire of July 4, 1866. Again, it was rebuilt, and this tour reflects the development of Portland and the contributions made by prominent citizens to the arts, business, and city life.

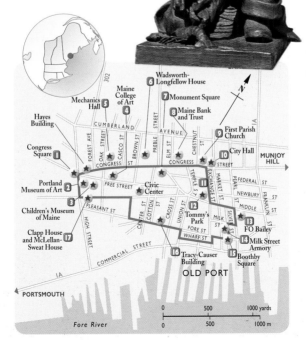

147

The Wadsworth-Longfellow House was the first brick house to be built in Portland

i *Congress Square (summer only); Convention and Visitors Bureau of Greater Portland, 305 Commercial Street*

▶ *Start at Congress Square.*

❶ Congress Square
This busy five-street intersection is the scene of many summer events including concerts. On the corner of Congress and Free streets is the Hayes Building, described as a flatiron building because of its wedge-shape. Built in 1826, it is one of the recognized icons of Portland.

❷ Portland Museum of Art
The I. M. Pei firm's brick colonnaded building (1983), right on the square, makes an impressive addition to the L. D. M. Sweat Memorial Galleries and rotunda, built in 1911. It houses one of New England's finest art collections and contains pieces by well-known Maine and American painters. You will also find the Joan Whitney Payson Collection of Impressionist and Post-Impressionist works here. One of the best known is Auguste Renoir's *Confidences*. A romantic tête-à-tête, this is a sensitive portrait of one of his favorite models, Margot Legrand.

❸ Children's Museum of Maine
Next door to the art museum, in a former Greek Revival church, is one of the best museums of its kind in New England. The Children's Museum of Maine really is for all ages. Even toddlers have their own play area, and older children can play at pretend in "Our Town," with its market, fire truck, lobster boat, bank, farm and animal hospital. For the technically minded, there are lots of interactive exhibits and other things to fire the imagination, including

the star lab, space shuttle and TV studio. A wonder from the 19th century is a camera obscura, one of only seven in the world. A camera obscura is a dark room where images of objects from outside are projected onto a wall. It may sound simplistic in these days of "virtual reality," but this effective, primitive use of light and lens led to still and motion picture cameras.

▶ *Leave Congress Square and walk north on Congress Street to No. 522.*

❹ Maine College of Art
Cherubs still frolic on the outside of the Porteous, Mitchell and Brown department store, once the largest in town. Gutted completely in 1995, it has been rebuilt as the new Maine College of Art.

▶ *Look across Congress Street.*

❺ Mechanics Hall
This impressive, Italianate, granite-fronted building, with its statues of Archimedes and Vulcan, is the home of the Maine Charitable Mechanic Association. Dedicated in 1851 to "informing and cultivating the mind and training up a race

of mechanics (skilled workmen) of sound moral principle and intellectual power," it still sponsors lectures, maintains an extensive library, and offers free technical drawing classes.

▶ *Continue along Congress Street to No. 485.*

❻ Wadsworth-Longfellow House
Three generations of one of the city's most distinguished familes lived here, behind the wrought-iron fence. In 1785, General Peleg Wadsworth, a hero of the Revolution and state senator, built this house, now the oldest surviving residence in Portland, and the first to be constructed of bricks. The bricks were shipped in from Philadelphia.

Wadsworth's grandson, the poet Henry Wadsworth Longfellow, grew up here. His childhood flute is on show, and the house is furnished much as he would have remembered it as an adult. "Often I think of the beautiful town that is seated by the sea; often in thought go up and down the pleasant streets of that dear old town, and my youth comes back to me." Next door, the Center for Maine History has changing exhibitions about the state.

SPECIAL TO...

Henry Wadsworth Longfellow (1807–82) is America's best-loved 19th-century poet. *The Battle of Lovell's Pond*, his first published verses, appeared in the *Portland Gazette* when he was only 12 years old. His best-known works tell all-American tales such as *The Song of Hiawatha* and *Paul Revere's Ride*, but his popularity was not limited to the United States. He had a following in England that included Queen Victoria and, after his death, he was the first American to be commemorated with a bust in Poet's Corner at Westminster Abbey.

Portland's impressive City Hall

▶ *Continue on Congress Street.*

7 Monument Square

This space, originally the town's Market Square, is named for Our Lady of Victories Monument. The monument is a Civil War memorial built in 1891, with money raised by local soldiers and sailors.

In recent years, the farmers' market has been revived, with stalls set out on Wednesdays in the summer and fall. Summer also brings noontime concerts; in December, the city's Christmas tree lights up the square and on New Year's Eve, crowds gather to watch the fireworks.

▶ *Look to the corner of Congress and Elm streets.*

8 Maine Bank and Trust

Portland's first skyscraper, built in 1910 in the Beaux Arts style, was at that time New England's tallest building. Unlike traditional structures of the period, where the exterior walls supported the building, this was constructed with a steel skeleton, allowing greater height. Inside, the marble lobby soars to a ceiling at least three stories

high. The impression is of solidity and security – perfect for a bank building.

▶ *Continue on Congress Street to No. 425.*

SPECIAL TO...

Congress Street leads to Munjoy Hill, perhaps a derivation of the French *Mont Joie*. Here, the 221-foot (67m) high Portland Observatory was erected in 1807, as a signal tower. Communication by flags announced the identity of approaching merchant ships and enabled the docks to be prepared for their arrival. Views from the top are spectacular.

Nearby is the Eastern Promenade. Turn right for the bandstand. Here, the panorama encompasses Portland Harbor, the best deep-water port north of New Jersey. Watch for an oil tanker or a cruise ferry coming from Nova Scotia. Don't try to count the islands in Casco Bay; supposedly, there are 365 of them, hence the name, the Calendar Islands.

---

9 First Parish Church

Founded in 1674, this church predates any other house of worship in Portland. The second building on the site took several hits during the British bombardment of the town in 1775. Inside, a cannon ball still lodges within the chain supporting the magnificent 600-pound (273kg) cut-glass chandelier. The 1794 clock and 1804 bell were saved and incorporated into the present building, rebuilt of granite in 1826.

▶ *Continue on Congress Street past the Frost Gully Gallery, the oldest commercial art gallery, and a useful stop for art lovers interested in living Maine artists.*

10 City Hall

The granite used to build the City Hall was quarried locally in Maine, but the design is based on the classic French *hôtel-de-ville*. Inside is a 3,000-seat auditorium, where the Portland Symphony Orchestra often gives concerts. This is the third municipal headquarters to be located here: the first was destroyed by the Great Fire of 1866; its successor by another blaze in 1908.

▶ *Turn right on Exchange Street.*

⑪ Exchange Street
Exchange Street leads into the six-square-block Old Port Exchange area, the oldest part of the city. Warehouses and offices have now become boutiques, art galleries, and ethnic restaurants. Look closely and you'll see another reminder of British shelling in 1775: the cannon ball embedded in the Colesworth building, on the right, just past the entry to the parking garage. Peer through the windows of F. Parker Reidy's restaurant, almost across the street, to see the open safe and original brick walls of the Old Portland Savings Bank.

▶ *Continue to the intersection with Middle Street.*

⑫ Tommy's Park
The *trompe-l'oeil* by two Portland artists on the wall represents architectural elements of the 19th-century marble post office which once stood across the street in what is now the postage-stamp size Post Office

Park. In this sunny spot, the granite boulders represent the many islands of Casco Bay, just outside Portland Harbor.

▶ *Turn left on Middle Street and walk two blocks to the intersection with Pearl Street.*

⑬ F. O. Bailey
Now the home of a well-respected firm of antiques sellers and auctioneers, this was one of the first buildings put up after the Great Fire of 1866. Look for the architect's autograph on the base of the left corner pilaster, on the Middle Street side.

▶ *Continue towards the harbor on Pearl Street. After a block, turn right on cobblestoned Milk Street. Straight ahead is the Regency Hotel.*

⑭ Milk Street Armory
It is no coincidence that the Regency Hotel, between Silver and Market streets, resembles a fortress. This was originally the armory, and was very active in the late 19th to mid-20th

centuries. It also had a tradition of hospitality, as it was the site of musical events and impressive balls. The contemporary dolphin fountain was originally offered to, and rejected by the city fathers. Shunted around town, it stood on a variety of sites until it was finally bought by the hotel.

▶ *Turn left on Silver Street.*

⑮ Boothby Square
At the intersection of Silver and Fore streets is Boothby Square. Directly in front is a row of old buildings, including the 1792 Sam Butts House and Store. It is the second-oldest surviving post-revolutionary house in Portland.

On your left is the 1868 granite U.S. Customs House. In the impressive interior, it is easy to imagine merchants sitting down to negotiate the tariffs on a cargo of molasses being unloaded at the wharf, just down the street.

▶ *Turn right on Fore Street, pass the granite-fronted 1828*

Mariner's Church and turn left immediately onto the cobbled Moulton Street. Turn right on Wharf Street, go right on Union Street, then left at the light on Fore Street. On the corner of Cotton Street is the Tracy-Causer Building.

16 Tracy-Causer Building

Note the old street sign on this building, one of the few survivors of the Great Fire of 1866. The city's Landmarks Association successfully campaigned for its preservation and restoration in 1996. On the harbor side stand some of the few remaining warehouses from the "Golden Age" of the 19th and early 20th centuries. Straight ahead is Portland's second flatiron building, now full of artists' studios, used and rare book stores, and the Danforth Gallery, exhibiting alternative art.

▶ *Continue through the five-street intersection onto Pleasant Street. Immediately past the first parking garage, turn right and go up the alley and stairs to Spring Street. On the right is the Civic Center. Cross the street and turn left.*

17 Clapp House and McLellan-Sweat House

The Great Fire did not reach this area, so these two impressive merchants' homes still stand. The Maine College of Art has offices in Clapp House, a Greek Revival mansion. Major Hugh McLellan's grand Federal house was given to the Portland Society of Art, in 1908, by Mrs. Lorenzo de Medici Sweat, along with funds to build a "proper" art museum.

▶ *Turn right on High Street. Across the street is another Federal brick residence, now a private club, built by McLellan's brother, also a successful merchant and auctioneer. Return to Congress Square, at the end of the block.*

RECOMMENDED TRIPS

Portland's waterfront is busy with both working fishermen and pleasure boats. In summer, as many as 50 trips go out each day to whale watch or bird watch, to poke around the islands of Casco Bay, or to visit explorer Admiral Peary's former home on Eagle Island. Ferries run a regular service up to Nova Scotia in Canada.

The Portland skyline at dawn, as seen from Back Cove

2 DAYS • 268 MILES • 431KM

Mountains &
Lakes of Maine

Nature lovers and sports fans head for the lakes and mountains, just as vacationers did 150 years ago when they came by railroad to escape the summer heat of more southerly states. Winter also brings visitors, such as downhill and cross-country skiers.

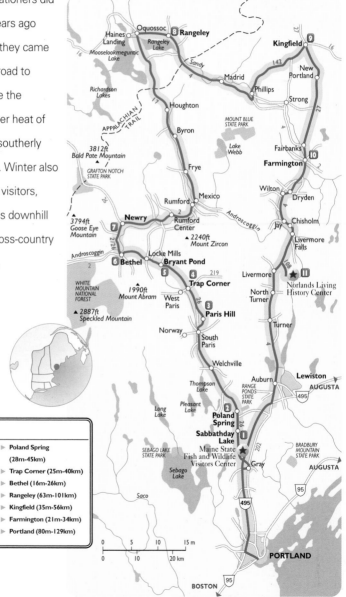

Haines Landing
Oquossoc — **8** Rangeley
Rangeley Lake
Mooselookmeguntic Lake
Sandy
Madrid
Kingfield — **9**
New Portland
Richardson Lakes
Houghton
Phillips
Strong
APPALACHIAN TRAIL
Byron
MOUNT BLUE STATE PARK
3812ft Bald Pate Mountain
GRAFTON NOTCH STATE PARK
Frye
Lake Webb
Fairbanks
Farmington — **10**
Wilton
Dryden
3794ft Goose Eye Mountain
Newry — **7**
Rumford
Mexico
Rumford Center
Androscoggin
Chisholm
Jay
Livermore Falls
Androscoggin
6 **Bethel**
Locke Mills
Bryant Pond
2240ft Mount Zircon
WHITE MOUNTAIN NATIONAL FOREST
219
1990ft Mount Abram
5
4 **Trap Corner**
Livermore
11 ★
Norlands Living History Center
2887ft Speckled Mountain
West Paris
North Turner
3 **Paris Hill**
Norway
South Paris
Turner
Welchville
Thompson Lake
Auburn
RANGE PONDS STATE PARK
Lewiston
AUGUSTA
495
Long Lake
Pleasant Lake
2 **Poland Spring**
ITINERARY
PORTLAND ▶ Poland Spring (28m-45km)
POLAND SPRING ▶ Trap Corner (25m-40km)
TRAP CORNER ▶ Bethel (16m-26km)
BETHEL ▶ Rangeley (63m-101km)
RANGELEY ▶ Kingfield (35m-56km)
KINGFIELD ▶ Farmington (21m-34km)
FARMINGTON ▶ Portland (80m-129km)
1
Sabbathday Lake
★ Maine State Fish and Wildlife Visitors Center
SEBAGO LAKE STATE PARK
Sebago Lake
Gray
BRADBURY MOUNTAIN STATE PARK
AUGUSTA
95
Saco
495
0   5   10   15 m
0   10   20 km
PORTLAND
BOSTON
95

i 305 Commercial Street

▶ *Leave Portland on I–495 (the Maine Turnpike), turning off on Exit 11 at Gray (18m/29km). Follow **Route 26** north for 8 miles (13km) to Sabbathday Lake.*

BACK TO NATURE

North of Gray is the Maine Wildlife Park. For those who are not heading out into the wilderness areas of the state, this is a wonderful place to get a close look at moose, bears, deer, and porcupines. This is not a zoo; the animals brought here were orphaned or injured.

❶ Sabbathday Lake

A cluster of white buildings plus a large red brick house mark Sabbathday Lake Village, the home of the Shakers, the religious community founded in 1782 by Mother Ann Lee, who voyaged from Manchester, England. Some 30 years later, the Shaker movement had grown to around 7,000, with settlements in New England, Ohio, and Kentucky.

This is the last remaining group. Less than a dozen men and women live here, following the credo "Put your hands to work and your heart to God." They aim for self-sufficiency through farming, tending the orchards, knitting, and printing. During the summer, outsiders are invited to join the Sunday services at 10am in the Meeting House, with its plain wooden benches. On other days, visitors can tour some of the buildings, including the museum, with examples of ingenious labor-saving inventions.

▶ *Follow **Route 26** to Poland Spring.*

❷ Poland Spring

The popularity of bottled mineral waters may seem a recent phenomenon but Poland Spring water has been prized for over a century. When its "healing" powers became known, the spring attracted visitors, a hotel was built, and the area developed into a summer resort. The hotel is long gone but its "library" building remains. This is now the Maine State Building from the Chicago Expo in 1893, moved and reconstructed here as an attraction for visitors. It is a museum recalling the grand old days when holidaymakers came, complete with their servants, for a month or two in the summer. Poland Spring water is still bottled nearby, but it is now owned by Perrier.

▶ *Continue on **Route 26** north for 17 miles (27km) through South Paris, where the Celebration Barn Theater puts on performances of vaudeville, mime, and juggling in the summer. Turn right to Paris Hill.*

❸ Paris Hill

Few Americans remember Hannibal Hamlin, Vice-President during Abraham Lincoln's first term. His home is the most impressive structure in this cluster of pristine white Federal and Victorian houses on the summit of a hill. Admire the vistas across the valley and to the White Mountains to the west, then tour the tiny library in the former jail. Built in 1822, it is entirely of granite, including the floors. Ask to see the jail door

keys, and to hear how a fat prisoner became stuck while trying to escape.

▶ *Continue and rejoin **Route 26** and drive north to the junction of **Routes 26** and **219**. On the east side of the road is a turn-off for Snow Falls Gorge, where there is a picturesque waterfall, picnic tables, and nature trails.*

❹ Trap Corner

"Rockhounds" and gemologists from all over New England know Oxford County because it is rich in minerals and gemstones such as tourmaline, amethyst, and quartz.

At the junction of Routes 26 and 219 is Perham's, a landmark since 1919. As well as a shop selling local finds, and the museum, this is where modern-day prospectors can get maps of nearby quarries and information about panning for gold in the Rangeley area.

▶ *Continue on **Route 26**.*

❺ Bryant Pond

The people of Maine are renowned for their stubbornness. This town enjoyed making telephone calls the old-fashioned way, and made national headlines with its campaign to keep its hand-cranked phone system, the last one in the country. They lost their battle in 1983, but the

Reflections at Bryant Pond

antiquated telephone technology is the focus of what must be one of the smallest museums in New England.

▶ *Take* **Route 26** *to Bethel.*

❻ Bethel
Founded on the Androscoggin River, the community nearly died after the Revolution. Railroads brought revitalization in the mid-19th century. As well as benefiting agriculture and timber businesses, the trains

Main picture: the covered bridge at Newry
Inset: one of Bethel's attractive houses; blueberry leaves in Acadia National Park

carried tourists. Now, vacationers come by car to what is a four-season resort. In winter, cross-country and downhill skiers head for Mount Abram and Sunday River, with its 110-trail network over eight different peaks.

In summer, the chairlift up the slope provides bird's-eye views of the White Mountains as well as a great hike down. There is also camping, canoeing, mountain biking, fishing, and swimming.

ℹ️ *18 Mayville Road, Route 2*

▶ *Leave Bethel on* **Routes 26** *and* **2***, and drive 5 miles (8km) north to Newry.*

SCENIC ROUTES

About 10m (16km) northwest of Newry is Grafton Notch State Park, where the park road has been designated a "Maine Scenic Highway." Moose can be sighted during dawn and dusk hours, while views of Bald Pate Mountain, plus Screw Augur Falls epitomize the beauties of the Carrabassett region. The Appalachian Trail crosses the road here. This hiking route starts in Georgia and follows the Appalachian Mountains all the way to Mount Katahdin in northeast Maine.

7 Newry

Just off the road is the Artist's Covered Bridge, much-painted and photographed long before the film *The Bridges of Madison County* lent cachet to similar bridges in Iowa. This one was built in 1872, over the Sunday River. More than just a scenic spot, it has popular swimming holes as well.

▶ *Continue on scenic **Route 2** north to the paper mill town of Rumford and cross the river at the mighty Pennacook Falls to Mexico, where much of the country's paper for books is made. Take **Route 17** north towards Oquossoc, then turn east on **Route 4** to Rangeley.*

8 Rangeley

Wilderness and isolation are the hallmarks of the Rangeley region, surrounded by mountains and punctuated by more than 40 bodies of water. The village boasts of being halfway between the North Pole and the Equator, but there is nothing halfway about the winters. A dog-sled postal service used to deliver letters to households cut off by snow; now, snowmobiles provide access to homes and businesses, but they are also raced for fun. Other winter sports include snow-shoeing, dog-sledding, and ice-fishing, as well as cross-country and down-hill skiing. The slopes here are less crowded than at most other resorts. When summer comes, there is fishing for landlocked salmon and trout, canoeing, hiking, and golfing.

There are also two museums. The Rangeley Lakes Historical Society, once a jail, recalls the 19th-century era of lake steamers and lodges that catered to New Yorkers escaping the heat of the city. More unusual is the Wilhelm Reich Museum, the home of the controversial Austrian psychoanalyst who studied with, then broke from, Sigmund Freud. Reich emigrated to the U.S.A. and eventually settled in Rangeley, to pursue "orgonomy, the science of the life energy." His writings and inventions were all

to do with sexual energy and personality analysis. In 1956, he was found guilty of violating Food and Drug Administration laws. He died, in prison, a year later. A museum preserves his library, memorabilia, and surviving inventions.

i Rangeley Lakes Region Chamber of Commerce, PO Box 317

▶ *Leave Rangeley via Route 4 south. Note that Smalls Falls, in the Sandy River Gorge, has a good swimming hole, plus a waterfall, picnic site, and hiking trails. At Phillips, take Route 142 northeast to Kingfield.*

9 Kingfield
What do violins, automobiles, and cameras all have in common? They fascinated the ingenious minds of F. O. and F. E. Stanley, twin brothers who lived here a century ago. Their most profitable discovery was a

photographic process which they sold to a company that later became Kodak. Car fans know them for their Stanley Steamers, made by the Stanley Motor Carriage Company. One of their racing cars set a speed record of 127.66mph (204.3km/h) in 1906, and it remained unbroken for many years. The brothers also made fine violins. The Stanley Museum tells their story and displays their inventions, along with photographs taken by their sister, Chansonetta Stanley Emmons.

▶ *Take Route 27 south through New Portland, stopping to see the amazing 1841 engineering feat, the Fireproof Wire Bridge, suspended across the Carrabassett River. Rejoin Route 4 and head for Farmington.*

10 Farmington
It is hard to imagine that this agricultural valley produced an international opera star. A simple farmhouse, just outside Farmington, was the birthplace in 1857 of Lillian Norton. As Madame Nordica, she triumphed in Europe and was the first American woman to take Wagnerian roles at the Bayreuth Festival. Returning to the States, her "liquid purity, exceptional range, and magnificent power" charmed New York critics during numerous seasons at the Metropolitan Opera House. The Nordica Memorial Homestead displays her costumes, annotated scores, and other memorabilia.

A branch of the University of Maine is here, continuing a tradition of education dating back to 1788 when the school was founded. The Red School House Museum recalls those days.

i Greater Farmington Chamber of Commerce, 30 Main Street

▶ *Continue on Route 4. At the junction with Route 2 at Wilton is the Western Maine Mountains Chamber of*

View over Step Falls, Grafton Notch State Park

Commerce. Route 4 leads through Dryden, Jay, and Livermore Falls, recognized long before arriving by the sulphurous smell of the paper mills. Take Route 108 east for the Norlands Living History Center.

11 Norlands Living History Center
Anyone who has ever wanted to go back in time should book in for a day or a weekend on this extensive farm. With a new name and a new character, adults and children participate in 19th-century life, cooking on a cast iron stove, harvesting grain, or tending the vegetable garden. They even sleep on rope beds. In the morning, breakfast is oatmeal porridge and pancakes.

Those who prefer to dip, rather than immerse themselves in history, can take a guided tour to learn about farming in the old days and the Washburn family, who spawned diplomats, congressmen, journalists, and businessmen, all in one generation.

▶ *Follow Route 4 to Auburn and then take I–495 south (Maine Turnpike) for the return to Portland.*

GETTING AROUND

Whether you use your own car or a rental car, driving is perhaps the best way to see New England. The forested hills, winding river valleys, and historic New England towns and villages are most accessible and best appreciated when seen from a car traveling at moderate speed on secondary roads (see **Motoring**, pages 159–60). But other means of transportation are available as well.

By Car

Within New England, you'll normally drive only an hour or two to your next destination. From Boston, it's only an hour's drive to Providence, Plymouth, Manchester, or Portsmouth; about two hours to Hartford, Portland, Mystic, or Cape Cod; about three hours to New Haven, the Berkshires, southern Vermont, Boothbay Harbor, or New Hampshire's White Mountains; and only about four hours to New York City or central Vermont. Five hours takes you from Boston to the resort and national park at Bar Harbor, Maine.

By Recreational Vehicle

Among the most pleasant ways to tour the country is in a recreational vehicle (motor home). RVs come in all sizes and shapes, and usually sleep four to six people comfortably, include a full kitchen (with cooking range, refrigerator, and running water), and are air-conditioned; some even have a shower!

Hundreds of campgrounds in New England can provide electrical, water, and sewer hookups for $15 to $20 per night. Some RVs can operate for several days without hookups. In an RV, you're completely independent, and for families with young children it can be a very cost-effective way to tour New England.

Renting an RV has its disadvantages as well. Rentals are fairly expensive, and you should work out estimated budgets for a trip in an RV versus a trip using a rental car and hotels before making your final decision. When figuring costs, keep in mind that RVs use a lot more fuel than passenger cars. During the busy summer months, many of New England's choicest campgrounds fill up early in the day. You may have to reserve in advance, which takes some of the fun out of footloose travel. Finally, New England is a region with many delightful country inns. If you've gone to the expense of renting an RV, you may not feel that you can pay to stay in an inn very often.

For more information on RVs, contact the Recreation Vehicle Industry Association, 1896 Preston White Drive, PO Box 2999, Reston, Virginia 22090-0999 (tel: 703/620–6003; fax 703/591–0734); for $5 they'll send you a 40-page catalog listing locations, services, and rates of the various RV rental agencies. The Recreation Vehicle Rental Association, 3930 University Drive, Fairfax, Virginia 22030 (tel: 703/591–7130) is another good source. RV America has a comprehensive website (www.rvamerica.com). Call Go Camping America (tel: 800/47–SUNNY) for a very helpful, free 16-page camping vacation planner.

By Plane

The larger cities, such as Boston, Providence, Hartford, Portland, and Burlington, all have good air service provided by the larger domestic airlines. Numerous regional "feeder" airlines fly between the larger and smaller cities, and many regional carriers connect to New York City.

Almost all the small regional airlines operate in conjunction with larger national and international airlines. The regional airlines' flights are included in the flight schedules of such airlines as American, Delta, Continental and USAir. Call these airlines for information on flights, fares, and cities served.

By Train

Amtrak (tel:1–800/USA–RAIL) operates trains connecting Boston with Springfield and Pittsfield, Massachusetts, and Albany, New York; Hartford, New Haven, New London, and Mystic, Connecticut; Providence, Rhode Island; and (via Springfield) Brattleboro, White River Junction, and Montpelier, Vermont; and Montréal, Québec. There is no interstate train service northeast of Boston to Maine or central and eastern New Hampshire, but buses run from Amtrak's terminus at Boston's South Station to Portsmouth, New Hampshire, and to major cities and towns in eastern Maine.

Trains on routes between Boston and points south and west are fast and frequent, but to get to points in Vermont from Boston, connections are not good and service is infrequent.

By Bus

Bus services are quite good in New England.

Bonanza Bus Lines (tel: 401/751–8800 or 1–888/751–8800), South Station Bus Terminal, 700 Atlantic Drive, runs from Boston to Cape Cod (Falmouth and Woods Hole) and Fall River (Massachusetts), and Newport and Providence (Rhode Island). Other routes run from Providence to central and western Connecticut and the Berkshires of Massachusetts, and from Providence to Cape Cod.

Concord Trailways (tel: 603/228–3300 or 1–800/639–3317) is the line to take to New Hampshire. Buses start at Logan Airport and the Peter Pan Trailways Terminal in Boston, then head north to Concord,

Laconia and North Conway, Plymouth, Waterville Valley, and Franconia. Another route goes to Alton and Wolfboro.

Greyhound (tel: 800/231–2222, with its terminal at South Station in Boston, operates many of the long-distance routes in New England, and connects the region with the rest of the country.

Peter Pan Trailways (tel: 617/426–7838 or 800/343–9999), at the Peter Pan Trailways terminal in Peter Pan Plaza, opposite Amtrak's South Station, runs between Boston and Albany, Amherst, Bridgeport, Danbury, Hartford, Holyoke, Lee, Middletown, New Britain, New Haven, New York City, Northampton, Norwalk, Pittsfield, Springfield, Sturbridge, Waterbury, and Worcester. Other routes connect Springfield, Massachusetts, with Bradley International Airport and Hartford, Connecticut.

Plymouth & Brockton Street Railway Co. (tel: 508/746–0378), Peter Pan Trailways Terminal in Dewey Square, is the one to take from Boston to Plymouth, Sagamore, Hyannis, Barnstable, and Provincetown on Cape Cod.

Vermont Transit Lines (tel: 802/862–9671, or 800/231–2222 in Vermont), Greyhound Terminal, in collaboration with Greyhound Lines, operates a comprehensive network.

HEALTH SERVICES

All New England cities have hospitals; blue signs bearing a white H mark the way. Boston is one of the most renowned medical centers, with dozens of hospitals and medical facilities.

To use most of these facilities, however, you'll need health insurance, since prices for services are astronomical.

HITCHHIKING

Hitchhiking is not a good way to get around New England, either within cities or between cities and towns. It's illegal to hitchhike on expressways. Incidents of robbery and violence by driver or hitcher, though few in number, mean most motorists won't stop.

HOLIDAYS

(LWE = long weekend, including Monday)

1 January – New Years Day;
Third Monday in January – Martin Luther King Day (LWE);
Second weekend in February – Lincoln's Birthday (LWE);
Third weekend in February – Washington's Birthday (LWE);
(Presidents Week, linking the two weekends, is often a school holiday);
First Tuesday in March – Town Meeting Day (Vermont);
Third Monday in April – Patriots' Day (Massachusetts and Maine, LWE);
Easter;
Last weekend in May – Memorial Day (LWE);
4 July – Independence Day;
Second Monday in August – Victory Day (Rhode I, LWE);
16 August – Bennington Battle Day (Vermont);
First Monday in September – Labor Day (LWE);
Second Monday in October – Columbus Day (LWE);
First Tuesday in November – Election Day (some states);
11 November – Veteran's Day;
Fourth Thursday in November – Thanksgiving Day;
25 December – Christmas Day.

LIQUOR LAWS

The minimum age for drinking varies by state, but in most it's 21 years. A few towns in New England, such as Rockport, Massachusetts, are "dry," which means that no shop, restaurant, or hotel may sell liquor, but it's not illegal to bring in your own liquor and serve yourself.

Restaurants have either a full liquor license (liquor, wine, and beer), a wine and beer license, or no license. Some unlicensed restaurants let you bring your own; others don't.

It's illegal to drink alcohol in public areas, such as streets and parks or on benches. Drink/ driving laws are very strict: don't take risks.

MOTORING
Driving

In many places outside major cities, cars are permitted to turn right on a red light after stopping, if it is safe to do so.

Freeways and toll roads make travel easy, whereas side roads are often narrow and winding. Use particular care in winter.

You should always have your driving license with you.

Speed limits, licensing of drivers, and all other rules governing automobile use are set by each state's legislature.

Car Rental

To rent a car in New York or New England, you must be at least 21 years of age (though most major agencies require you to be at least 25) and have a valid driver's license. A credit or charge card is almost always a necessity.

Some companies may insist that non-U.S. residents have an International Drivers Permit.

If your own auto insurance covers damage to a rental car, you needn't purchase Collision Damage Waiver (CDW) or Loss Damage Waiver (LDW).

The major New England airports have national car rental chains. Some handy phone numbers are:
Alamo (tel: 800/327–9633)
Avis (tel: 800/230–4898)
Budget (tel: 800/527–0700)
Dollar (tel: 800/800–4000)
Hertz (tel: 800/654–3131)
National (tel: 800/227–7368)
Thrifty (tel: 800/367–2277).

Breakdowns

Car rental companies will advise drivers of what to do in the case of a breakdown. However, the American Automobile Association ("Triple A") has reciprocal arrangements with many other motoring organizations around the world, so it is worth checking with your own association before leaving home. The AAA nationwide, toll-free number is 800–AAA–HELP. In case of a breakdown, lift up the hood, as a signal, and remain in the car. Only open doors and windows to police in a patrol car.

Accidents
All accidents should be reported to the police. Exchange names, addresses, driver license number, and insurance details. Non-U.S. residents who have caused, or are held responsible for an injury, should insist on contacting their embassy or consulate.

Safety Belts
The use of safety belts is required by law. Throughout the United States, infants and small children (under 5) are required by law to be placed in child safety seats secured by seat belts. Child safety seats are available from car-rental firms at a small extra charge.

Speed Limits
The speed limit in New England is 55 to 65mph (88 to 105km/h). In cities and built-up areas, it is 20 to 40mph (32 to 64km/h), and 15mph (24km/h) in school zones. Speed limits are strictly enforced. When a school bus stops, all traffic must do the same.

Police use radar to detect speeding drivers.

In many states, it's illegal to mount or to use a radar detector. If you are caught speeding in Connecticut and you have a radar detector in your car (whether or not it's connected or in use), fines may total upward of $300.

Road Maps
New England maps are sold in the region's bookstores and gas stations. Maps of each state drawn with greater detail are available, sometimes for free, from official state tourism departments by mail, or from state roadside information centers located on major highways near state borders.

For addresses of the state tourism offices, see **Visitor Information** on page 162.

NEW ENGLAND CALENDAR OF EVENTS
For up-to-date information on events throughout New England, buy the Thursday edition of the *Boston Globe*, which carries a separate calendar section with detailed listings on all sorts of happenings.

January
• *Warm up to Winter* in the Farmington Valley with lots of special events. Late Jan–late Mar.
• *Brookfield Ice Harvest* includes ice-sculpture and ice-cutting competitions. Tel: 802/276–3959. End Jan.

February
• The maple sugaring season begins, continuing through March; look out for demonstrations throughout the region.
• *Newport Winter Festival* offers ten days of fun, with events all over the city. Tel: 401/849–8048.
• *Connecticut Flower and Garden Show* transforms Hartford's Expo Center into lovely gardens. Tel: 860/529–2123. Mid-Feb.

March
• *Boston Massacre Reenactment*. Tel: 617/720–3290. Early Mar.
• *Irish Cultural Week* in Boston, including the St. Patrick's Day Parade. Tel: 978/459–0561 or 617/536–4100. Mid-Mar.

April
• *Boston Marathon*, the oldest marathon in America and largest single-day sporting event in New England. Tel: 617/236–1652 or 508/435–6905. Mid-Apr.
• *Battle of Lexington and Concord reenactment*. Tel: 781/861–0928. Mid-Apr.
• *New Hampshire Music Festival*, with concerts at various venues. Tourist offices will have details. Early–mid-Apr.

May
• *Dodge Dealers Grand Prix* at Lime Rock Park; largest sports-car race in North America. Tel: 800/RACE–LRP. Late May.
• *Mystic Lobsterfest* at Mystic Seaport includes a traditional outdoor lobster bake, music and activities. Tel: 860/572–5315. Late May.
• *Civil War Event* at Hammonasset Beach State Park includes mock battles, music and historic re-creations. Tel: 203/481–2393. Early May.

June
• *Yale-Harvard Regatta* on the Thames River in New London. Tel: 617/495–4848. Early Jun.
• *Newport International Film Festival*. Tel: 401/848–9443. Early Jun.
• *International Festival of Arts and Ideas* in New Haven; street theater, concerts, childrens events, historic tours. Tel: 203/489–1212. Mid-Jun–early Jul.
• *Boston Harborfest* celebrates the city's maritime history with concerts, fireworks and historic reenactments. Tel: 617/227–1528. Late Jun–early Jul.
• *Vermont Morgan Field Day* at Shelburne; with Morgan horses, and other entertainment. Tel: 802/985–4944. Late Jun.
• *Great Schooner Race* at Rockland. Over 20 tall ships. Tel: 800/807–WIND. Late Jun.

July
• *Independence Day* celebrations everywhere, with parades, fireworks and festivities. Pittsfield has one of America's largest parades (tel: 413/443–9186) and the Boston Pops put on a spectacular outdoor concert with fireworks (tel: 617/266–1492).
• *Wolfman Weekend* at Lincoln is the ultimate in silliness, with wolfman lookalike, growling and pie-eating contests and all kinds of games. Tel: 603/745–8913. Mid-Jul.
• *Riverfest* at Hartford and East Hartford includes big-name entertainers and spectacular fireworks over the river. Tel: 860/713-3131.

August
• *Newport Folk Festival*. Tel: 401/847–3700. Second week in Aug.
• *League of New Hampshire Craftsmen Fair* at Newbury. Tel: 603/224–3375. Early Aug.

- *Boston Caribbean Carnival*, with street parade, music, food and crafts. Tel: 617/534–5832.
- *Carnival Week* in Provincetown includes a lavish costume parade. Tel: 508/487–2313 or 800/637–8696. Late Aug.

September
- *Harwich Cranberry Harvest Festival* week-long celebration includes a beach party, country-western jamboree, fireworks and a parade. Tel: 508/432–6389 or 800/441–3199. Mid-Sep.
- *Woodstock Fair* is a traditional agricultural fair. Tel 860/928–3246. Early Sep.
- *African American Parade* in Hartford has marching bands, colorful floats, and other entertainment. Tel: 860/242–1734. Late Sep.
- *Heritage Festival* in Providence brings together some 30 ethnic groups to celebrate their culture with music, dance, food and arts and crafts. Tel: 401/222–2669.

October
- Fall Foliage and Harvest Festivals, pumpkin events and Halloween all come to the fore during October. Tourist offices will have full details.
- *Chowderfest* at Mystic offers delicious clam or corn chowder with a riverside setting and spectacular foliage. Tel: 860/572–5315 or 888/9–SEAPORT. Early Oct.
- *Haunted Happenings* at Salem. Halloween is when the town can really capitalize on its witchcraft heritage. Tel: 978/744–0013. End Oct.
- *Head of the Charles Regatta* in Cambridge, one of the biggest rowing events in the world. Tel: 617/864–8415. Late Oct.

November
- *Thanksgiving* is a big feature of the oldest communities of New England, notably at Plymouth, where it all began. Tel: 508/746–2334. Late Nov.
- *Festival of Light* at Hartford continues into the new year and centers on Constitution Plaza, lit by 200,000 bulbs. Tel: 860/728–3089. Late Nov–early Jan.

December
- *Christmas* is the focus, of course, with seasonal celebrations everywhere. Bethlehem in Connecticut is appropriately busy. Tel: 203/266–5557.
- *Boston Common Tree Lighting* has more than 50 illuminated trees, with choral accompaniment. Tel: 617/635–4505.
- *Holiday Tree Festival* at North Conway lasts for two weeks; over 100 decorated trees. Tel: 603/356–7031.
- *Reenactment of the Boston Tea Party* includes a fife and drum march to the Tea Party Ship. Tel: 617/338–1773. Mid-Dec.

NEWSPAPERS/ MAGAZINES
Each of the larger cities in New England has its own daily newspaper. The *Boston Globe* and the *Boston Herald* are distributed throughout New England, as is the *New York Times*, and, in most cities, the *Washington Post*. The national newspapers *USA Today* and the *Christian Science Monitor* are also available. You can buy the *International Herald Tribune* at Boston's Logan Airport and at some newsstands in large cities.

POST OFFICES
Most post offices are open Monday through Friday from 8am to 5pm and Saturday from 8am to noon or 2pm. A few major post offices stay open until 5.30 or 6pm, and the post office at Boston's Logan Airport stays open until midnight. To receive mail at a post office, have it sent to you c/o General Deliveries (Poste Restante) in the town where you'd like to pick up your mail. Specify the name of the post office where you'd like to pick up your mail; if in doubt, write "Main Post Office." You'll need to show identification, such as a passport or driver's license, to pick up your mail.

SAFETY
Whenever you're traveling in an unfamiliar city or country, stay alert and keep a close eye on your possessions.

TAXES
Taxes on hotel rooms, restaurant meals, some transportation services, and purchases in general are levied by each state and by some cities. Taxes on rooms, meals, and other purchases (which can be as high as 11 or 12 per cent) are not included in the price.

TIPS FOR SPECIAL TRAVELERS
Families
Museums, amusement attractions, whale-watch trips, and most other sights offer reduced admission rates for children or good-value family tickets.

Some attractions (outdoor concerts, state parks, beaches, and so forth) charge admission "per car," so families can pay as little as solo travelers.

Often a family of four or even five can stay in the same hotel room. Most modern hotels and motels allow children to stay for free with their parents if the parents pay the normal two-person rate (not a special discount rate) and the children use the room's existing beds. If a rollaway bed is necessary, there will be a small charge ($10 to $20) for it. The age permissible for children under the "family plan" varies; for some plans, there is no age limit. Some inns follow the same policy, but some don't accommodate children at all.

A good source of information for family travel is *Frommer's New England with Kids*.

Seniors
Senior discounts are readily available throughout New England at museums, parks, attractions, and some hotels and on Amtrak trains, so make sure to carry some convincing form of photo identification.

It's best to request discounts on hotel rates, train and plane fares, and rental-car fees when you make your reservation, not when you're paying for the services. For more information about senior discounts in general and for a good-as-gold discount card, contact the American Association of Retired Persons (AARP), 601 E Street, NW, Washington, D.C. 20049 (tel: 1-800/424–3410).

Travelers with Disabilities

All of New England's major hotels and most museums and stores, as well as other large institutions, have, by law, to be, accessible to visitors in wheelchairs or on crutches. However, many of the smaller country inns and bed-and-breakfast houses are not accessible or not fully accessible. The best plan is always to call ahead to determine whether the level of accessibility is sufficient for your requirements.

Vermont Department of Tourism and Marketing and the New Hampshire Office of Travel and Tourism (see **Visitor Information**) offer information about accessible facilities and events. Amtrak trains are accessible to travelers with disabilities, but not all Amtrak stations are; ask about this when you make your train reservations, and also inquire about help with your baggage, special seating, and other assistance. There's a bonus: Amtrak grants discounts of 25 percent (off the normal coach fare) to adult disabled travelers and 50 percent (off normal children's fares) to disabled travelers aged 2 to 12. For full information, ask for a copy of Amtrak's annual Travel Planner from Amtrak, National Railroad Passenger Corp., 400 N. Capitol Street NW, Washington, D.C. 20001 (tel: 800/USA–RAIL).

VISITOR INFORMATION

State tourism offices:
Connecticut Office of Tourism, 505 Hudson Street, Hartford, CT 06106 (tel: 860/270–8080);
Maine Office of Tourism, 325B Water Street, Hallowell, ME 04347 (tel: 207/623–0363);
Massachusetts Office of Travel & Tourism, 10 Park Plaza, Suite 4510, Boston,

Massachusetts 02116 (tel: 617/973–8500;
New Hampshire Office of Travel & Tourism, 172 Pembroke Road (P.O. Box 1856), Concord, New Hampshire 03302 (tel: 603/271–2343);
Rhode Island Tourism Division, 1 West Exchange Street, Providence, Rhode Island 02903 (tel: 401/222–2601 or 800/556–2484);
Vermont Department of Tourism and Marketing, 6 Baldwin Street, 4th Floor, Drawer 33, Montpelier, Vermont 05633 (tel: 802/828–3237).

WHEN TO GO
Climate

Without doubt, the best times to tour New England are summer (June through August), and autumn (September and October), unless you're coming for skiing.

The Seasons

Coming very late and staying very briefly, spring tends to be a disappointment, but the week or two of spring days in the normal year are a delight, with cool temperatures in the evening and just the perfect degree of warmth during the day. In the countryside the thaw brings "mud time," between the last frosts and spring planting, and this is the slowest season for tourist facilities, with many country inns, resorts, and amusements closed for a few weeks.

By mid-June, summer is on its way and, despite the region's northerly and coastal location, it can be pretty hot and sometimes humid. When it's 85°F (or even up to 95°F) and humid, head for the beaches, the islands, the mountains, lakes, and riverbanks.

Autumn is undoubtedly New England's glory, its finest season, and if you have a choice of vacation times, this is the one to pick. Although you may have to forsake swimming, the famous fall foliage is a worthy substitute; it's at its peak,

usually in late September and mid-October. Days are still warm and very pleasant, nights a bit chilly but not uncomfortably so. This is the time for fresh apple cider, pumpkins and squash, fresh cranberries and apple orchards.

If you're heading to New England specifically to enjoy the fall foliage, you *must* book early. To be sure of catching the "peak color," you can call a special hotline number in each state to find out about fall-foliage (see pages 102–3).

Most tourist resorts and inns stay open through September and often to mid-October. Those that stay open all year sometimes close for two weeks or so from mid-October to early December. By Thanksgiving (November 25), everyone's getting in shape for the ski season.

After a period of chilly weather in October, New England usually gets a respite, with a short period of warm weather known as "Indian summer," which can occur in later October or November. It's not dependable and may be brief, but it's glorious all the same.

Winter, as they say, depends: snow might begin as early as November, but the first flurries usually come in mid-December. January through March is guaranteed cold and snowy, and the skiing may be quite good through April; gray snowy days alternate with brilliant, crisp, sunny days when the air is very cold but the sun's warmth makes it pleasant.

None of this applies to Mount Washington in New Hampshire, of course. This "highest peak in New England" is reputed to have the worst weather in all of the 50 states, and New Englanders take a delight in exchanging horror stories of the latest report: winds in excess of 150 miles per hour (the record is 231mph), temperatures of -40°F, and windchill factors that don't seem earthly.

ACCOMMODATIONS

Following is a selection of hotels which can be found along the routes of each tour. Prices are based on a standard double room.

$	under $70
$$	$70 to $110
$$$	$110 to $150
$$$$	over $150

TOUR I
CONCORD
Best Western at Historic Concord $$
Route 2 and Elm Street, Concord MA 01742. Tel: 978/369–6100 or 800/528–1234.

Colonial Inn $$–$$$$
48 Monument Square, Concord MA 01742. Tel: 978/369–9200 or 800/370–9200.

TOUR 2
NEWBURYPORT
Clark Currier Inn $$–$$$$
45 Green Street, Newburyport MA 01950. Tel: 978/465–8363 or 800/360–6582.

Morrill Place Inn $$
209 High Street, Newburyport MA 01950. Tel: 978/462–2808.

IPSWICH
Whittier Motel $–$$
120 County Road, Whittier's Corner, Ipswich MA 01938. Tel: 978/356–5205.

TOUR 3
PROVINCETOWN
Brass Key $$–$$$$
67 Bradford Street, Provincetown MA 02657. Tel: 508/487–9005 or 800/842–9858.
Closed early Nov–late Mar.

Breakwater Motel $–$$
Route 6A, Provincetown MA 02657. Tel: 508/487–1134 or 800/487–1134.

ORLEANS
Governor Prence Motor Inn $$
66 Route 6A at Route 28, Orleans MA 02653. Tel: 508/255–1216 or 800/342–4300.

TOUR 4
GREENFIELD
Brandt House $$–$$$$
29 Highland Avenue, Greenfield MA 01301. Tel: 413/774–3329 or 1–800/235–3329.

CHARLEMONT
Charlemont Inn $
Box 316, Charlemont MA 01339. Tel: 413/339–5391.

WILLIAMSTOWN
The House on Main Street $$
1120 Main Street, Williamstown MA 01267. Tel: 413/458–3031.

TOURS 5 and 6
BOSTON
463 Beacon Street Guest House $$
463 Beacon Street, Boston MA 02115. Tel: 617/536–1302.

Harborside Inn $$$
185 State Street, Boston MA 02116. Tel: 617/723–7500 or 888/723–7565.

Oasis Guest House $–$$
22 Edgerly Road, Boston MA 02115. Tel: 617/267–2262.

Susse Chalet Boston Lodge $$
800 Morrissey Boulevard, Boston MA 02122. Tel: 617/2879100 or 800/886–0056.

TOUR 7
CAMBRIDGE
A Friendly Inn $–$$
1673 Cambridge Street, Cambridge MA 02138. Tel: 617/547–7851.

Best Western Homestead Inn $$$
220 Alewife Brook Parkway, Cambridge MA 02138. Tel: 617/491–8000 or 800/528–1234.

Harding House $$–$$$
288 Harvard Street, Cambridge MA 02139. Tel: 617/876–2888.

TOUR 8
HARTFORD
Goodwin Hotel $$
Goodwin Square, 1 Haynes Street, Hartford CT 06103. Tel: 860/246–7500 or 800/922–5006.

Ramada Inn–Capitol Hill $–$$
440 Asylum Street, Hartford CT 06103. Tel: 860/246–6591.

TOUR 9
NEW HAVEN
Grand Chalet Inn $$–$$$
400 Sargent Drive, New Haven CT 06511. Tel: 203/562–1111 or 800/5-CHALET.

New Haven Hotel $$–$$$
229 George Street, New Haven CT 06510. Tel: 203/498–3100.

Three Judges Motor Lodge $
1560 Whalley Avenue, New Haven CT 06515. Tel: 203/389–2161.

TOUR 10
KENT
Chaucer House $$–$$$
88 North Main Street (Route 7), Kent CT 06757. Tel: 860/927–4858.

LAKEVILLE
Inn at Iron Masters $$–$$$
229 Main Street (Route 44), Lakeville CT 06039.
Tel: 860/435–9844.

Interlaken Inn, Resort & Conference Centre $$–$$$
Route 112, Lakeville CT 06039. Tel: 860/435–9878 or 800/222–2909.

TOUR II
OLD LYME
Bee & Thistle Inn $$–$$$
100 Lyme Street, Old Lyme CT 06371. Tel: 860/434–1667 or 800/622–4946.

Old Lyme Inn $$–$$$
85 Lyme Street, Old Lyme CT 06371. Tel: 860/434–2600 or 800/434–5352.

MYSTIC
Harbour Inne & Cottage $$–$$$
15 Edgemont Street, Mystic CT 06355. Tel: 860/572–9253.

TOUR 12
PROVIDENCE
Day's Hotel on the Harbor $$
220 India Street, Providence
RI 02903. Tel: 401/272–5577.

Old Court $$
144 Benefit Street, Providence
RI 02903. Tel: 401/751–2002.

Providence Biltmore $$$
11 Dorrance Street, Providence
RI 02303. Tel: 401/421–0700.

TOUR 13
NEWPORT
Cliffside Inn $$-$$$
2 Seaview Avenue, Newport
RI 02840. Tel: 401/847–1811 or
1-800/845–1811.

Francis Malbone House
$$-$$$
392 Thames Street, Newport
RI 02840. Tel: 401/846–0392.

Ivy Lodge $$-$$$
12 Clay Street, Newport
RI 02840. Tel: 401/849–6865.

TOUR 14
BENNINGTON
Molly Stark Inn $-$$
1067 Main Street, Bennington
VT 05201. Tel: 802/442–9631 or
1-800/356–3076.

South Shire Inn $$$
124 Elm Street, Bennington
VT 05201. Tel: 802/447–3839.

TOUR 15
CHESTER
Chester Inn $$$
On The Green, PO Box 589,
Chester VT 05143.
Tel: 802/875–2444 or 1-888/
CHESINN.

MARLBORO
Whetstone Inn $-$$
South Road, Marlboro
VT 05344. Tel: 802/254–2500.

TOUR 16
QUECHEE
Herrin House Inn $$$-$$$$
PO Box 312, Quechee
VT 05059. Tel: 1-800/616–4415.

Quechee Inn $$-$$$$
Mashland Farm, Main Street,

Quechee VT 05059.
Tel: 1-800/235 3133.

WOODSTOCK
Woodstock Inn $$$
14 The Green, Woodstock
VT 05091-1298. Tel: 802/457–
1100 or 1-800/448–7900.

TOUR 17
WATERBURY CENTER
Black Locust Inn $$-$$$$
5088 Waterbury-Stowe Road,
Waterbury Center VT 05677.
Tel: 802/244–7490.

MIDDLEBURY
Middlebury Inn $$-$$$
14 Court House Square,
Middlebury VT 05753-0798.
Tel: 802/388–4961.

TOUR 18
PORTSMOUTH
Anchorage Inn
417 Woodbury Avenue,
Portsmouth NH 03801. Tel:
603/431–8111 or 800/370– 8111.

Susse Chalet Inn
650 Borthwick Avenue
Extension, Portsmouth NH
03801. Tel: 603/436–6363 or 1-
800/5–CHALET.

TOUR 19
JACKSON
Carter Notch Inn $-$$
Carter Notch Road, Box 269,
Jackson NH 03846.
Tel: 603/383–9630 or 800
794–9434.

GLEN
Covered Bridge House $
Route 302, Glen CT 03838.
Tel: 603/383–9109 or
800/232–9109.

NORTH CONWAY
Nereledge Inn $
River Road, off Main Street
(Route 16), North Conway
NH 03860. Tel: 603/356–2831.

TOUR 20
WOLFEBORO
Brookside Cottage $
PO Box 247, 396 Gov.
Wentworth Highway, Melvin
Village, Wolfeboro NH 03894.
Tel: 603/544–6162.

WEIR'S BEACH
Cozy Inn $
12 Maple Street, Weir's Beach,
NH 03246. Tel: 606/366–4310.

MEREDITH
Nutmeg Inn $$
80 Pease Road, Meredith
NH 03253. Tel: 603/279–8811.

TOUR 21
BELFAST
Penobscot Meadows Inn $-$$
Tel: 207/338–5320.

CAMDEN
Nathaniel Hosmer Inn $$
4 Pleasant Street, Camden
ME 04843. Tel: 207/256–or
800/423–4012.

Swan House $$-$$$
49 Mountain Street (Route 52),
Camden ME 04843.
Tel: 207/236–8273 or 800/207–
8275.

ROCKLAND
Trade Winds Motor Inn $-$$
2 Park View Drive, Rockland
ME 04841. Tel: 207/596–6661.

TOUR 22
PORTLAND
Inn at St John $-$$$
939 Congress Street, Portland
ME 04102. Tel: 207/773–6481
or 800/636–9127.

SOUTH PORTLAND
Merry Manor Inn $$-$$$
700 Main Street, South Portland
ME 04106. Tel: 207/774–6151.

TOUR 23
LEWISTON
Farnham House Bed and
Breakfast $-$$
520 Main Street, Lewiston
ME 04240. Tel: 207/782–9495.

RANGELEY
Hunter Cove on Rangeley
Lake $$- $$$
Mingo Loop Road, Rangeley
ME 04970. Tel: 207/864–3383.

Rangeley Inn $$
PO Box 160, Main Street,
Rangeley ME 04970.
Tel: 207/864–3341 or 800/666–
3687.

Practical Information

The addresses, telephone numbers and opening times of the attractions mentioned in the tours, including the telephone numbers of the Tourist Information Offices are listed below tour by tour.

TOUR 1

[i] Cambridge Visitor Information Booth, Harvard Square, Cambridge MA 02138. Tel: 617/441–2884.

[i] Lexington Visitor Center, 1875 Massachusetts Avenue, Lexington MA 02473. Tel: 781/862–1450.

[i] Minute Man Visitor Center, Route 2A, Lexington MA 02473. Tel: 978/369–6993.

[i] Concord Chamber of Commerce, Heywood Street, Concord MA 01742. Tel: 978/369–3120.

[i] North Bridge Visitor Center, 174 Liberty Street, Concord MA 01742. Tel: 978/369–6993.

1 Museum of Our National Heritage
33 Marrett Road, (Route 2A) Lexington. Tel: 781/861–6559. Open Mon–Sat 10–5, Sun 12–5.

2 Munroe Tavern
1322 Massachusetts Avenue, Lexington. Tel: 781/674–9238. Open Apr–Oct daily for tours.

3 Lexington
Buckman Tavern
1 Bedford Street. Tel: 781/862–5598. Open Mar–early Dec, Mon–Sat 10–4, Sun 1–4.

Hancock-Clarke House
36 Hancock Street. Tel: 781/861–0928. Open Apr–Oct daily for tours.

4 Minute Man National Historical Park
Route 2A, Lexington. Tel: 978/369–6993.

5 Concord
The Wayside
455 Lexington Road. Tel: 978/369–6975. Open Apr–Oct. Tours Tue–Sun 1, 2.30 ,4.

Orchard House
399 Lexington Road. Tel: 978/369–4118. Open Mon–Sat 10–4.30, Sun 1–4.30; shorter hours on winter weekdays. Closed first 2 weeks Jan.

Concord Museum
200 Lexington Road. Tel: 978/369–9763. Open Mon–Sat 9–5, Sun noon–5. Shorter hours in winter.

Ralph Waldo Emerson House
23 Cambridge Turnpike. Tel: 978/369–2236. Open mid-Apr–mid-Oct, Thu–Sun 10–4.30.

Sleepy Hollow Cemetery
Route 62, Concord. Tel: 978/371–6280.

Old Manse
269 Monument Street. Tel: 978/369–3909. Open mid-Apr–Oct, 10–5.

6 Walden Pond
Walden Pond State Reservation, Route 126. Tel: 978/369–3254.

7 Gropius House
68 Baker Bridge Road, Lincoln. Tel: 781/259–8098. Open Jun–mid-Oct, Wed–Sun. Some winter weekends. Phone for hours.

8 DeCordova Museum and Sculpture Park
51 Sandy Pond Road, Lincoln. Tel: 781/259–8355. Open Tue–Sun 11–5. Park open to 10pm in summer.

Recommended Trips
South Bridge Boathouse
496 Main Street, Concord. Tel: 978/369–9438. Open Apr–Oct daily.

TOUR 2

[i] Boston Common Visitor Information Center, 147 Tremont Street. Tel: 617/536–4100.

[i] Marblehead Information Booth,
Pleasant and Spring streets, Marblehead MA 01945. Tel: 781/631–2868.

[i] National Park Service Regional Visitor Service, New Liberty and Essex streets, Salem MA 01970. Tel: 978/740–1650.

[i] Stage Fort Park Information Center, Hough Avenue, Gloucester MA 01930. Tel: 978/281–8865.

[i] Rockport Chamber of Commerce, Upper Main Street, Rockport MA 01966. Tel: 978/546–6575.

[i] Newburyport Information Kiosk, Merrimac Street, Newburyport MA 01950. Tel: 978/462–6680.

2 Marblehead
Jeremiah Lee Mansion
161 Washington Street. Tel: 781/631–1069. Open mid-May–Oct, Mon–Sat 10–4, Sun 1–4.

3 Salem
Salem Witch Museum
Washington Square North. Tel: 978/744–1692. Open daily 10–5 (till 7pm Jul, Aug).

Salem Witch House
282 Rear of Derby Street. Tel: 978/740–92292. Open daily, Apr–Jun and Sep 9–6; Jul–Aug 9–9; Oct 9–midnight; Nov–Apr 10–5.

Witch House
310½ Essex Street. Tel: 978/744–0180. Open mid-Mar–Nov 10–4.30 (till 6pm Jul–Oct).

Pioneer Village
Forest River Park. Tel: 978/745–0529. Open May–Oct, Mon–Sat 10–5, Sun noon–5.

Peabody Essex Museum
East India Square. Tel: 978/745–9500. Open Mon–Sat 10–5, Sun noon–5. Closed Mon Nov–Mar.

Salem Maritime National Historic Site
174 Derby Street. Tel: 978/740–1680. Open daily 9–5.

6 Hammond Castle Museum
80 Hesperus Avenue,
Gloucester. Tel: 978/283–2080/7673. Open Mon–Fri 10–4.

7 Gloucester
Cape Ann Historical Museum
27 Pleasant Street. Tel: 978/283–0455. Open Tue–Sat 10–5. Closed Feb.

8 Rocky Neck and Beauport
Sleeper-McCann House Museum
75 Eastern Point Boulevard, Beauport, Gloucester. Tel: 978/283–0800. Open daily mid-May–mid-Oct.

9 Rockport
Rockport Art Association Gallery
12 Main Street. Tel: 978/546–6604.

10 Pigeon Cove
Paper House
52 Pigeon Hill. Tel: 978/546–2629. Open daily Jul–Aug or by appointment.

11 Essex
Shipbuilding Museum
28 Main Street. Tel: 978/768–7541. Open May–Oct, Mon–Sat 10–5, Sun 1–4.

12 Ipswich
John Whipple House
1 South Village Green. Tel: 978/356–2811. Open May–mid-Oct, Wed–Sat 10–4, Sun 1–4 (last tour 3).

John Heard House
54 South Main Street. Tel: 978/356–2811. Open May–mid-Oct, Wed–Sat 10–4, Sun 1–4 (last tour 3).

Castle Hill and Crane's Beach
290 Argilla Road. Tel: 978/356–4351, (beach) –4354. Call for details.

13 Plum Island and the Parker River National Wildlife Refuge
Plum Island Northern Boulevard, Newburyport. Tel: 978/465–5753.

14 Newburyport
Custom House Maritime Museum
25 Water Street. Tel: 978/462–8681. Open Apr–Dec, Mon–Sat 10–4, Sun 1–4.

Cushing House Museum
98 High Street. Tel: 978/
462–2681. *Open May–Oct,
Tue–Fri 10–4, Sat 11–2.*

For History Buffs
Abbot Hall
188 Washington Street.
Tel: 781/631–0000. *Open
Jun–Oct, daily 8–6;
Nov–May, weekdays 8–6.*

Special to…
**The House of the Seven
Gables**
54 Turner Street. Tel: 978/
744–0991. *Open daily 10–
5 (noon–5 Sun Dec–Apr).*

Woodmans of Essex
121 Main Street, Essex.
Tel: 978/768–6451 and
800/649–1773. *Open
summer 11–10; closes
8/9pm in winter.*

Recommended Walks
Halibut Point State Park
Off Route 127, Rockport.
Tel: 978/546 2997.

Back to Nature
Wolf Hollow
144 Essex Road, Route
133. Tel: 978/356–0216.

For Children
**Moby Duck Amphibious
Sightseeing**
75 Essex Avenue,
Gloucester. Tel: 978/281–
3825. *Daily from 10am.*

The *Adventure*
Jodrey State Fish Pier,
Route 128. Tel: 508/281–
8079. *Open late May–early
Sep, Thu–Sun 10–4.*

---

i Cape Cod Chamber of
Commerce, Hyannis MA
02601. Tel: 508/362–3225.

i Cape Cod Canal
Chamber of Commerce,
70 Main Street, Buzzards
Bay MA 02532.
Tel: 508/759–6000.

i Yarmouth Chamber of
Commerce, 657 Route 28,
East Yarmouth MA 02675.
Tel: 508/778–1008.

i Dennis Chamber of
Commerce, Routes 134/28,
West Dennis MA 02760.
Tel: 800/243–9920.

i Brewster Chamber of
Commerce, Town Hall,
2198 Main Street,
Brewster MA 02631.
Tel: 508/255–7045.

i Eastham Information
Center, Route 6, Eastham
MA 02642. Tel:
508/255–3444.

i Wellfleet Chamber of
Commerce Information
Booth, off Route 6, South
Wellfleet MA 02663.
Tel: 508/349–2510.

i Provincetown
Chamber of Commerce,
307 Commercial Street,
Provincetown MA 02657.
Tel: 508/487–3424.

i Chatham Information
Booth, 533 Main Street,
Chatham MA 02633.
Tel: 508/945–5199.

2 Sandwich
Thomas Dexter Grist Mill
Water Street.
Tel: 508/888–4910 (town
hall). *Open mid-Jun–mid-
Sep, Mon–Sat 10–4.15.*

Hoxie House
18 Water Street. Tel: 508/
888–1173. *Open mid-Jun–
Sep, Mon–Sat 10–5, Sun 1–5.*

**Thornton W. Burgess
Museum**
4 Water Street (Route
130). Tel: 508/888–6668.
*Open Apr–Oct, Mon–Sat
10–4, Sun 1–4.*

3 Barnstable
Sturgis Library
Route 6A. Tel: 508/362–
6636. *Call for hours.*

4 Yarmouth
**Captain Bangs Hallet
House**
11 Strawberry Lane. Tel:
508/362–3021. *Open Jun,
Sun 2–4; Jul–Sep, Wed–Fri
and Sun 2–4.*

**Thatcher House and
Winslow-Crocker House**
250 Route 6A. Tel: 508/362
–4385. *Open Jun–mid-Oct,
Tue, Thu, Sat, Sun noon–5.*

5 Dennis and East
Dennis
**Josiah Dennis Manse
Museum**
Nobscusset Road and

Whig Street, Dennis.
Tel: 508/385–2232. *Open
Jul–Aug, Tue and Thu 2–4.*

Cape Playhouse
Main Street, Dennis.
Tel: 508/385 3838. *Open
summer Mon–Sat evenings,
matinees Wed and Thu.
Children's Theater Fri am.*

Cape Museum of Fine Arts
Route 6A, Dennis.
Tel: 508/385 4477. *Open
Tue–Sat 10–5, Sun 1–5.*

Scargo Hill Observation
Tower
Off Route 6A. *Open daily.*

6 Brewster
**Brewster Historical
Society Museum**
Route 6A, Spruce Hill.
Tel: 508/896–8495.

**New England Fire and
History Museum**
1439 Main Street, Route
6A. Tel: 508/896–5711.
*Open May–Sep 10–4;
weekends in fall.*

8 Eastham
**Captain Edward Penniman
House**
Fort Hill Road. Tel: 508/
255–3421. *Undergoing
restoration; phone for details.*

**Cape Cod National
Seashore**
Salt Pond Visitor Center,
Route 6. Tel: 508/255–
3421 or 349–3785.

Oldest Windmill
Opposite Town Hall.
Open Jun–Sep, daily 10–5.

12 Provincetown
**Pilgrim Monument and
Provincetown Museum**
High Pole Hill. Tel:
508/487–1310 or
800/247–1620. *Open daily.
Closed Jan, Feb.*

13 Chatham
Railroad Museum
Depot Road. Tel: 508/945–
2493. *Open mid-Jun–mid-
Sep, Tue–Fri 1–4.*

Special to…
Sandwich Glass Museum
129 Main Street.
Tel: 508/888–0251. *Open
Apr–Oct, daily 9.30–5;
Nov–Dec and Feb–Mar,
Wed–Sun 9.30–4.*

Cranberry World Visitors
Center
225 Water Street,
Plymouth. Tel: 508/747–
2350. *Open daily May–Nov.*

For Children
Heritage Plantation
Pine and Grove streets.
Tel: 508/888 3300. *Open
early May–Oct, daily 10–5.*

**Green Briar Nature
Center & Jam Kitchen**
6 Discovery Hill Road, East
Sandwich. Tel: 508/888–
6870. *Open Jan–Mar,
Tue–Sat 10–4; Apr–Dec,
Mon–Sat 10–4, Sun 1–4.*

**Cape Cod Museum of
Natural History**
Route 6A, Brewster.
Tel: 508/896–3867. *Open
Tue–Sat 9.30–4.30, Sun
12.30–4.30.*

Scenic Route
**Cape Cod Central
Railroad**
252 Main Street, Hyannis.
Tel: 508/771–3800. *Open
late May–Oct , Tue–Sun
10–4 (check last train
times). Also Mon holiday
weekends.*

---

i Greater Springfield
CVB, PO Box 15589,
Springfield MA 01115.
Tel: 413/787–1548.

i Riverfront Park
Information Center, West
Columbus Avenue,
Springfield MA 01115.

i Stockbridge
Information Booth, Main
Street, Stockbridge
MA 01262.

i Lenox Chamber of
Commerce, 75 Main
Street, Lenox MA 01240.
Tel: 413/637–3646.

i Berkshire Hills Visitors
Bureau, Berkshire
Common Level Plaza,
Pittsfield MA 01201.
Tel: 413/443–9186.

i RSVP Tourist
Information Booth, Park
Square, Pittsfield MA
01201.

[i] Tourist Information Office
[12] Number on tour

[i] Williamstown Chamber of Commerce, Routes 2 and 7, Williamstown MA 01267. Tel: 413/458–4922.

[i] Shelburne Falls Village Information Center, 75 Bridge Street, Shelburne Falls MA 01370. Tel: 413/625–2544.

[i] Pioneer Valley Tourist Information Center, Routes 5 and 10, South Deerfield MA 01342. Tel: 413/665–7333.

[i] Northampton Area Visitors Center, 99 Pleasant Street, Northampton MA 01060. Tel: 413/584–1900.

[2] **Great Barrington**
Aston Magna Festival
St. James Church. Tel: 413/528–3595. *Open Jul–Aug.*

[5] **Stockbridge**
Red Lion Inn
Main Street.
Tel: 413/298–5545.

Norman Rockwell Museum
Route 183. Tel: 413/298–4100. *Open daily 10–5 (closes 4 winter weekdays). Studio open May–Oct only.*

Chesterwood
Off Route 183.
Tel: 413/298–3579. *Open May–Oct, daily 10–5.*

Naumkeag
Prospect Hill Road.
Tel: 413/298–3239. *Open May–Oct, daily 10–5.*

Berkshire Botanical Garden
Junction Routes 183 and 102. Tel: 413/298–3926. *Open May–Oct, daily 10–5.*

[6] **Tanglewood**
Tanglewood Music Festival
Route 183, Lenox. Tel: 413/637–5165. *Jul and Aug.*

[7] **Lenox**
The Mount–Edith Warton Restoration
Plunkett Street. Tel: 413/637–1899. Shakespeare and Company Tel: 413/637–1199. *Restoration work in progress; phone for details.*

[8] **Arrowhead**
780 Holmes Road, Pittsfield. Tel: 413/442–1793. *Open Jun–Oct. Rest of year by appointment only.*

[9] **Hancock Shaker Village**
Junction Routes 20 and 41, Pittsfield. Tel: 413/443–0188. *Open Apr–Nov, daily 9.30–5 (closes 3pm early in season).*

[10] **Williamstown**
Sterling and Francine Clark Art Institute
225 South Street. Tel: 413/458–9545. *Open Tue 10–5; also Mon Jul and Aug.*

Williams College Museum of Art
Main Street. Tel: 413/597–2429. *Open Tue–Sat 10–5, Sun and holiday Mon 1–5.*

Williamstown Theatre Festival
Williams College. Tel: 413/597–3400. *Open Jun–Aug.*

[11] **North Adams**
Massachusetts Museum of Contemporary Art
87 Marshall Street. Tel: 413/664–4481. *Open Jun–Oct, daily 10–5 (to 7 Fri and Sat); winter, Tue–Sun 10–4.*

[13] **Deerfield**
The Street (off Routes 5 and 10). Tel: 413/774–5581. *Open daily 9.30–4.30.*

Emily Dickinson House
280 Main Street, Amherst. Tel: 413/542–8161. *Limited opening. Make reservation.*

Special to...
Basketball Hall of Fame/Naismith Memorial
1150 West Columbus Avenue, Springfield. Tel: 413/781–6500. *Open daily 9–6 (9–8 Wed, Fri and Sat in spring and summer).*

For Children
Six Flags New England
Route 159, Agawam. Tel: 413/786–9300. *Open May–Oct, daily 10–10/11; winter weekends, times vary.*

Magic Wings Butterfly Conservatory and Garden
Routes 5 and 10, South Deerfield. Tel: 413/665–2805. *Open all year daily.*

For History Buffs
Colonel John Ashley House
Cooper Hill Road, Ashley Falls. Tel: 413/229–8600. *Open May-mid–Oct, Sat, Sun and holidays 10–5.*

Back to Nature
Barthlomew's Cobble
Weatogue Road off Route 7A, Ashley Falls. Tel: 413/229–8600. *Open daily sunrise–sunset. Museum 8.30–4.30, closed holidays.*

Pleasant Valley Wildlife Sanctuary
472 West Mountain Road. Tel: 413/637–0320.

TOUR 5

[i] Boston Common Visitor Information Center, 147 Tremont Street. Tel: 617/536–4100.

[i] Boston National Historical Park Visitor Center, 15 State Street. Tel: 617/242–5642.

[i] Charlestown Navy Yard Visitor Center. Constitution Road, Charlestown. Tel: 617/242–5601.

[2] **State House**
Beacon Street. Tel: 617/727–3676. *Tours weekdays and Sats 10–4.*

[8] **Globe Corner/Old Corner Bookstore**
1 School Street. Tel: 617/367–4000.

[9] **Old South Meeting House**
310 Washington Street. Tel: 617/482–6439. *Open daily.*

[10] **Old State House**
Corner of State and Washington streets. Tel: 617/720–3290/3285. *Open daily 9.30–5.*

[11] **Faneuil Hall**
Merchants Row. Tel: 617/242–5675/5642. *Open daily 9–5.*

[12] **Union Oyster House**
41 Union Street. Tel: 617/227–2750.

[15] **Paul Revere's House**
19 North Square.

Tel: 617/523–2338. *Open daily 9.30–4.15 (5.15 summer).*

[18] **USS Constitution**
Pier 1, Charlestown Navy Yard. Tel: 617/242–5670/5671. *Open daily 9.30–5.30.*

[19] **Bunker Hill Monument**
Monument Square, Charlestown. Tel: 617/242–5641. *Open daily 9–4.30.*

Special to...
Omni Parker House
60 School Street.
Tel: 617/227–8600 or 800/THE OMNI.

TOUR 6

[i] Boston Common Visitor Information Center, 147 Tremont Street. Tel: 617/536–4100.

[i] Boston National Historical Park Visitor Center, 15 State Street. Tel: 617/242–5642.

[1] **New England Aquarium**
Central Wharf. Tel: 617/973–5200. *Open daily 9–5 (later some evenings).*

[3] **Faneuil Hall**
See Tour 5.

[6] **The Harrison Gray Otis House**
141 Cambridge Street. Tel: 617/227–3956. *Open Tue–Sun 11–5.*

[7] **Black Heritage Trail**
Abiel Smith School
46 Joy Street. Tel: 617/725–0022. *Open daily 10–4. Closed Sun in winter.*

African Meeting House
8 Smith Court.
Tel: 617/742–5415. *Open daily 10–4.*

[8] **Nichols House Museum**
55 Mount Vernon Street. Tel: 617/227–6993. *Call for opening hours.*

[13] **John Hancock Tower**
John Hancock Observatory
200 Clarendon Street,

Practical Information

[i] Tourist Information Office
[12] Number on tour

60th floor. Tel: 617/572–6429.

Special to…
Durgin-Park
340 Faneuil Hall Marketplace. Tel: 617/227–2038.

Scenic Routes
Boston Duck Tours
Depart from Prudential Center, Boylston Street.
Tel: 617/227–5296. *Apr–Nov, half-hourly from 9am.*

TOUR 7

[i] Cambridge Visitor Information Booth, Harvard Square, Cambridge MA 02139.
Tel: 617/441–2884.

[i] Harvard University, 26 Oxford Street, Cambridge MA 02138. Tel: 617/495–3045. Museums and tours.

[i] Harvard Information Center, Holyoke Center Arcade, 1350 Massachusetts Avenue, Cambridge MA 02138. Tel: 617/ 495–1573.

[6] **Carpenter Center for the Visual Arts**
24 Quincy Street. Tel: 617/495–4351 for film times.

[7] **Fogg and Busch-Reisinger Art Museums**
32 Quincy Street.
Tel: 617/495–9400. *Open Mon–Sat 10–5, Sun 1–5.*

[8] **Arthur M. Sackler Museum**
485 Broadway. Tel: 617/495–9400. *Open Mon–Sat 10–5, Sun 1–5.*

[9] **Annenberg Memorial Hall**
45 Quincy Street. Tel: 617/496–2222. *Opening very limited; phone for details. Transepts open daily noon–6.*

[10] **Museums of Natural History**
26 Oxford Street.
Tel: 617/495–8206. *Open Mon–Sat 9–5, Sun 1–5.*

[13] **Brattle Street**
Cambridge Historical Society
Hooper-Lee Nichols

House, 159 Brattle Street.
Tel: 617/547–4252. *Open Tue and Thu 2–5.*

[14] **Longfellow House National Historic Site**
105 Brattle Street. Tel: 617/876–4491. *Closed for renovation; phone for details.*

TOUR 8

[i] Hartford Civic Center, 1 Civic Center Plaza, Hartford CT 06103.
Tel: 860/728–6789.

[2] **Old State House**
800 Main Street.
Tel: 860/522–6766. *Open Mon–Fri 10–4, Sat 11–4. Closed last 2 weeks Aug.*

[3] **Travelers Tower**
1 Tower Square Tel: 860/277–4208. *Tours mid-May–Oct, Mon–Fri 10–3.*

[4] **Wadsworth Atheneum**
600 Main Street.
Tel: 860/278–2670. *Open Tue–Sun 11–5.*

[7] **Bushnell Park Carousel**
Jewell Street. Tel: 860/987–5900. *Open mid-Apr–mid-May, Sat–Sun 11–5; mid-May–Aug, Tue–Sun 11–5.*

[8] **State Capitol**
210 Capitol Avenue.
Tel: 860/240–0222.
Tours Mon–Fri 9.15–1.15 (2.15 Jul–Aug); also Sat 10.15–2.15 Apr–Oct.

[9] **Museum of Connecticut History**
231 Capitol Avenue.
Tel: 860/566–3056. *Open Mon–Fri 9.30–4.*

[10] Mark Twain House
351 Farmington Avenue.
Tel: 860/493–6411. *Open Mon–Sat 9.30–5, Sun noon–5. Closed Tue Jan–May and mid-Oct–Nov.*

[11] **Harriet Beecher Stowe House**
Farmington Avenue at Forest Street. Tel: 860/525–9317. *Open Mon–Sat, 9.30–4, Sun noon–4. Closed Mon, mid-Oct–Nov and Jan–May.*

[12] **Connecticut Historical Society**
1 Elizabeth Street.
Tel: 860/236–5621.
Open Tue–Sun, noon–5; Library Tue–Sat 10–5.

[13] **Noah Webster House**
227 South Main Street, West Hartford.
Tel: 860/521–5362. *Open Thu–Tue 1–4; extended hours in summer.*

Back to Nature
Elizabeth Park Rose Garden
Prospect Avenue.
Tel: 860/242–0017. *Open daily dawn–dusk.*

For Children
Science Center of Connecticut
950 Trout Brook Drive, West Hartford.
Tel: 860/231–2824. *Open Mon–Sat 10–5 (8pm Thu), Sun noon–5.*

TOUR 9

[i] Greater New Haven Convention and Visitors Bureau, 59 Elm Street, New Haven CT 06510.
Tel: 203/777–8550.

[i] Yale University Visitor Information Center, 149 Elm Street, New Haven CT 06520. Tel: 203/432–2300.

[5] **Yale University Art Gallery**
1111 Chapel Street at York Street. Tel: 203/432–0600. *Open Tue–Sat 10–5, Sun noon–6. Closed major holidays.*

[6] **Yale Center for British Art**
1080 Chapel Street.
Tel: 203/432–2800. *Open Tue–Sat 10–5, Sun noon–5. Closed major holidays.*

[7] **Yale Repertory Theatre**
Corner of Chapel and York streets. Tel: 203/432–1234. *Open Sep–May.*

[11] **Beinecke Rare Book Library**
121 Wall Street
Tel: 203/432–2977. *Open*

Mon–Fri 8.30–5, Sat 10–5. Closed holidays and Sat in Aug.

TOUR 10

[i] Hartford Civic Center, 1 Civic Center Plaza, Hartford CT 06103.
Tel: 860/728–6789.

[i] Litchfield Hills Information Booth, Route 202, On-the-Green, Litchfield CT 06759. No phone.

[i] Chamber of Commerce, Main Street, Salisbury CT 06068.
Tel: 860/435–0740.

[1] **Litchfield**
Tapping Reeve House and Law School
Route 63 South.
Tel: 860/567–4501. *Open Tue–Sat 11–5, Sun 1–5.*

Litchfield Historical Society Museum
7 South Street.
Tel: 860/567–4501. *Open mid-Apr–mid-Nov, Tue–Sat 11–5, Sun 1–5.*

[3] **Lake Waramaug**
Hopkins Vineyard
25 Hopkins Road, New Preston. Tel: 860/868–7954.
Open May–Dec, Mon–Sat 10–5, Sun 9–5; Jan–Feb, Fri–Sat 10–5, Sun 11–5; Mar–Apr, Wed–Sat 10–5, Sun 11–5.

[6] **Kent**
Sloane-Stanley Museum and Kent Furnace
Route 7. Tel: 860/927–3849. *Open mid-May–Oct, Wed–Sun 10–4.*

Connecticut Antique Machinery Association Museum
Route 7. Tel: 860/927–0050. *Open May–Sep, Sat–Sun 10–5.*

[8] **Cornwall Bridge to West Cornwall**
Clarke's Outdoors
163 Route 7, West Cornwall. Tel: 860/672–6365. *Open mid-Mar–Dec.*

[9] **Lime Rock Park**
Routes 7 and 112, Lakeville. Tel: 860/435–5000.
Regular meets Apr–Nov.

[i] Tourist Information Office
[12] Number on tour

[11] Salisbury
Chaiwalla
1 Main Street. Tel: 860/
435–9758. *Open Mon–Sat.*

Harney & Sons
23 Brook Street, Lakeville.
Open Mon–Sat.

Special to…
White Flower Farm
Route 63. Tel: 860/567–
8789. *Open daily 9–6;
Nov–Mar 10–5.*

The Silo
44 Upland Road, New
Milford. Tel: 860/355–0300.
Open Wed–Mon 10–5.

Cornwall Bridge Pottery
Route 7, between junc-
tions with Routes 45 and
4. Tel: 860/672–6545. *Open
daily 9–5.*

Recommended Walks
Kent Falls State Park
Route 7. Tel: 860/927–3238.
Open daily 8am–dusk.

TOUR 11

[i] Greater New Haven
Convention and Visitors
Bureau, One Long Wharf
Drive, New Haven CT
06511. Tel: 203/777–8550.

[1] Branford
Nathaniel Harrison House
124 Main Street. Tel: 203/
488–4828. *Phone for hours.*

[3] Guilford
Henry Whitfield State
Museum
248 Old Whitfield Street.
Tel: 203/453–2457. *Open
Feb–mid-Dec, Wed–Sun
10–4.30, or by appointment.*

Hyland House
84 Boston Street.
Tel: 203/453–9477. *Open
Jun–Aug, Tue–Sun 10–4;
Sep–mid-Oct, weekends only
10–4.*

Thomas Griswold House
171 Boston Street.
Tel: 203/453–3176. *Open
mid-Jun–mid-Sep, Tue–Sun
11–4 or by appointment.*

[4] Madison
Hammonasset Beach
State Park
Route 1. Tel: 203/245–
2785. *Open daily 8–sunset.*

[5] Old Saybrook
General William Hart
House
350 Main Street. Tel: 860/
388–6148. *Hours limited;
phone for details.*

[6] Essex
Griswold Inn
36 Main Street.
Tel: 860/767–1776.

Connecticut River
Museum
67 Main Street, Steamboat
Dock. Tel: 860/767–8269.
Open Tue–Sun 10–5.

Pratt House
19 West Avenue.
Tel: 860/767–0681. *Open
Jun–early Sep, Sat–Sun 1–4.*

[7] East Haddam
Goodspeed Opera House
Route 82. Tel: 860/873–
8668. *Open Apr–Dec,
Wed–Sun.*

Nathan Hale Schoolhouse
Main Street. Tel: 860/873–
9547. *Phone for hours.*

[8] Gillette Castle
Gillette Castle State Park
67 River Road. Tel:
860/526–2336. *Open
Jun–mid-Oct, Fri–Sun 10–5.*

[9] Old Lyme
Florence Griswold
Museum
96 Lyme Street. Tel: 860/
434–5542. *Open Jun–Dec,
Tue–Sat 10–5, Sun 1–5.
Rest of year Wed–Sun, 1–5.*

Lyme Academy of Fine Art
84 Lyme Street.
Tel: 860/434–5232. *Open
Tue–Sat 10–4, Sun 1–4.*

[10] New London
Hempsted House
11 Hempsted Street. Tel:
860/443–7949 or 247–
8996. *Open mid-May–mid-
Oct, Thu–Sun noon–4.*

US *Eagle*
US Coast Guard Academy,
Mohegan Avenue. Tel: 860/
444–8270. *Open Fri–Sun
1–5 when in port. Museum
May–Oct, daily 1–5.*

Lyman-Allyn Art Museum
625 Williams Street.
Tel: 860/443–2545. *Open
Tue–Sat 10–5, Sun 1–5.*

Monte Cristo Cottage
325 Pequot Avenue. Tel:
860/443–0051. *Open Jun–
Sep, Tue–Sat 10–5, Sun 1–5.*

Eugene O'Neill Theater
305 Great Neck Road,
Waterford.
Tel: 860/443–5378.

[11] USS *Nautilus*
Naval Submarine Base, 1
Crystal Lake Road,
Groton. Tel: 860/694–3174
or 800/343–0079. *Open
daily 9–5, Tue 1–5; Nov–
mid-May 9–4, closed Tue.*

[12] Noank
Abbott's Lobster-in-the-
Rough
117 Pearl Street. Tel: 860/
536–7719. *Open Apr–Aug,
daily; weekends to mid-Oct.*

[13] Mystic
Mystic Seaport
75 Greenmanville Avenue.
Tel: 860/572–5315. *Open
daily 9–5, winter 10–4.*

Mystic Aquarium
55 Coogan Boulevard.
Tel: 860/572–5955. *Open
daily 9–5 (6pm Jul–Sep).*

Olde Mistick Village
Coogan Boulevard (Route
27). Tel: 860/536–4941.
*Open Mon–Sat 10–6 (8pm
in summer), Sun noon–5.*

[14] Stonington
Old Lighthouse Museum
7 Water Street. Tel: 860/
535–1440. *Open May–Oct,
Tue–Sun 10–5; Jul–Aug daily.*

Scenic Routes
The Essex Steam Train
and Riverboat Ride
Valley Railroad, 1 Railroad
Avenue (off Route 9). Tel:
860/767–0103. *Open
May–Dec; call for schedule.*

Special to…
Pequot Museum and
Research Center
110 Pequot Trail, Mashan-
tucket. Tel: 800/411–9671.
Open Wed–Mon 10–6.

For History Buffs
U.S. Cotton House and
Museum
150 Bank Street, New
London. Tel: 860/447–
2501 or 442–7848. *Hours
limited; phone for details.*

For Children
Science Center of East
Connecticut
33 Gallows Lane, New
London. Tel: 860/442–
0391. *Open Tue–Sat 10–6,
Sun 1–5.*

Ocean Beach Park
1225 Ocean Avenue, New
London. Tel: 860/447–
3031. *Open late May–early
Sep, daily 9am–11pm.*

TOUR 12

[i] Waterplace Park,
Providence, RI 02903.
Tel: 401/274–1636 or
800/233–1636.

[3] Rhode Island School
of Design
Museum of Art
224 Benefit Street.
Tel: 401/454–6500. *Open
Wed–Sun 10–5 (8pm Fri).*

Woods-Gerry Gallery
62 Prospect Street.
Tel: 401/454–6141. *Open
Mon–Sat 10–4, Sun 2–5;
closed Mon Feb 21–Jun 1.*

[4] Providence
Athenaeum
251 Benefit Street. Tel: 401/
421–6970. *Open Mon–Fri
8.30–5.30 (Sat from 9.30).
Oct–May Sun only 1–5.
Closed Sat in summer.*

[5] David Winton Bell
Gallery
264 College Street.
Tel: 401/863–2952. *Open
Mon–Fri 11–4, Sat and Sun
1–4.*

[6] Libraries
John Hay Library
Prospect and College
streets. Tel: 401/863–2146.
Open Mon–Fri 9–5.

[7] Brown University
45 Prospect Street,
College Hill. Tel: 401/863–
1000. *Tours Mon–Fri at 10,
11, 1, 3 and 4 (from
Admissions Office); Sat 10,
11 and noon during fall.*

[8] Benefit Street
Governor Stephen
Hopkins House
Benefit/Hopkins streets.
Tel: 401/421–0694. *Open
Apr–Dec, Wed and Sat 1–4.*

⑩ John Brown House
52 Power Street.
Tel: 401/331–8575. *Open Tue–Sat 10–5, Sun noon–4. Closed Mon, except holidays.*

⑬ The Arcade
65 Weybosset Street.
Tel: 401/598–1199. *Open Mon–Fri 10–6, Sat 10–4.*

ⓘ Gateway Visitors Center, 23 America's Cup Avenue, Newport RI 02840. Tel: 401/849–8049.

❶ Brick Market Building
Museum of Newport History
Thames Street/Washington Square. Tel: 401/846–0813. *Open May–Oct, Mon and Wed–Sat 10–5, Sun 1–5.*

❹ Wanton-Lyman-Hazard House
17 Broadway.
Tel: 401/846–0813. *Phone for opening times.*

❺ Touro Synagogue
85 Touro Street. Tel: 401/847–4794. *Open May–Jun and early Sep–mid-Oct Mon–Thu 1–3; Jul–early Sep, Sun–Thu 10–4, Fri 10–3; mid-Oct–Apr, Sun 1–3.*

❻ The Newport Historical Society
82 Touro Street. Tel: 401/846–0813. *Open mid-Jun–Aug, Tue–Sat 9.30–4.30; Sep–mid-Jun, Tue–Fri 9.30–4.30, Sat 9.30–noon.*

⑩ The Redwood Library and Athenaeum
50 Belleville Avenue.
Tel: 401/847–0292. *Open Mon–Sat 9.30–5.30.*

⑪ Newport Art Museum
76 Bellevue Avenue.
Tel: 401/848–8200. *Open Jun–Aug, daily 10–5; Sep–May, Tue–Sun, shorter hours.*

⑫ Newport Casino and the International Tennis Hall of Fame
194 Bellevue Avenue.
Tel: 401/849–3990. *Open*

daily 10–5. Call for details during tournaments.

⑬ Kingscote Mansion
Bellevue Avenue.
Tel: 401/847–1000. *Open May–Oct daily 10–5.*

⑭ The Elms
Bellevue Avenue.
Tel: 401/847–1000. *Open daily 10–5.*

⑮ Château-sur-Mer
Bellevue Avenue.
Tel: 401/847–1000. *Open May–Oct daily 10–5.*

⑯ The Breakers
Ochre Point Avenue.
Tel: 401/847–1000. *Open late Mar–Dec, daily 10–5 (stables May–Oct).*

⑰ Rosecliff
Bellevue Avenue.
Tel: 401/847–1000. *Open May–Oct, daily 10–5.*

⑱ The Astors' Beechwood Mansion
580 Bellevue Avenue.
Tel: 401/846–3772. *Open mid-May–Oct, daily 10–5; Nov–Dec 19 closes at 4; Feb–mid-May, weekends only.*

⑲ Marble House
Bellevue Avenue.
Tel: 401/847–1000. *Open late Mar–Dec, daily 10–5.*

⑳ Belcourt Castle
657 Bellevue Avenue.
Tel: 401/846–0669. *Open most of the year; phone for details.*

㉑ Hammersmith Farm
Harrison Avenue (Ocean Drive). Tel: 401/846–7346. *Open Apr–mid-Nov daily.*

Special to…
Fort Adams State Park
Ocean Drive.
Tel: 401/847–2400. *Open daily dawn–dusk.*

Museum of Yachting
Tel: 401/847–1018. *Open mid-May–Oct, daily 10–5, winter by appointment.*

Scenic Routes
Cliff Walk
Memorial Boulevard.
Tel: 401/849–8048. *Open all year.*

ⓘ Veterans Memorial Drive, Route 7, Bennington VT 05201. Tel: 802/447–3311.

❶ The Bennington Museum
West Main Street. Tel: 802/447–1571. *Open daily Jun–Oct 9–6; Nov–May 9–5.*

❹ Bennington Battle Monument
Monument Circle, Old Bennington, off Route 9.
Tel: 802/447–0550. *Open mid-Apr–Oct, daily 9–5.*

❺ Hemming's Sunoco Station
Tel: 802/447–9652. *Open daily 7am–10pm.*

❻ Historic Bennington Railroad Station
Bennington Station Restaurant. Tel: 802/447–1080.

❽ Potters' Yard
324 County Street.
Tel: 802/447–7531.

⑪ Park-McCullough House
Park and West streets, North Bennington. Tel: 802/442–5441. *Open late May–late Oct, Thu–Mon, tours on the hour 10–3.*

ⓘ Veterans Memorial Drive, Bennington VT 05201. Tel: 802/447–3311.

ⓘ The Green, Chester. No telephone.

❶ Arlington
Norman Rockwell Exhibition
Route 7A. Tel: 802/375–6423. *Open May–Oct, daily 9–5; Nov–Apr, daily 10–4.*

❷ Mt Equinox
Equinox Mountain Inn
Skyline Drive, Manchester.
Tel: 802/362–1113 or 800/868–6843. *Open May–Oct 8am–10pm.*

American Museum of Fly Fishing
Route 7A, Manchester.
Tel: 802/362–3300. *Open daily 10–4.*

❸ Hildene
Robert Todd Lincoln's Hildene
Route 7A, Manchester.
Tel: 802/362–1788. *Open mid-May–Oct, 9.30–5.30.*

❻ Bromley Mountain Ski Area
Bromley Mountain, Route 11. Tel: 802/824–5522.

❽ Weston
Vermont Country Store
Route 100. Tel: 802/824–3184. *Open Mon–Sat 9–5 (6pm Jul–Oct).*

Weston Village Store
Route 100. Tel: 802/824–5477.

Weston Playhouse
On the Green.
Tel: 802/824–5288. *Open late Jun–mid-Oct.*

❾ Ludlow
Okemo Mountain Resort
77 Okemo Ridge Road.
Tel: 802/228–4041.

⑩ Chester
Fullerton Inn
40 Common, Chester.
Tel: 802/875–2444.

Green Mountain Railroad
54 Depot Street, Bellows Falls. Tel: 800/707–3530. *Open late Jun–mid-Oct, daily 9–5.*

⑪ Grafton
Grafton Village Cheese Company
Tel: 800/472–3866. *Open Mon–Fri 8–4, weekends and holidays 10–4.*

Village Store
Tel: 802/843–2348. *Open Mon–Sat.*

⑫ Newfane
Historical Society
Museum of Windham County
Tel: 802/365–4148. *Open Wed–Sun noon–5.*

⑬ Brattleboro
Museum and Art Center
Tel: 802/257–0124. *Open mid-May–Nov, Tue–Sun noon–6.*

Naulakha
Dummerston. Tel: 802/254–6868 for rental details.

Special to…
Orvis
Route 7A. Tel: 802/362–3750. *Open daily.*

TOUR 16

i Central Vermont Chamber of Commerce, PO Box 336, Barre VT 05641. Tel: 802/229–4571.

i Rutland Chamber of Commerce, at Routes 4B and 7, Rutland VT 05701. Tel: 802/775–0831.

1 Norman Rockwell Museum
Route 4E. Tel: 802/773–6095. *Open daily 9–6.*

2 Bethel
White River National Fish Hatchery
Route 107, Gaysville. Tel: 802/234–5400. *Open daily 8–3.*

3 Quechee and Quechee Gorge
Simon Pearce Glass
Main Street. Tel: 802/295–2711. *Open daily 9–9.*

4 Woodstock
Marsh-Billings-Rockefeller National Historic Park
Route 12. Tel: 802/457–3368. *Open late May–Oct, daily 10–5.*

Billings Farm Museum
Route 12. Tel: 802/457–2355. *Open late May–Oct, daily 10–5; Nov, Dec weekends.*

6 Plymouth
Coolidge Homestead and the Wilder House
Tel: 802/672–3772. *Open daily 9.30–5.30 (weekdays only during off season).*

Plymouth Cheese Factory
Tel: 802/672–3650. *Open daily 9.30–5.*

Green Mountain Sugar House
Echo Lake, Route 100N, Ludlow. Tel: 800/643–9338. *Open daily 9–6.*

Special to…
Crowley Cheese
Healdville. Tel: 802/259–2340. *Cheese shop open daily; factory open Mon–Fri.*

Recommended Walks
Green Mountain Club
Route 100 between Stowe and Waterbury. Tel: 802/244–7037. *Open daily 9–5.*

For History Buffs
Joseph Smith Birthplace Memorial
Dairy Hill Road. Tel: 802/763–7742. *Open daily 9–5.*

TOUR 17

i Lake Champlain Regional Chamber of Commerce, 60 Main Street, Burlington VT 05401. Tel: 802/863–3489.

i Addison County Chamber of Commerce, 2 Court Street, Middlebury VT 05753. Tel: 802/388–7951, 800/733–8376.

i Stowe Area Association, Main Street, Stowe VT 05672. Tel: 888/253–4849.

1 Shelburne
Shelburne Farms
1611 Harbor Road. Tel: 802/985–8686. *Open mid-May–mid-Oct, daily 10–5.*

Shelburne Museum
Route 7. Tel: 802/985–3346. *Open daily 10–5 (in winter reservations recommended).*

Vermont Teddy Bear Company
Route 7. Tel: 802/985-3001, ext.1800). *Tours Mon–Sat 9.30–4, Sun 10.30–4.*

2 Charlotte
Vermont Wildflower Farm
4750 Shelburne Road. Tel: 802/985–9455. *Open May–late Oct, daily 10–5.*

3 Ferrisburgh
Rokeby Museum
4334 Route 7. Tel: 802/877–3406. *Open mid-May–mid-Oct, Thu–Sun.*

4 Vergennes
Lake Champlain Maritime Museum
4472 Basin Harbor Road. Tel: 802/475–2022. *Open mid-May–mid-Oct, daily 10–5.*

5 Middlebury
Sheldon Museum
1 Park Street. Tel: 802/388–

2117. *Open Mon–Fri 10–5; May–Oct also Sat 10–4.*

Vermont State Craft Center at Frog Hollow
1 Mill Street, Frog Hollow. Tel: 802/388–3177. *Open summer Mon–Sat 9.30–5.30, Sun noon–5; winter, Mon–Sat 10–5.*

6 East Middlebury
Waybury Inn
Route 125. Tel: 802/388–4015, 800/348–1810.

8 Warren
Sugarbush Resort
Tel: 802/583–6300.

9 Waitsfield
Vermont Icelandic Horse Farm
The Common Road. Tel: 802/496–7141. *Open daily.*

10 Waterbury
Ben and Jerry's Ice Cream Factory
Route 100, Waterbury. Tel: 802/244–5641. *Open Jun–Oct, daily 9–5 (to 8pm Jul–Aug; to 6pm Sep–Oct); Nov–May 10–5.*

Green Mountain Chocolate Co.
Route 100, Waterbury Center. Tel: 802/244–8356. *Open daily.*

Cold Hollow Cider Mill
Route 100. Tel: 802/244–8771, 800/327–7537. *Open daily 8–6 (Jul–Oct 8–7).*

11 Stowe
Stowe Mountain Resort
5781 Mountain Road. Tel: 802/253–3000.

For Children
Spirit of Ethan Allen II
Burlington Boathouse, Burlington. Tel: 802/862–8300. *Boat trips May–Oct daily.*

Waterfront Boat Rentals
Shelburne. Tel: 802/864–4858.

Special to…
University of Vermont Morgan Horse Farm
74 Battell Drive, Weybridge, off Route 23. Tel: 802/388–2011. *Open May–Oct, daily 9–4.*

TOUR 18

i 500 Market Street, Portsmouth NH 03802. Tel: 603/436–1118.

3 John Paul Jones House
Corner Middle and State streets. Tel: 603/436–8420. *Open Jun–mid-Oct, Mon–Sat 10–4, Sun noon–4.*

5 Rundlet-May House
364 Middle Street. Tel: 603/436–3205. *Open Jun mid-Oct, Wed–Sun 11–5.*

7 Governor Langdon House
143 Pleasant Street. Tel: 603/436–3205. *Open Jun–mid-Oct, Wed–Sun 11–5.*

10 Wentworth Gardner House
50 Mechanic Street. Tel: 603/436–4406. *Open Jun–mid-Oct, Tue–Sun 1–4.*

12 Strawbery Banke
Marcy Street, On the Waterfront. Tel: 603/433–1106. *Open mid-Apr–Oct, 10–5.*

13 Warner House
Corner of Daniel and Chapel streets.
Tel: 603/436–5909. *Open Tue–Sat 10–4, Sun 1–4.*

Moffatt-Ladd House
154 Market Street.
Tel: 603/436–8221. *Open mid-Jun–mid-Oct, Mon–Sat 10–4, Sun 2–5.*

Recommended Trip
Vaughan Cottage Memorial and Celia Thaxter Museum
Star Island. No telephone. *Open summer, museum daily 1–3, Vaughan Reading Room 8am–10pm.*

For Children
USS *Albacore*
Albacore Park, 600 Market Street. Tel: 603/436–3680. *Open May–mid-Oct, daily 9.30–5.30.*

TOUR 19

i Chamber of Commerce booth, exit 28, off I-83. Tel: 603/536–1001, 800/386–3678.

Practical Information

i Tourist Information Office
12 Number on tour

i Visitors Center, North Woodstock NH 03262, exit 32 off I-93.
Tel: 603/745–8720 or 800/FIND–MTS.

1 North Woodstock
Clark's Trading Post
Route 3, Lincoln. Tel: 603/745–8913. *Open late Jun–Sep daily; weekends spring and fall.*

2 Franconia Notch
Franconia Notch State Park
Tel: 603/823–5563.

The Flume Visitor Center
Route 3. Tel: 603/745–8391. *Open mid-May–Oct (weather permitting) daily 9–5 or 5.30.*

Cannon Mountain Aerial Tramway
I-93. Tel: 603/823–8800. *Open mid-May–Oct daily.*

3 Franconia
Robert Frost Place
Ridge Road, Franconia. Tel: 603/823–5510. *Open Jun weekends, Jul–mid-Oct, Wed–Mon 1–5. Closed Tue.*

6 Mount Washington
Mount Washington Auto Road at Great Glen
Route 16, Gorham. Tel: 603/466–3988. *Open mid-May–late Oct (weather permitting).*

Great Glen Trails
Tel: 603/466–2333.

Mount Washington State Park
Tel: 603/466–3347.

Mount Washington Museum
Tel: 603/466–3988. *Open daily 8–6.*

8 Glen
Heritage-New Hampshire
Route 16. Tel: 603/383–9776. *Open mid-Jun–Oct 9–5.*

Story Land
Route 16. Tel: 603/383 4293. *Open daily mid-Jun–Sep 9–6 (spring and fall weekends only 10–5).*

9 North Conway
Conway Scenic Railroad
Route 16. Tel: 603/356–

5251. *Open daily mid-May–late Oct, weekends, spring, fall.*

Weather Discovery Center
Route 16. Tel: 603/356–2137. *Open daily 10–5.*

11 Lincoln
Whale's Tale
Route 3. Tel: 603/745–8810. *Open early Jun–Sep, daily 10–6.*

Hobo Railroad
Main Street. Tel: 603/745–2135. *Open late Jun–mid-Oct, daily; weekends mid-May–mid-Jun.*

For History Buffs
New England Ski Museum
Franconia Notch Parkway, exit 2. Tel: 603/823–7177, 800/639–4181. *Open Jun–Oct, daily noon–5; Dec–Mar, Thu–Tue noon–5.*

Scenic Routes
Mount Washington Cog Railway
Route 302, Bretton Woods. Tel: 603/278–5404. *Open May–Oct.*

For Children
Six Gun City
Route 2, Jefferson.
Tel: 603/586–4592. *Open mid-Jun–mid-Sep, daily 9–6; weekends 9.30–5 in spring.*

Special to…
The Jackson Ski Touring Foundation
PO Box 216, Jackson
Tel: 603/383–9355.

TOUR 20

i Lakes Region Association, Exit 23 off Route 93. Tel: 1–800/60–LAKES.

1 Ashland
Pauline Glidden Toy Museum
Pleasant Street. Tel: 603/968–7289 or 7023. *Open afternoons, Jul, Aug.*

4 Moultenborough
Castle in the Clouds
Route 171. Tel: 603/476–2352.

Loon Center and Markus Wildlife Sanctuary
Lees Mill Road. Tel:

603/476–5666. *Open Mon–Sat 9–5.*

5 Wolfeboro
Libby Museum
Route 109. Tel: 603/569–1035.

Wentworth State Park
Route 109. Tel: 603/569–3699.

Wright Museum
77 Center Street. Tel: 603/569–1212. *Open May–Oct, daily 10–4; Nov and Feb–Apr, Sat 10–4, Sun noon–4.*

6 Alton Bay
Ellacoya State Beach
Route 11, Gilford.
Tel: 603/293–7821.

8 Meredith
Annalee Doll Museum
44 Reservoir Road, off Route 104. Tel: 603/279–6542. *Open late May–mid-Oct, daily 9–5.*

Back to Nature
Squam Lakes Natural Science Center
Route 113, Holderness.
Tel: 603/968–7194. *Open daily May–Oct.*

Scenic Rides
Mount Washington Cruises
Weirs Beach. Tel: 603/366–5531. *Cruises late May–late Oct.*

Winnipesaukee Railroad
Tel: 603/279–5253. *Open May–Oct, Mon–Sat 10–4, Sun noon–4; Nov–Apr, Sat 10–4, Sun noon–4.*

TOUR 21

i Convention and Visitors Bureau of Greater Portland, 305 Commercial Street, Portland ME 04101. Tel: 207/772–5800.

i Brunswick Chamber of Commerce, 59 Pleasant Street, Brunswick ME 04011. Tel: 207/725–9787.

i 45 Front Street, Bath ME 04530. Tel: 207/443–9751.

i Damariscotta Region Information Bureau, Route 1, Damariscotta ME 04543. Tel: 207/563–3175 or 3176.

i Harbor Park, Rockland ME 04841. Tel: 207/596–0376.

i Public Landing, Camden ME 04843. Tel: 207/236–4404.

i Main Street, Belfast ME 04915. Tel: 207/338–5900.

1 Brunswick
Peary-MacMillan Arctic Museum
Hubbard Hall, Bowdoin Campus. Tel: 207/725–3416. *Open Tue–Sat 10–5, Sun 2–5.*

Bowdoin College Museum of Art
Upper Park Row, Walker Art Building. Tel: 207/725–3275. *Open Tue–Sat 10–5, Sun 2–5.*

2 Bath
Maine Maritime Museum
243 Washington Street.
Tel: 207/443–1316. *Open daily 9.30–5.*

3 Wiscasset
Wizard of Odds and Ends
7 Main Street. Tel: 207/882–7870. *Open Jun–Dec daily.*

Musical Wonder House
18 High Street. Tel: 207/882–7163. *Open May–Oct daily 10–5.*

Castle Tucker
Lee Street at High Street.
Tel: 207/882–7364. *Open Jul–mid-Oct. Tours hourly Wed–Sun 11–4.*

Nickels-Sortwell House
Main Street. Tel 207/882–6218. *Open Jun–Sep, Wed–Sun, tours hourly 11–4.*

Lincoln County Museum and Old Jail
Federal Street. Tel: 207/882–6817. *Open Jul–Aug, Tue–Sun 11–4.30.*

4 Damariscotta
Chapman-Hall House
Main Street. Tel: 207/882–6172. *Open mid-Jun–mid-Sep, 1–5. Closed Mon.*

5 Colonial Pemaquid/Fort William Henry
Off Route 130.
Tel: 207/677–2423. *Open*

late May–early Sep, daily 9.30–5.

6 Pemaquid Light and Fisherman's Museum
End of Route 130. Tel: 207/677–2494. *Open Jun–mid-Oct, daily 10–5 (11 on Sun).*

8 Thomaston
General Henry Knox Museum
Montpelier, junction Routes 1/131. Tel: 207/354–8062. *Open late May–Sep, Tue–Sat 10–4, Sun 1–4, last tour leaves at 3.*

Maine Watercraft Museum
4 Knox Street Landing. Tel: 207/354–0444. *Open late May–Oct.*

9 Rockland
Farnsworth Art Museum and Wyeth Centre
352 Main Street. Tel: 207/596–6457. *Open late May–Oct, Mon–Sat 9–5, Sun 1–5; Nov–late May, Tue–Sat 10–5, Sun 1–5.*

10 Rockport
Opera House
7 Central Street.
Tel: 207/236–2823.

Maine Photographic Workshop
Central Street. Tel: 207/236–8581.

Maine Coast Artists Gallery
162 Russell Avenue. *Open Tue–Sat 10–5, Sun noon–5.*

11 Camden
Conway Farm House
Tel: 207/236–2257. *Open Jul–Aug, Tue–Fri 10–4.*

13 Pownalborough Courthouse
Route 128, off Route 27.
Tel: 207/882–6817.

Special to…
L.L. Bean
95 Main Street, Freeport.
Tel: 207/865–4761, 800/221–4221.

Ernie's Drive-In
18 Bath Road, Brunswick.
Tel: 207/729–9439.

Moody's Diner
Route 1, Waldoboro.
Tel: 207/832–7785.

Olson House
Hathorn Point Road, Cushing. Tel: 207/596–6457. *Open Jun–mid-Oct, daily 11–4.*

Recommended Trips
Monhegan Island
Maine State Ferry Service, 517A Main Street, Rockland. Tel: 207/596–2202.

For Children
Owl's Head Transportation Museum
Next to Knox County Airport, off Route 73. Tel: 207/594–4418. *Open daily 10–5 (4 Nov–Mar). Restoration Shop also Thu 6.30–9pm.*

The Riding Centre at Mount Pleasant Farm
Union. Tel: 207/785–4628. *Open daily in summer, weekends in spring.*

Scenic Route
Maine Coast Railroad
51 Water Street, Wiscasset. Tel: 207/882–8000. *Open late May–mid-Oct weekends (daily mid-Jun–early Sep) 11–4.*

TOUR 22

| i | Convention and Visitors Bureau, 305 Commercial Street, Portland ME 04101. Tel: 207/772–5800

2 Portland Museum Of Art
7 Congress Square. Tel: 207/775–6148. *Open daily 10–5 (Thu–Fri till 9). Closed Mon mid-Oct–late May.*

3 Children's Museum of Maine
142 Free Street. Tel: 207/828–1234. *Open Mon–Sat 10–5 (8pm Fri), Sun noon–5. Closed Mon, Tue in winter except vacations.*

4 Maine College Of Art
97 Spring Street.
Tel: 207/775–3052.

6 Wadsworth-Longfellow House
487 Congress Street.
Tel: 207/879–0427. *Open Jun–Oct, daily 10–5.*

Center for Maine History
485 Congress Street. Tel: 207/879–0427. *Open daily 10–5/6 (Tue–Sat winter).*

9 First Parish Church
425 Congress Street. Tel: 207/773–5747. *Open by appointment.*

10 City Hall
389 Congress Street.
Tel: 207/874–8300. *Open weekdays 8–4.30.*

Portland Symphony
Tel: 207/842–0800.

11 Exchange Street
F. Parker Reidy's
83 Exchange Street. Tel: 207/773–4731. *Open daily.*

13 F. O. Bailey
141 Middle Street. Tel: 207/774–1479.

14 Milk Street Armory
Portland Regency Hotel, 20 Milk Street.
Tel: 207/774–4200.

15 Boothby Square
U.S. Customs House
312 Fore Street.
Tel: 207/780–3326. *Open weekdays 8–4.30.*

16 Tracy-Causer Building
20–36 Danforth Street.
Tel: 207/775–6245.
Call for times.

Special to…
Gritty McDuff's
396 Fore Street.
Tel: 207/772–2739.

Portland Observatory
138 Congress Street. Tel: 207/772–5547. *Closed for renovation; phone for details.*

TOUR 23

| i | Convention and Visitors Bureau, 305 Commercial Street, Portland ME 04101. Tel: 207/772–5800.

| i | Maine Tourism Association Welcome Center, 18 Mayville Road, Route 2, Bethel ME 04217. Tel: 207/824–4582.

| i | Rangeley Lakes Region Chamber of Commerce, PO Box 317, Rangeley ME 04970. Tel: 207/864–5364.

| i | Greater Farmington Chamber of Commerce, 30 Main Street, Farmington ME 04938.
Tel: 207/778–4215.

1 Sabbathday Lake
Sabbathday Lake Village
Route 26, New Gloucester
Tel: 207/926–4597. *Open late May–mid-Oct, Mon–Sat 10–4.30.*

2 Poland Spring
State of Maine Building
Tel: 207/998–4142. *Open Jun–Sep, weekends; Jul–Aug, daily.*

4 Trap Corner
Perham's of West Paris
194 Bethel Road, Routes 26 and 219. Tel: 207/674–2341. *Open daily 9–5.*

8 Rangeley
Rangeley Historical Society Museum
Main Street. Tel: 207/864–3317. *Open mid-Jun–mid-Sep, Mon–Sat 10–noon.*

Wilhelm Reich Museum
Dodge Pond Road, off Route 4/16. Tel: 207/864–3443. *Open Jul–Aug, Tue–Sun 1–5; Sep, Sun 1–5.*

9 Kingfield
Stanley Museum
School Street. Tel: 207/265–2729. *Open Tue–Sun 1–4 (Tue–Fri Nov–Apr).*

10 Farmington
Nordica Memorial Homestead
Holley Road. Tel: 207/778–2042. *Open Jun–early Sep, Tue–Sun 10–1, 2–5.*

Red School House Museum
Routes 2 and 4. Tel: 207/778–4215. *Open Tue–Fri 9–4.*

11 Norlands Living History Center
290 Norlands Road, Livermore Falls. Tel: 207/897–4366. *Open Jul–Aug, daily 10–4; Sep–Oct, weekends.*

Back to Nature
Maine Wildlife Park
Route 26. Tel: 207/657–4977. *Open mid-Apr–mid-Nov, 9.30–5.30.*

Index & Acknowledgments

The Automobile Association
wishes to thank the following libraries and photographers for their assistance in the preparation of this book.

MARY EVANS PICTURE LIBRARY 8a, 8b, 56a, 56/7; TOM MACKIE 5, 59, 83, 84, 92, 94/5, 95, 102/3, 103a, 118/9, 120/1, 136/7, 136, 142, 143, 144/5, 153, 154/5, 154b, 157, 165; MAINE OFFICE OF TOURISM 147, 148, 149; GENE PEACH/THE PICTURE CUBE 51; PICTURES COLOUR LIBRARY LTD 9, 10, 17, 103b; SPECTRUM COLOUR LIBRARY 6, 11, 42, 44, 82/3, 97; THE STOCK MARKET 12 (Michele Burgess 1993), 20 (Kunio Owaki 1988), 26/7 (Jean Miele MCMXCII), 28 (B O Zaunders 1991), 31 (ChromoSohm/Sohm MCMXCIV), 32/3 (Brownie Harris 1992), 33 (Lance Nelson), 58 (O'Rourke 1986), 62b (Ed Bohon 1986), 63 (Audrey Gibson 1986), 72/3 (Lance Nelson), 72 (Sonya Jacobs 1985), 74/5 (Kunio Owaki 1987), 79 (John Madere), 81 (James Marshall), 85 (Craig Hammell 1993), 92/3 (Craig Hammell 1993), 116 (Mark E Gibson 1987), 126 (James Blank), 150/1 (Randy Ury 1992); ZEFA PICTURES LTD 34, 37, 38, 49b, 68, 86/7, 91, 96, 105, 108/9, 111, 138, 139a, 146.

All remaining pictures are held in the Association's own library (AA PHOTO LIBRARY) with contributions from:
R HOLMES 2, 14/5, 18, 29b, 30, 34/5, 36, 39b, 40, 41, 43, 45, 47, 50a, 53, 54, 55, 60, 61, 62a, 66, 76, 78/9, 122, 123b, 124, 125, 130/1, 132/3, 140; J LYNCH 13, 19a, 19b; M LYNCH 4, 7, 23, 24, 25, 27, 29a, 39a, 49a, 50b, 52, 64, 65, 67, 70, 80, 86, 88, 89, 98, 99, 100, 101, 106, 106/7, 110, 112/3, 113, 114, 115, 117, 120, 123a, 127, 129, 131, 132, 135, 139b, 145, 154a; J WILLIAMS 57.

Contributors
Copy editors: Larry Dunmire, Karen Bird   **Indexer:** Marie Lorimer
Thanks also to **Penny Phenix** for her updating work on this book.